PATTERNS OF FOREIGN INFLUENCE IN THE CARIBBEAN

The Royal Institute of International Affairs is an unofficial body which promotes the scientific study of international questions and does not express opinions of its own. The opinions expressed in this publication are the responsibility of the author.
The Institute wishes to thank the following who read the manuscript on behalf of the Research Committee: Alan Angell, Professor Hugh Thomas, and Adam Watson.

Patterns of Foreign Influence in the Caribbean

Edited by
EMANUEL DE KADT

Published for
THE ROYAL INSTITUTE OF
INTERNATIONAL AFFAIRS
by
OXFORD UNIVERSITY PRESS
LONDON NEW YORK TORONTO

1972

Oxford University Press, Ely House, London W. 1

GLASGOW NEW YORK TORONTO MELBOURNE WELLINGTON
CAPE TOWN SALISBURY IBADAN NAIROBI DAR ES SALAAM LUSAKA
ADDIS ABABA BOMBAY CALCUTTA MADRAS KARACHI LAHORE DACCA
KUALA LUMPUR SINGAPORE HONG KONG TOKYO

ISBN 0 19 214988 1

Printed in Great Britain by
The Camelot Press Ltd, London and Southampton

Contents

Abbreviations not explained in the text   vi

Preface   vii

1 Introduction
  EMANUEL DE KADT   1

2 The Caribbean and the Outside World: Geopolitical
  Considerations
  PETER R. ODELL   18

3 The Ex-Colonial Society in Jamaica
  DOUGLAS HALL   23

4 Foreign Influence in Guyana: The Struggle for Independence
  COLIN V. F. HENFREY   49

5 The French Antilles and their Status as Overseas Departments
  GUY LASSERRE AND ALBERT MABILEAU   82

6 The Dutch Caribbean and its Metropolis
  HARRY HOETINK   103

7 Cuba and the Super-Powers
  ROBIN BLACKBURN   121

8 The Social Structure of Guatemala: the Internal Dynamics of US
  Influence
  BRYAN ROBERTS   148

9 The United States and the Caribbean
  LINCOLN GORDON   170

Contributors to this volume   181

Index   183

Map   *at end*

95761

Abbreviations not explained in the text

AID	Agency for International Development
CIA	Central Intelligence Agency
ECLA	(UN) Economic Commission for Latin America
EEC	European Economic Community
FT	*Financial Times*
GDP	Gross Domestic Product
IDS	Institute of Development Studies, University of Sussex
IRBMs	Intermediate Range Ballistic Missiles
LA Handbook	*Latin America and the Caribbean: a Handbook*, ed. by Claudio Véliz (1968)
LAFTA	Latin American Free Trade Association
NYT	*New York Times*
OAS	Organization of American States
OLAS	Organization for Latin American Solidarity

Preface

THIS book has been long, over-long in the making. Its origins lie in a series of meetings of the Chatham House Latin American seminar in 1967–8, focused on the theme of foreign influence in the Caribbean. Most of the papers presented there were revised by their authors in the light of comments during the discussions; as is usual in such circumstances, some took longer over this than others. More delays occurred, mainly because of the unavoidable interference of other work; a postal strike in 1970 caused us to fall further behind schedule. These delays have meant that many papers have had to be brought up to date more than once. Dr Lincoln Gordon's contribution is undoubtedly the one for which it is most necessary to bear in mind the original date of writing (mid-1968). 'Bringing up to date' would have had to involve, in this case, rewriting. But as his essay is so clearly based on his *personal* acquaintance with US policy, its value is, I believe, no less now than it was when originally written. Now that the book is at last to see the light of day, I wish to thank the contributors for their patience and forbearance.

Alan Angell, Hugh Thomas, and Adam Watson read the entire, now much changed, volume for Chatham House. Their comments were most helpful. Alan Angell has been my colleague at Chatham House throughout the gestation period of this book, and I am especially grateful for his help and encouragement. I should also like to thank Dudley Seers, who commented extensively and constructively on an earlier version of the Introduction.

Hermia Oliver was rapporteur of the original seminar series. As time lapsed, and papers had to be revised, it was she who undertook most of the work involved, which included a considerable amount of research. She greatly lightened the task of authors and editor by incorporating the often substantial draft revisions into the text, and carefully edited the final version of the book for the printers. I am sure the authors would wish to join me in thanking her warmly for her help.

Angela Hepner and then Diana Greenfield typed and re-typed the whole book, and I am also indebted to Diana Greenfield for helping with research for the Introduction. The index was prepared by Mrs Helen Baz. Mrs Joan White translated the first version of the chapter on the French Antilles. Peter Odell prepared the map of the region.

Sincere thanks are, finally, due to the Ford Foundation. Without its generous financial assistance to the Chatham House Latin American programme this book would not have been produced.

November 1971   EMANUEL DE KADT

I Introduction

EMANUEL DE KADT

THROUGHOUT its history the Caribbean has never been left alone. Outside influences have always been very diverse, and the way in which they have made themselves felt has no doubt changed. But the geographical situation of the region as well as its natural resources have captured and held the interest of outside powers and outside entrepreneurs ever since the Americas entered world history.

This book attempts to discuss some of the main kinds of external influence on (or interference with) some of the countries of the region and to capture something of their historical, economic, and social diversity. At the outset I should, however, state with some emphasis that it makes no pretence at comprehensiveness. It does not attempt to discuss the relations between the Caribbean and the countries of Latin America or the prospects for increasing integration of the Caribbean countries in regional organizations. Many territories in the Caribbean where foreign influence has been of importance are not dealt with. This applies particularly to some of the islands of the British Commonwealth Caribbean of especial interest to a United Kingdom audience—Trinidad, the Bahamas and Bermuda, the Leeward and Windward Islands—and also to Haiti and the Dominican Republic and Puerto Rico. These omissions regrettably reflect limitations imposed by the fact that most of the papers were originally presented in a series of seminars at Chatham House (and later revised). As the Contents reveal, this book discusses in detail only Jamaica, Guyana, the French and Dutch Antilles and Surinam, Cuba and Guatemala. It is necessary also to state that many contributions are 'essays' rather than 'papers', and that some discuss topics on which people have strong views and which easily give rise to controversy. Perhaps it is worth repeating at the beginning of this Introduction what is said in small print before the title page: that the opinions expressed in this book (including my own) are the responsibility of the authors alone, and that they are in no way attributable to Chatham House.

The contributors examine their subjects from a variety of disciplinary viewpoints: history rubs shoulders with economics, political science, geography, and sociology. Perhaps there is a slight bias towards the last, because of my own professional background. Despite these disparate approaches, significant common features do, however, emerge. An obvious point, but one often overlooked, is made early on by Peter Odell: many of the Caribbean states are small. They are mini-states, or even micro-states, and as such they are more susceptible to various forms of influence from abroad than nations whose territory or population are larger, who can strive for greater economic independence, meet more of their own needs, and mobilize more resources of all kinds when faced either by pressures from abroad or alien dominance within. The dependence of such small states on the economically and politically more powerful nations of the world is an almost inevitable fact. Questions nevertheless arise as to how the hitherto widespread negative effects of such dependence can be eliminated or at least mitigated, and how a truly constructive and mutually beneficial relationship can develop with powerful governments as well as with an expatriate private sector, and especially with the now almost ubiquitous multinational corporations.

Two other broad themes recur throughout the volume. The first is the stress laid on economic factors in most of the papers. The second refers to the implications of the strategic importance which the region has had in the eyes of successive US governments, especially since the building of the Panama Canal at the turn of the century. Of course, the momentous changes in military strategy brought by developments in the nuclear and missile fields have made the Panama Canal much less relevant. Nevertheless, a strategic orientation to the area was maintained. This was much strengthened by the ideology of the cold war, which helped to convert considerations about the internal socio-political structure of nations swiftly into quasi-military ones.

Before the building of the Canal the United States on the whole did not play a particularly active role in the area, despite the formulation of the Monroe doctrine (mainly aimed at keeping European conflicts from spreading to the Americas) in 1823.[1] That is not to say that the United States did not pursue an active policy in the Caribbean before its first intervention in the Dominican Republic in 1904. The Spanish–American War and its effect on Cuba (the Platt amendment, under which the United States first intervened in Cuba in 1906, was formulated in 1901) need only be mentioned as a very important example to the contrary. But the emergence of American intervention as a matter of almost normal

[1] For a short historical survey of American policy in the Caribbean see Herbert L. Matthews, 'Diplomatic Relations', in American Assembly, *The United States and Latin America*, ed. by Matthews (New York, 1963). A very useful reference book, which contains chapters on the individual countries as well as one on 'foreign influence', is Sir Harold Mitchell, *Caribbean Patterns* (Edinburgh, 1967).

expectation under certain circumstances dates from the first third of this
century. After the second world war debt-collection by gunboat became
taboo, but concern for material matters lurked not far beneath the surface
where intervention was justified by reference to the danger of a communist take-over. So Franklin D. Roosevelt's Good-Neighbour Policy
appears, in restrospect, as something of an interlude.

It is very difficult to disentangle economic, ideological and strategic
motives during the years of the cold war. At the time of the most serious
confrontation between the United States and the Soviet Union (before
the nuclear balance was established) the fear of a Russian military presence
in the Americas must have been considerable. And yet, before this had
become a reality with the turn to Marxism–Leninism of the Cuban
Revolution, *military* justifications for intervention always sounded a little
thin. There is no better example than the overthrow of the Arbenz
government in Guatemala in 1954. The role played in that connection
by the CIA marked the increasingly active involvement of that agency
as a kind of ideological watchdog in the continent. The fact that the
CIA always appears to have been given a good deal of freedom in its
actions is a reminder of the need to distinguish clearly between different
domestic forces in the United States, when speaking of American
influence, interference, or interests.

In his contribution to this volume Lincoln Gordon in fact suggests
that the Caribbean is regarded not only by American policy-makers and
government agencies as belonging to the American 'sphere of influence',
but that this view is widespread among the American public, which would
not tolerate a 'second Cuba' in the area. As the competence of the public
at large to reason from strategic premises is obviously limited, the weight
of ideological factors in this view must be considerable. I have little
doubt that this has also been the case among statesmen and government
officials. OAS justifications of (collective) intervention in defence of the
institutions of representative democracy has always seemed to me to be
rather flimsy. After all, those justifications have been invoked only to
deal with threats from the left, but never either to cope with threats
from the right or to propose a forcible change in the very undemocratic
status quo in so many of the Republics.

What the contributions to this book do bring out is that this ideological
definition of the situation is not divorced from the operation of genuine
interests. It may be absurd to tar all radical movements or governments in
the area with the brush of communism, and still more ridiculous to
ascribe to them potentially hostile military motives.[2] But the privileges

[2] Even the presence of Russian troops in Cuba can hardly be considered a military threat to
the US, though the presence of IRBMs obviously could.

and advantages enjoyed by foreign (and that means mainly American) business firms in most of the area, their very dominance,[3] could well be threatened once local governments start to pursue a policy of economic development and of distributive social justice by means other than the wholesale encouragement of private enterprise, and of indiscriminate private foreign investment. It is true that the explicit defence of the private interests of American citizens or corporations is no longer acceptable in the United States as a goal of American foreign policy. But intervention, military or otherwise, justified with reference to the upholding of democratic forms of government or of the military integrity of the hemisphere, can usefully fulfil the same function.[4] Repeated allusions in the following chapters to the importance of American, or international, business corporations in the Caribbean economies make such continuing interventionism as does exist much more comprehensible—even where direct American interests are not involved. In the Caribbean, as in most of Latin America, a significant part of the private sector of the economy—generally comprising the most dynamic industries—has developed such close links with foreign corporations that even embarking upon a course of *capitalist* economic nationalism would have profound consequences for the structure of the economy. Changes in a socialist direction, even where direct American involvement is minimal, would, of course, pose a much more serious threat to the regional interests of the international capitalist system.

Although the United States figures conspicuously on the pages of virtually all the following chapters, none of the contributors is primarily concerned with US military intervention in the area. But military influence operates in more subtle ways than through direct military incursions. Alarmed by the possibility of 'another Cuba', disturbed not only by active (though small) guerrilla movements in various countries, but also by potentially violent forms of mass unrest, considerable emphasis came to be placed in Latin America (including various Caribbean countries) on 'counter-insurgency' training of the armed forces. American military advisers, either on the spot or in training camps abroad, have pushed their Latin counterparts towards re-defining in military terms

³ For an up-to-date review of American economic interests (both in terms of trade and of investments) in the Caribbean, see L. F. Manigat, 'Les États-Unis et le secteur caraïbe de l'Amérique latine', *R. française de sci. pol.*, June 1969.

⁴ It would not be particularly helpful (though no doubt more precise) to restrict oneself in this connection to cases involving the actual dispatch of armed forces: somewhere within the range of actions from the landing of troops, through the establishment of military missions, to the making of strong diplomatic representations, perfectly acceptable behaviour between sovereign states begins to shade into an exercise of power which is considered improper at least by some significant sections of opinion in the dependent society.

situations which were fundamentally of a social or economic nature: opinions or activities which challenged the *status quo* have come to be regarded as subversive, and subversion has called for a military or paramilitary response.[5] Examples of this chain of events can be found in much of the continent; Bryan Roberts refers to it in his chapter on Guatemala, and he deplores the consequent polarization of positions (the vicious circle of violence and counter-violence) which makes it ever more difficult to arrive at solutions.

But these military reinterpretations are not the prime concern of our contributors. They write rather of foreign influence, a much more diffuse subject, something less easy to grasp or to define, or to be 'objective' about. For while there is no obvious reason to suggest that foreign influence is in any way inherently 'bad', the statement that their country is being 'subjected to foreign influence' draws at least mildly disapproving reactions from most people. That tone of disapproval in fact also finds its way into the following pages.

Yet certain problems emerge in this type of discussion. Perhaps not all forms of foreign influence are equally undesirable. If that is so, then we need criteria to enable us to compare the different kinds of effects. Such criteria are not easy to formulate. If *some* foreign influence in small states seems in any case inevitable, it may be worthwhile to try to shape the form such influence is going to take. The case of Cuba is instructive in this regard. Various contributors note that Cuba escaped American domination only to fall into the clutches of the Soviet Union, on whom the Cubans have become dependent to the tune of $1 m. per day. But Robin Blackburn argues that their freedom of manœuvre has remained considerable, and that Cuba can hardly be regarded as a docile 'satellite'. This raises the question whether from the dominated country's point of view economic dependence upon another state is more or less 'desirable' than the operation of economic influence through the presence of a foreign-dominated sector in the economy. The arguments for preferring the latter are fairly strong, at least *in abstracto*. While little can be done to force a more powerful nation to modify its foreign policy, legislation can be introduced to bend the activities of foreign corporations to suit the host country's interests.[6]

In practice, however, governments are frequently either loath to antagonize entrepreneurial groups, or are unable to muster the expertise

5 See I. L. Horowitz, 'The Military Elites', in S. M. Lipset & A. Ferrari, *Elites in Latin America* (New York, 1967). See also Horowitz, ed., *The Rise and Fall of Project Camelot* (Cambridge, Mass., 1967).
6 The experience of Chile after the assumption to power of President Allende will be worth watching in this respect.

necessary to deal with them as equals—a situation that occurs especially in dealings with large international companies.[7] They are also often found soft-pedalling the foreign-investment issue because of its short-term balance-of-payments implications.[8] Moreover, the influence of a powerful foreign economic enclave on the economic structure as well as on consumption patterns often results from many small decisions made at the level of the individual firm. These may concern the types of technology imported, the amount of employment created, or the sort of product produced—not to speak of the institutional framework itself of capitalist enterprise. Cuba may have difficulties over the kinds of goods she can purchase because of her economic dependence upon the Soviet Union, and this obviously puts her in an unenviable position. But she may well be freer to reject the *social* implications of that country's economic system than a comparable dependence upon free-enterprise capitalism would imply. If this sounds absurd to many (has not Cuba adopted Marxism–Leninism, lock, stock, and barrel?), they should reflect on Cuba's difficulties. Partly, of course, these have arisen out of defective planning—all too centralized, and yet piecemeal decision-making, and a bureaucratic machine often without effective contact with the grass-roots. But partly those difficulties arise out of the Cuban rejection not only of the profit motive (a rejection she shares with other socialist countries), but also of all material incentives, a rejection which flies in the face of Soviet economic doctrine. A comparison of Blackburn's chapter on Cuba with the chapter on Guatemala, in which Bryan Roberts concentrates precisely on those rather less tangible social effects, is instructive.

Andre Gunder Frank's prescription for development—isolate yourself if you want to develop—may be an over-simplification and an over-statement, impossible to achieve in practice without a revolution, and even then only at a cost which may in retrospect be unacceptable to most.[9] But to the extent that underdevelopment *is* a result of structural linkages between the less developed and the more developed, to the extent that dependence in a capitalist world market system does favour the transfer of resources from the poor to the rich—as it incidentally also does in a socialist international economic system, where unequal power relationships are just as important—a very much less permissive policy towards

[7] For a trenchant discussion of this problem see Dudley Seers, 'Big Companies and Small Countries: a Practical Proposal', *Kyklos*, xvi/4 (1963). Constantine V. Vaitsos examines this situation in the context of technological transfers: 'Bargaining and the distribution of returns in the purchase of technology by developing countries', IDS *Bull.*, Oct. 1970.

[8] See B. van Arkadie, 'Private Foreign Investment: Is It Useful?', ibid., May 1970. Cf. also, in the same issue, the paper by Maurice Zinkin, 'The Role of Private Investment Overseas'.

[9] *Capitalism and Underdevelopment in Latin America* (New York, 1967).

foreign firms may well be called for on the part of many governments in the Caribbean area.

In this connection, a recent paper by Albert O. Hirschman is of interest.[10] In it, he proposes a number of novel schemes for 'divestment' in Latin America, i.e. the transfer to local ownership and control of existing foreign-held investments, and concludes (with a nationalist-bourgeois equivalent to Frank's socialist proposal) that a measure of insulation from the advanced economies would be beneficial to Latin America. His view that international companies might well be willing to look at such apparently rather startling ideas is shared by Hans Singer. In a perceptive analysis of the needs and expectations of multinational corporations in a foreign environment he points out that 'the foreign company is interested in clear-cut, dependable and familiar situations'.[11] Hence, he feels, no great advantages attach to negotiating with a government unable to understand or pursue its own interests. In the short run very high profits could be made, but there would surely be a 'rude awakening' later.

In the Caribbean, it seems, many foreign companies have not yet taken the point. But perhaps the host governments can more easily than is commonly thought persuade them to let their activities be determined by *mutual* advantages. For such persuasion to be successful, governments will have to co-operate on a regional basis to a much greater degree than has hitherto been the case. Such co-operation would also be beneficial on occasions of negotiations over government aid, but that would, no doubt, be much harder to achieve.

A few paragraphs are called for at this point on a fairly recent development in the Caribbean, not dealt with explicitly by any of the contributors: the establishment of the Caribbean Free Trade Area, CARIFTA, in May 1968 to provide a form of economic integration for the territories of the Commonwealth Caribbean.[12]

Looking at CARIFTA on its second anniversary, one reporter felt that it is 'destined to be the economic transformation of the Commonwealth Caribbean'.[13] CARIFTA has created a wider protected market of 4·5 m. consumers for its members; it also helps to create a sense of

[10] *How to Divest in Latin America, and Why* (Princeton Univ., Nov. 1969).

[11] H. W. Singer, 'The Foreign Company as an Exporter of Technology', IDS *Bull.*, Oct. 1970.

[12] The original members of CARIFTA were: Antigua, Barbados, Dominica, Grenada, Guyana, Jamaica, Montserrat, St Kitts–Nevis–Anguilla, St Lucia, St Vincent, and Trinidad and Tobago. Since then British Honduras has joined.

[13] Victor Hinkson, 'CARIFTA; Two Years Later', *New Commonwealth*, no. 5, 1970. This paragraph also draws on other, unsigned, articles in the same issue.

solidarity on other fronts. For example, conferences of Caribbean heads of government and missions to protect the interests of the Caribbean Commonwealth in sugar, bananas, and shipping have sought to advance common interests. The mission to the Common Market in September 1969 served to inform EEC members of the position of the Caribbean Commonwealth and cleared a number of important issues with the United Kingdom. Another of CARIFTA's achievements was the tripartite currency arrangement which was concluded late in 1969 between the central banks of the major trading partners to facilitate the exchange of currencies and the financing of transactions within the CARIFTA area.

It is clear that the association has been of considerable benefit to certain territories, such as Jamaica, Guyana, and Trinidad and Tobago, stimulating the expansion of both agricultural and industrial production.[14] But the picture does not appear so bright from the point of view of its smaller and least developed members. Lacking raw materials, capital, and skilled labour, they find it more difficult to attract investment and industry.

The Windwards and the Leewards, for example, have claimed that CARIFTA has brought them no benefits and they are being exploited through it by the more industrialized members. They complain that manufactured goods imported from Port-of-Spain, Kingston, or Bridgetown cost more than similar items previously brought in from Hong Kong, Japan, or even Britain. It is widely accepted that CARIFTA has not achieved its aim 'to ensure that the benefits of the agreement are equitably distributed among member territories'. In the first two years Jamaica's exports to sister territories increased by some 60 per cent, Trinidad and Tobago's by more than 30 per cent, and the others, for the most part, by under 10 per cent.[15]

The establishment by sixteen Commonwealth Caribbean countries, with Britain and Canada, of the Caribbean Development Bank (which started operating early in 1970), will no doubt help to iron out some of the inequalities that have arisen in the wake of CARIFTA. Its capital of US$50 m. (to which Britain and Canada have contributed US$10 m. each) is likely to be put to work disproportionately in the smaller and least developed territories, which are most in need of infrastructural investments, without which neither tourism nor industry can be expected

---

[14] Jamaica, for example, doubled her exports to the area in the first 18 months after CARIFTA was established. In 1969 13 new industries were set up there, and in early 1970 she was able to boast of some 1,000 industries, ranging from electronics to matches. By the end of 1968 Trinidad and Tobago had nearly 400 industries, including a motor vehicle assembly plant, with another one being planned. See John Bradley, 'Investments in the Caribbean', *FT* Survey, 4 Feb 1970, for further details.

[15] *FT*, 9 July 1970.

to develop. Apparently, the Bank is already flooded with applications for loans from the smaller islands, especially for the construction of deep water ports and for hotel schemes.[16]

It is hard to disagree with the views expressed in a *Financial Times* article that the CARIFTA countries must develop stronger links and that the political leaders must begin to think in regional terms if CARIFTA is not to break up or merely degenerate into a quadripartite trade pact between Jamaica, Trinidad, Guyana, and Barbados. That article criticizes the widely differing taxation levels, financial and monetary policies, and above all the rival incentive schemes which have resulted in island-hopping by foreign investors and revenue losses for the islands, and it emphasizes the urgent need for CARIFTA politicians to sit down and plan the economic development of their islands jointly and selectively. Because of their reluctance to do this, proposals to harmonize tax incentives to investors have been shelved, and so has the UN Industrial Development Organization catalogue of new factories tailored to meet the import demands of the whole region.[17] Now that a Commonwealth Caribbean Regional Secretariat has been formed more attention might be paid to these matters in future—but the political obstacles to effective joint action appear to remain daunting.

Moves towards regional co-operation and integration run directly counter to one political formula which continues to be favoured by some of the smaller British Caribbean islands as well as by the dependencies of two other European powers, France and the Netherlands. That is the formula of political association or even assimilation with the metropolis, involving a degree of internal political autonomy but also full integration into the economic system of the 'mother country'. It is very doubtful, for example, if a fully independent Curaçao would have found economic assistance from international (or North American) sources on the scale provided by the Netherlands after the large-scale automation of the oil refineries. Freedom of migration, though its effects may be tempered by high transport costs, is a considerable asset in economies where unemployment is high—as the disassociated West Indies have found to their detriment after Britain raised the barrier to (coloured) immigration in 1962. Harry Hoetink deals in this volume with the Dutch Caribbean; Guy Lasserre and Albert Mabileau discuss the French Antilles. In both cases considerable attention is devoted to the political and economic

[16] See *FT*, 30 Jan. & 4 Feb. 1970, *Keesings Contemporary Archives* 1969–70, No. 23830A, and the article by Sir Arthur Lewis, President of the Bank, in the *FT* survey on 'Investments in the Caribbean', 14 Jan 1971.
[17] *FT*, 29 July 1970.

B

issues which have arisen in the course of the search for a satisfactory formula of association. In both cases, too, a careful analysis is presented of the underlying *social* structure, and of the varying extent to which different groups or strata oppose or favour, or stand to benefit from, the ties with the metropolis. Inequalities in this respect seem to be considerably more pronounced in the French case than in that of Curaçao or even Surinam: Lasserre and Mabileau give us to understand that the benefits of departmental status accrue mainly to the upper classes, who maintain their privileges in the French Antilles much as do their counterparts in many other Latin American societies.

The unusual solution to decolonization in the French and Dutch dependencies stands in notable contrast to the process which marked Guyana's road to independence. Colin Henfrey's interpretation of events there focuses on the interaction between internal social and political forces and external pressure. Henfrey's approach is particularly fruitful when he looks at the situation in Guyana in 1953, compares this with the position at the end of the 1960s, and asks whether from the constellation of internal forces in the former year one could have predicted the course of events leading to Independence in 1966. He thereby makes clear that as a result of decisions taken in the first place by the British government a chain reaction occurred with political and social consequences which, in Henfrey's view, were extremely damaging to the interests of Guyana—in terms of social structure, political attitudes, and economic development. Whatever one's assessment of the socio-economic potential by the end of the 1960s, it would be hard for anyone to deny that the thirteen-year period leading up to 1966 was marked by lost chances, political frustrations, economic stagnation if not retrogression, and the emergence of highly undesirable and almost totally 'unnecessary' racial strife—though the most recent developments are more encouraging from an economic as well as practical point of view than one might have been inclined to expect at the turn of the decade.

A number of points made in other papers in this volume shed further light on the Guyanese developments. Surinam, despite the presence of expressly ethnic parties, has not—at least so far—developed a pattern of essentially racial politics. Perhaps the Dutch experience with religious political parties participating in coalition governments has made a positive adjustment to (and by) a 'Hindustani' party easier. Perhaps the emergence of the racial split in Guyana, though certainly in no way *desired* by British officials or Ministers, was useful from the British point of view, if only in so far as it pushed firmly into the background the earlier predominant rejection of Guyana's social past, and of the structures this had bequeathed.[18]

But it was perhaps less that opposition in itself than the manner in which it expressed itself that caused the British back-pedalling on de-colonization, and the considerable US pressure obviously brought to bear on the British government. Douglas Hall, in his discussion of the Jamaican scene, draws attention to the effects of the cold war on his country, and laments that this resulted in a polarized world-view which attempted to suggest that two, and only two, basic models were available to the hitherto non-aligned nations. This made it extremely difficult to devise an institutional framework more relevant to conditions in ex-colonial societies. When the West Indian Federation was set up, its con-stitution was copied almost entirely from western examples. A political system emerged which, outwardly at least, looked remarkably like that which prevailed in Britain. Pressures to choose the western model of representative democracy (and free enterprise) were obviously greater in the Caribbean than in some other parts of the world, for reasons that have already been indicated. So too was suspicion of social and political forms which looked as if they might have been taken straight out of Moscow's copybook, but also of other kinds of radical adventures, or even of vaguely socialist experimentation. Guyana's misfortune was that her electorate, in 1953, was united enough to spawn a virtual one-party system—and this at the height of the cold war. Apart from the danger perceived to British interests, it must have seemed, in American eyes, to pose a potential threat to Venezuelan oil at about the same time that developments in Guatemala could be interpreted as being dangerous to the safety of the whole Central American peninsula and the Panama Canal.

But in Guatemala, too, as Bryan Roberts is at pains to point out, the real threat was neither a military nor an international one. It was a threat of internal social change, which came to be identified with 'communism' by outside powers as well as by those in the country itself whose interests were bound up with the *status quo*, and whose thinking was dominated by cold-war categories. (Even in the early 1970s appeals to the over-simplifications of the 1950s are still remarkably effective among sections of the Latin American military and of the US government machine,

---

[18] Sir Harold Mitchell's interpretation of the switch to proportional representation by Duncan Sandys at the Constitutional Conference in 1963 is that it was meant to break the dominance of racially determined political behaviour by forcing the need for government by coalition and by encouraging the emergence of new parties (*Caribbean Patterns* (Edinburgh, 1967), p. 211). Henfrey sees it as a solution which hardened racial voting by making the entire country one constituency, thus eliminating the cross-pressures generated in racially mixed constituencies (below, p. 71).

notably the CIA but also the Pentagon, and substantial sectors of the Latin American middle classes). And in Guatemala the very pervasiveness of North American interests, their integration into the social and economic structures of the country and their capacity to operate as part of those structures, made attempts at change particularly problematical. Cultural patterns imported from the Northern hemisphere expanded as part of a process of economic penetration in a society characterized by great inequalities and the predominance of vertical (patron–client) relations. A challenge to that traditional structure first by Arévalo, then by Arbenz, in an attempt to bring about a greater measure of distributive justice through the creation of alternative bases of power for the least privileged, came to be defined as heralding the advent of communism. This definition was both stimulated and welcomed by the all-pervasive foreigners and foreign groups in the country.

The often doubtful nature of the benefits of foreign influence on culture and economy emerges clearly in the following chapters. The importation of patterns of consumption and production from affluent societies—something to which I will return later—and the penetration, especially via technical assistance missions, of educational patterns which are possibly appropriate to industrial societies, but are hardly relevant to developing countries, give rise to problems throughout the Caribbean. Moreover, experience indicates that in those countries where foreign penetration has been most widespread, its very success contributes to propping up the existing social and economic framework. The main benefits accrue to those social classes whose incomes enable them to purchase the goods produced by foreign companies, and whose life-styles make them especially receptive to the appeals of the Sirens of the affluent enclave. The impact on the poorest part of the population, especially in the countryside, is frequently above all to strengthen the forces which keep them poor and marginal to economy as well as to society.[19]

Interesting, from this point of view, is the way tourism is of considerable economic importance. In fact, it often appears as one of the very few potentially promising sectors in small countries whose natural resources are extremely limited. But in the Caribbean stimulating the

[19] There is, by now, a considerable literature in economics as well as sociology on the dynamics of regional inequalities, sometimes referred to as 'internal colonialism'. For an early, but still very valuable, statement see G. Myrdal, *Economic Theory and Underdeveloped Regions* (London, 1958). See also P. Gonzalez Casanova, 'Internal Colonialism and National Development', in I. L. Horowitz and others, eds, *Latin American Radicalism* (New York, 1969), and J. Cotler, 'The Mechanics of Internal Domination and the Dynamics of Social Change in Peru', *Studs. in Compar. Internat. Dev.*, iii/12, 1967–8. The work of Gunder Frank is also relevant in this context; see n. 9 above.

tourist trade still means, to a large extent, promoting the influx of Americans. This in turn puts a premium on policies, internationally as well as internally, which are well received by US public opinion; as Peter Odell puts it, tourism makes for 'friendship' between these countries and the United States. And at least in the tourist areas a pattern of consumption must be made possible which meets the minimum requirements of the tourists. This may even involve large-scale importation of foodstuffs, unless local agriculture can take up the challenge of diversification—a question that often hinges on the need for agrarian reform.

Tourism on a large scale can, however, have more far-reaching effects on the social and economic fabric of society. At best it can substantially contribute to economic development, its effects making themselves felt through many sectors of the economy, and reaching a large proportion of the population. But tourism can also give rise to a kind of enclave-economy, where relatively high wages are paid by mainly foreign-owned, and what is worse, foreign-run enterprises. A tourist trade which is *seen* to be in the hands of foreigners may give rise to serious doubts on the part of the local population, making tourism economically and socially less desirable in their eyes. It may also become culturally suspect if, on the one hand, it leads to the stimulation of patterns of behaviour and consumption regarded as alien intrusions, while on the other it promotes those aspects of the local scene which do not enjoy undivided local approval. Havana as the playground—or the whorehouse—of the North Americans was perhaps an extreme example, but it stands as a warning to other countries in the area.

However, a small Caribbean island which has no viable economic alternative to trying to attract foreigners to its palm-lined beaches may have to pay the price of forgoing the freedom to make major decisions about its own future. Dependence on the tourist trade means dependence on foreigners and foreign tastes—even though, of course, those foreign tastes include a taste for the exotic which the host country can assiduously cultivate. Mexico has done so for decades. Nevertheless, a *major* dependence on tourism almost automatically creates the need to adopt certain patterns of consumption, production—and importation—directly copied from the developed world. Here little can be done by legislation or regulation. Unless you make the country attractive to foreign tourists (and for the bulk of the tourist market this means making the resort like home in terms of comforts and amenities), tourists will not come, or come back. There is no easy or obvious way out of the dilemma. It is most serious for the smallest countries, which cannot absorb the possible negative effects as successfully as a larger country, with a more diversified economy.

In some ways foreign firms resemble tourists. Their natural inclination is to make the best of the rather special 'amenities' of the host country (cheap labour, favourable legislation, and inadequate tax inspectors, rather than sunshine) and then to operate under the economic and cultural assumptions of their country of origin. Goods such as juke-boxes or air-conditioners may be demanded by tourists, but foreign firms manufacturing these products abroad may create local demand through advertising and sales promotion. In the French Antilles, it is suggested later in this volume, the patterns of behaviour and consumption of affluent France, imported by the local élite, underscore the already existing inequalities; they become part of a structure of privilege, and their resistance to change suggests that only the most ruthless and radical policies could effect this. Even the 'Black Power riots' in Trinidad become less mysterious when seen in this light, though, of course, the wider economic problems, the lack of an outlet through emigration, and the very high unemployment rate among young people were further factors (not unrelated to the structure of privilege and its international anchoring).[20] Clearly, if in future the more obviously undesirable effects of the free operation of foreign companies are to be checked, governments in the area will need to have a much clearer idea about the kinds of products they wish to have produced on their soil, and about the kinds of demands to be stimulated by billboard or other means. They will also have to reflect upon the kinds of existing—but 'mute'—demands that should have priority claims to being met. Thus, for example, foreign collaboration may be essential as well as invaluable in producing buses and commercial vehicles, but the wholesale transplantation of the cult of the private motor car may have to be much more closely questioned.

In most countries of the Caribbean, as in other developing areas, the percentage of the population fully participating in the market for manu-factured consumer goods is still very limited. Yet the billboards which greet one in the towns and on the highways of the Caribbean proclaim the virtues of products which even in the industrialized world are by no means within the reach of everyone, or which, though relatively inexpensive, are not of undisputed desirability. Cheap plastic sandals are seldom advertised: demand from the barefoot peasantry needs little stimulation, and few people would dispute the usefulness of this product (however much its impact on sandal-making craftsmen may be forgotten). But despite their irrelevance to any rational scheme of development planning, considerable sums are expended on promoting and advertising soft

[20] Stuart Hall in *New Society*, no. 403, June 1970.

drinks, washing machines, or detergents in the limited urban middle-class market.[21]

Two further topics need to be mentioned. The first is the effect on the developing economy of productive techniques imported by foreign enterprises. The other is the way in which the widespread intrusion of foreign capital influences the overall structure of the economy. Few would disagree with the proposition that money spent on washing machines is badly spent in an economy with considerable female unemployment (where in any case only a small percentage of the population can afford them). But consumer durables have further inconveniences. They usually have a high import content even when assembled locally, as many components cannot be produced by local industry. With balance-of-payments problems looming large in all but a few exceptional cases, this is a heavy price to pay. In addition, many of the products first developed in the industrial countries employ production methods with a capital-intensive technology, and therefore provide few jobs per unit of capital invested. Foreign firms, dependent upon machinery, production techniques, and know-how that come from the country where head office is situated, are never in a good position to take account of the special needs of a developing economy, and there is by now an abundant literature which suggests that those needs are special. Many contributors to this book explicitly mention the grave and disquieting growth of unemployment, but there is no doubt that the overwhelming majority of foreign firms are not very concerned with this problem and with their own contribution to aggravating it.[22] Government policies can, of course, be formulated to minimize the disadvantages and maximize the positive effects of foreign investment. But certain less desirable consequences of the presence of foreign firms are difficult to prevent. Capital-intensive technology is one of them; dependence for decisions on the head office is another.

This leads to the second, and last, point to be made in this context. Dependence upon the head office, which effectively means integration into the economy of the industrialized society, results in decision-making by the foreign firm or subsidiary which may not be in the best interests

[21] The difference between Jagan's People's Progressive Party and the coalition of Burnham's People's National Congress and d'Aguiar's United Force which took over after the elections of December 1964 is captured by John Hazard, when he wrote—approvingly—that the coalition's 'concept of a free society excludes dictation to individuals of consumption patterns'. In the free-enterprise view of the world only states 'dictate'; big corporations merely benevolently fill existing needs ('Guyana's Alternative to Socialist and Capitalist Legal Models', 16 *Am. J. Compar. Law* (1968), 515).

[22] These issues are examined at length for another Caribbean country, Colombia, in the recent report of the ILO mission on unemployment, *Towards Full Employment* (Geneva, 1970). See also the earlier cited issues of the IDS *Bull.*

of the economic development of the host country. Those interests may, for example, demand an export orientation—but the subsidiary is often discouraged from selling its products in competition with those manufactured by other subsidiaries of the same firm or by the parent corporation, or even expressly prevented from doing so. Or in a wider sense, those interests may demand activities which the foreign investor is not keen to develop; both Roberts and Blackburn make the point that foreign firms in Guatemala and Cuba were clearly guided, in a broad sense, by considerations of complementarity with the economy of the United States, or with the activities of branches of their own corporation elsewhere. In itself such complementarity is, of course, in no way 'wicked'— and in many cases it is unavoidable. But serious doubts arise when resources are left untouched or undeveloped merely because economic policies are dictated by the interests of the industrial countries on the one hand and the monopoly powers of foreign firms on the other.[23] The extraction of raw materials, such as bauxite in some countries in the Caribbean, and their processing abroad by other branches of vertically integrated international companies is a case in point; here the main profits as well as the main employment effects (direct and indirect) are generated outside the host country.

The picture with which we are left is not very encouraging. Most Caribbean countries have grave problems of economic development, to which solutions are by no means obvious. Greater co-operation or economic integration are often mooted as essential, but clearly the obstacles are many.[24] Caribbean nations will presumably continue to receive foreign aid (Britain has lately been providing between £7 m. and £8 m. per year in technical assistance and net capital aid),[25] though the mechanics and benefits of such aid need careful scrutiny, not only in respect of multilateral as opposed to bilateral agreements, but also in relation to such politically sensitive issues as the tying of aid to purchases from the

[23] There is, by now, a growing literature which deals with the consequences for developing countries of economic dependence. Apart from the neo-Marxist view of Gunder Frank, see e.g., Osvaldo Sunkel, 'Política nacional de desarrollo y dependencia externa', *Estudios internacionales* (Santiago), Apr. 1967, or F. H. Cardoso and Enzo Faletto, *Dependencia y desarrollo en América Latina* (Mexico, 1969). See also Sunkel and Pedro Paz, *El Subdesarrollo latinoamericano y la teoría del desarrollo* (Mexico, 1970).
[24] See the valuable analysis by Aaron Segal, 'Economic Integration and Preferential Trade: Caribbean Experience', *The World Today*, Oct, 1969.
[25] GB, Min. Overseas Development, *British Aid Statistics* (1970). The latest available figure for net capital *grants* and technical assistance (1969) for Central America and the islands of the Caribbean is £7.5 m. But it should be noted that approximately one-half of this amount (£4 m.) went to nine colonial mini-territories with a total population of 482,000 while a further third was granted to British Honduras (120,000 inhabitants). Hence British aid only reaches a minute proportion of the Caribbean population.

donor country, or the exclusion of local currency expenditures from aid agreements (thus reducing the direct effects on the aid recipient's economy, e.g. in terms of employment). One can also safely assume that private foreign investment (usually, quite erroneously, shown by donor countries as part of their aid effort) will be further stimulated and encouraged by governments in the area.

The view of the US government and public opinion that the Caribbean is, *par excellence*, in the American sphere of influence is likely to remain the dominant political fact, and this almost certainly rules out a 'Cuban-type' solution for these countries in the foreseeable future.

These are the realities with which the Caribbean countries are faced. Certainly not all influences coming from abroad are deleterious, and certainly the interests of Caribbean countries and foreign governments or investors are not always opposed. There is, among many persons concerned with aid policies in the developed world, a genuine desire to help, and even economic motivations (or the 'profit motive') do not necessarily lead to conflict, misallocation of resources, or 'exploitation'. But if the Caribbean and the outside world are really to become 'Partners in Development',[26] there is an urgent need to reappraise many schemes, unravel many political and social entanglements, and coolly analyse the social and economic implications of the existing arrangements and structures. Where governments are too bound up in the *status quo* this task will have to fall to others—those in opposition, in the universities, or even abroad. I hope that this book will contribute to a better understanding of some of the problems, and that, in that sense, it will be a beneficial foreign influence.

[26] Lester B. Pearson, *Partners in Development*, Report of the Commission on International Development of the World Bank (London, 1969).

2 The Caribbean and the Outside World: Geopolitical Considerations

PETER R. ODELL

ANY examination of a region's relationship with the outside world demands a definition of the region whose relationships are being examined. This is particularly so in the case of the Caribbean, whose limits are by no means self-evident. All the land areas literally emerging from the Caribbean Sea itself must quite obviously be included; but even this restrictive view of the Caribbean region produces so complex a political pattern of nation-states and dependencies and semi-dependencies, that there is already adequate scope for a study designed to sort out some of the complexities. So to limit the area, however, is tantamount to dealing with the centre of a jig-saw puzzle whilst forgetting about its edges, and besides the islands, one must also include the countries and territories bordering on the sea—in much the same way that reference to Mediterranean lands and civilizations deals with phenomena that have some coastal contact with the sea itself. This approach to defining the Caribbean region adds, to the islands, Venezuela and Colombia on the mainland of South America, the Caribbean-fronting countries and territories of the Central American isthmus, and the extreme south-west coast of the Yucatan peninsula of Mexico. An accident of history—the drawing of the post-independence boundary between the United States of Mexico and the United States of Central America—brings this part of present-day Mexico very peripherally into the Caribbean as defined. However, the unimportance of Yucatan at the present time and the non-Caribbean nature of Mexico proper make it infinitely more logical to consider Mexico as an outside power with which the Caribbean has relationships rather than as a part of the region. By contrast, significant parts of the national territories of the other two large countries included by this delineation of the region—Venezuela and Colombia—have Caribbean characteristics, and their inclusion is certainly not an anachronism.

This definition of the region does, however, strictly exclude two areas that cannot be omitted when other criteria are considered. One is the sovereign state of El Salvador, which happens not to have a Caribbean coastline but which is, of course, an integral part of the isthmus of Central

America and of its political and economic organization. Thus it certainly cannot be excluded. At the other extremity the eastern limit of the Caribbean Sea is marked by the line of the Lesser Antillean islands, running north-south, and by the island of Trinidad whose geological and other physical characteristics tie it in closely to the neighbouring mainland of Venezuela. However, this delimitation for the eastern and south-eastern boundary of the region omits the adjacent areas of mainland to the east—Guyana, Surinam, and French Guiana. Nevertheless, these territories do have important links with Caribbean phenomena—in, for example, their racially admixed populations, their colonial histories, and their dependence on plantation agriculture. Thus there appears to be little justification for accepting limits to the region which exclude them—although their inclusion does make the task of generalized description even harder and more complex. There is even something to be said for extending the boundary of the region still farther east, so as to include part, at least, of the Brazilian coastlands, whose settlement and development had much in common with large parts of the Caribbean region proper, but their exclusion can be justified on grounds similar to those used for justifying the exclusion of Yucatan. The heartland of Brazil is very much part of the outside world as far as the Caribbean is concerned, and through national ties the attention of north-east Brazilian coastlands have gradually turned effectively southwards. (See map at the end of this book.)

Thus defined, the area of study is shown in the end map. This also attempts to demonstrate aspects of the area's fragmentation in both physical and political terms. In geopolitical terms the internal form of the region can be recognized conceptually as a nodal area—albeit a very weak one—having the Caribbean Sea as its unifying and centralizing element. The unifying nature of the Sea—and of the accompanying maritime tropical climatic regime—operates, however, only as a backdrop to the disunity of the political set-up, with some fourteen nation states and eight dependencies of one kind or another. At a more generalized level one can establish[1] a division of the region into two parts: (1) a Euro-African Caribbean rimland (comprising the islands and most of the coastal periphery of surrounding areas); and (2) a Euro-Indian mainland with contrasting cultural attributes. Yet, when looking at external geopolitical relationships, such a division which, as West and Augelli show, has a good deal of validity in providing a basis for a study of the region's internal differentiation, is overshadowed by other considerations such

[1] After R. C. West and J. P. Augelli in *Middle America: its Lands and Peoples* (Englewood Cliffs, 1966).

as the incidence of national boundaries and the pre-existence of earlier colonial ties.

An appreciation of such relationships demands recognition of the nature of the territorial entities within the region. The high degree of Balkanization, except for Colombia and Venezuela, carries, as an inevitable corollary, the existence of units that are economically and politically weak and hence highly susceptible to outside pressures. In spite of this the tendency for the units to keep apart has remained stronger than any tendency towards integration or some other form of mutually advantageous co-operation, and in no other area of the world is there such a proliferation of small national units of government: the only hopeful feature of the situation arises from the fact that in this respect things are just about as bad as they can be, and that any political change can only be for the better. This judgement, however, should not be taken as an indication that change can necessarily be expected.

Finally, in introducing the Caribbean region one other phenomenon must be mentioned because of its significance for influencing the external relationships of the area. This is the Panama Canal which, having been dug through territory prized away from Colombia by the United States for the sole purpose of securing an uninhibited and sovereign right to construct the canal, has become the world's second most important man-made transport route. As such it enters into the political and economic calculations of all the great maritime nations, of all the states of the western part of Latin America whose contacts with the North Atlantic region are dependent upon it, of Brazil in the light of her growing contacts with Japan and, above all, of the United States, not only for sound commercial reasons but also for the flexibility it gives to that nation in her multi-oceanic naval strategy. The location of the Panama Canal 'deep' in the Caribbean gives each of these groups of interested parties an enhanced appreciation of the region's significance.

From this general background to the geopolitics of the region, one turns to look rather more closely at the development and importance of the various strands involved, and firstly, at that of European connections. It is ironical that the Caribbean, which not only had the first western-hemisphere connections with Spain, through the latter's earliest discoveries of Santo Domingo and other islands, but which was also the location of Spain's most recent colonies (viz. Cuba and Puerto Rico), should have been so little valued by the metropolitan power. In the early period the region, in contrast with Mexico and many countries of South America, offered little to Spain, and the local colonists were left to their own devices (which often included moving on to more attractive colonies on the mainland) and sometimes even to their fate. That fate, more often than not, consisted of being 'taken over' by another European nation, for several of these intervened to take advantage of Spain's pre-occupation elsewhere in the continent, and secured both influence and territory within the Caribbean. As a result there developed, from the seventeenth century onwards, a geographical extension of European conflicts to the Caribbean, so that many territories in the region changed hands, often several times. The strategic and political interests of different European nations were thus reflected locally. Later, once the pattern of ownership became fixed, the European nations also created contrasting developmental patterns arising from different motives in their colonization. For example, for Britain, the Caribbean territories were viewed in economic terms. They were solely and simply providers of tropical products grown mainly on plantations run by a white aristocracy. But for Spain the Caribbean colonies after the 1830s remained all that was left of her former empire in the western hemisphere and, in a period of increasing economic difficulty provided opportunities for continuing migration, thus establishing numerically much more significant European white populations in Cuba and Puerto Rico than in the other islands.

Before examining the current status of Caribbean-European relationships, it is necessary to touch on the involvement of the United States in the region—now the main element in the Caribbean's external geo-political relationships. This, in spite of present deceptive appearances, is a relatively recent phenomenon, as for most of the nineteenth century the United States did not see the extension of her domain over the Caribbean area as part of her 'manifest destiny'. Undivided attention was given to her own continental limits and to the realization of national unity within these limits. Ironically, however, it was this very theme in American historical geography that took the United States, towards the end of the nineteenth century, into the Caribbean area for the first time in pursuit of a very positive aim. The then recent achievement of the United States' continental-wide manifest destiny had made the country a two-ocean power, and thus posed the problem of mobility as far as movement between the Atlantic and the Pacific was concerned. Movement via Cape Horn was costly and time-consuming, Mexico's Isthmus of Tehuantepec railway solved some transhipment problems but not the crucial one of moving warships between the oceans. The growing importance of the American west in the last quarter of the nineteenth century accentuated the problem, and eventually the United States reversed her earlier policy of non-intervention in the Caribbean and made successful play for the right to build a canal, navigable for her ocean fleets, across the isthmus of

Panama. This barely disguised military intervention, and the permanent alienation of territory for the canal and its associated facilities, contrasts markedly with the hesitancy just a year or so earlier in US attitudes towards Cuba and Puerto Rico following the expulsion of Spain after the brief Spanish–American War of 1898. Thus it represents much more of a turning point in the geopolitical relations between the United States and the Caribbean than did this war with Spain, although the war did in fact bring Puerto Rico directly, and Cuba indirectly, under American hegemony. Between them, the 1898 war and the Panama incident put the United States in a stronger position *vis-à-vis* the Caribbean than any one of the other European powers which retained interests there. The continuing activities and adventures of such European powers in the area became, in any case, a source of increasing concern to the United States which, once she had dropped her inhibitions about intervention, sought to have her dominance in the area recognized and accepted unconditionally by all parties concerned.

In the first half of the twentieth century this implied that the United States should establish working relationships with the European interests in the large areas they still controlled, whilst elsewhere she had to persuade the independent nations that she could preserve their integrity without compromising their independence. The United States' participation in the two world wars, and the preoccupation of the European powers with these wars, helped significantly in achieving these objectives, which were accompanied by growing American involvement in the countries and territories concerned, including—since 1950—the former colonies as they secured their independence. With these newly independent nations the United States sought to establish good relations, and tried to ensure that their governments were of an acceptable kind. In this last respect there was some American reluctance until very recently to get involved in the domestic, electoral affairs of these and other nations in the region—a relic of the nineteenth-century policy of non-intervention. That reluctance was finally discarded at the beginning of the 1960s with the shock of realizing that what had happened in Cuba had occurred partly as a result of insufficient and ineffective American concern. The impact of Cuba on the US resolve *vis-à-vis* Caribbean nations is demonstrated in her action over the political developments in the Dominican Republic and in Guyana in 1965. In neither case did the United States permit a regime to come to power which she feared might remove the territories from American hegemony. Thus, by the mid-1960s, the United States was at last entirely convinced of the validity of the spheres-of-influence concept as far as the Caribbean was concerned. In her eyes no other nation has any significant interest in the area, or any chance of securing one, with the exception of the Soviet Union and her remaining links with Cuba, a situation which has arisen from the 'settlement' of the missile crisis in 1962. As the same settlement also implied the acceptance by both parties of the general idea of 'spheres of influence' on a world scale, as a means of restricting areas of friction, it seems unlikely that Cuba will remain outside the US sphere (or within the Soviet sphere) for more than a relatively short period. Her present status thus emerges as an accident of history and Cuba's return to the American system in the Caribbean, seems likely to be acceptable—and most probably welcome— to both the super-powers at an appropriate time.

After outlining the at first somewhat reluctant, but later rapid rise to geopolitical dominance of the United States in the Caribbean, it is necessary to return briefly to examine the continuation of European colonialism in the contemporary situation.

It has been suggested previously that little geopolitical significance can be attached to the few remaining European interests in the Caribbean. The formal political ties that remain do so either because of the special relationships which have evolved between metropolitan powers like France and the Netherlands and their former colonies, or because of special problems affecting the external position of certain territories. For example, one factor delaying the independence of Guyana for some years was the potential danger to an independent Guyana from neighbouring Venezuela, which had territorial claims to a large part of the British colony. And similarly British Honduras remains a colony because of Guatemala's claim to the whole of her national territory rather than for any other reason. Less formal political 'ties' arising from continuing relationships between European nations and their former colonies are given an appearance of importance in official pronouncements. They seem to be backed up in the continued existence of highly recognizable social phenomena such as the devotion to cricket in the former British West Indies. But in practice little effective contact or influence emerges out of such lip-service to 'historic ties', except possibly in one respect—the phenomenon of a reverse colonization arising from large-scale population flows from the former colonies to the metropolitan territory. Caribbeans seeking opportunities and jobs decided to take advantage of the previously forged colonial links—but, at least in the case of Britain, latterly to little avail. In the face of a rapidly increasing flow of migrants Britain quickly showed herself uninterested in continuing to accept responsibility for the peoples of the former colonies and curbed the migratory movement. The almost total absence of opposition to this curb in Britain serves to confirm the general lack of interest in the Caribbean by former colonial powers, whose economic motivations for continued contact are minimized now that in parts of Africa and Asia the generally larger ex-colonial territories are well able to 'compete' with the small former Caribbean colonies in producing tropical agricultural products and even minerals such as oil and bauxite. In general, in the absence of any major incentive to prevent it happening, the relationships between the metropolitan powers and their recent former colonies seem likely to become as tenuous as those currently existing between Spain and her considerably more important ex-colonial territories in the region.

As has already been stated, the one European power that does have effective relationships with colonial overtones is, of course, the new-comer to the Caribbean, the Soviet Union, in her new responsibility for Cuba. Ignoring some niceties of political theory, it is possible to argue a case for viewing basic Soviet behaviour towards Cuba as not greatly dissimilar from that of the United States before the Cuban revolution and break with the American system. Superficially at least one can see many parallels between the present Cuban economic dependence on the Soviet Union, both for export markets—particularly sugar—and for imports, and her previous dependence on the United States. Not only have Soviet markets replaced American markets, but they have moreover replaced them within the same sort of framework of long-term agreements not disadvantageous to the major powers. American machinery and American capital for the exploitation of resources and for industrial development have been replaced by Soviet machinery and Soviet financial assistance; all this to be serviced in much the same way as the previous US investment. Previously Cuba lacked choice in determining the source and cost of her oil imports because of the control of the oil trade by American companies; now she is unable to secure any but Soviet oil at price levels which reflect the relative bargaining strengths of the two parties concerned. Perhaps successes in other fields by the Cuban revolution ought to be set against the inability of Castro to steer his country out of her former colonial position into a more economically independent one. Instead, one colonialism has been replaced by another—and one that is, moreover, possibly less efficient, because the Soviet Union lacks experience in dealing with tropical territories, with their host of unfamiliar problems, agricultural and otherwise.

Aside from Cuba, and from the remnants of European colonization, the United States now fulfils, directly or indirectly, a role as the colonial power for the whole of the Caribbean. Politically, as already demonstrated, this involves virtually open intervention in order to secure types of government which she finds not unacceptable—and a clearly defined commitment by her to keep such governments in office. Though sometimes, as in the case of the US intervention in the Dominican Republic in 1965, this involves the use of military forces to keep out a government which appears too far to the left, it sometimes also involves the United States in restraining the activities of her own nationals (individuals or companies) when action on their part would involve the downfall of governments that she finds acceptable. An outstanding example of this dates from the late 1950s and early 1960s following the accession to power of the *Acción Democrática* government of Rómulo Betancourt in Venezuela. His government was left wing, but acceptable to the United States as it was reformist rather than revolutionary. Moreover, in the aftermath of Cuba's defection to the communist camp, the United States saw in Venezuelan stability the key to Caribbean stability. But the American oil companies in Venezuela interpreted the Betancourt government in rather a different light, since Betancourt, whilst in exile, had consistently advocated nationalizing the Venezuelan oil industry. On coming to power, he significantly increased the oil companies' tax obligations and encouraged and supported the wage and related demands of the oil workers. To the oil companies this seemed the not-so-thin edge of an eventual decision to expropriate. In 1950 the companies, when faced with a similar situation, had worked actively to help overthrow the offending regime. Now, in the light of the very rapid and continuous expansion of oil-industry activities in Venezuela throughout the 1950s, much more was at stake. The companies' inclination was thus to help secure the overthrow of the *Acción Democrática* government and the establishment of a regime more favourable to their activities. Their wealth and influence was certainly such that there was little doubt that this objective could have been achieved—particularly in circumstances in which the powerful military establishment in Venezuela was also becoming increasingly suspicious of the intentions of the Betancourt regime. To the United States the possibility of instability and/or an extremist regime—either of the right or, as a reaction to this, of the left—was a daunting prospect. Thus the State Department intervened with the oil companies concerned and 'persuaded' them to accept the political situation in Venezuela and to seek a *modus vivendi* with the *Acción Democrática* government. The companies responded to the pressure and limited their reaction to the new regime in Venezuela to restricting the rate of increase in oil offtake and new investment. This limited response by the companies did not prevent government revenues from the industry from continuing to rise, and it ensured that *Acción Democrática* had sufficient funds both to

C

'buy off' the military's suspicion of its intentions and to pursue its programme of social and economic measures designed to improve living
standards.

The power of American companies in all the countries of the Caribbean
region is, of course, one very important aspect of American 'imperialism'
in the area. But, as the foregoing example illustrates, the very great power
of the companies over the economy and, indirectly, over the politics of
individual countries can be tempered by the responsibility which the
United States as a nation now formally accepts for the whole region. It
would be wrong to assume that her national interests and the interests of
individual companies invariably and inevitably coincide. They did not
in Venezuela in the above example, and it seems not unreasonable to
speculate that there have been other cases where the US government has
acted as a restraining influence on the economic imperialism of individual
companies. For example, the United Fruit Company has significant
interests in many of the countries of the region, but it also has interests
elsewhere (in the production of bananas, for example) which could well
have been expanded at the expense of those in the Caribbean because of
uncertainties about developments in, say, Honduras. Similarly, the large
American aluminium companies have had corporate choice over decisions
as to where in the world they should expand output—and have been in
positions to take decisions which would adversely affect Caribbean
nations. The political and strategic interests of the US government in the
Caribbean seem certain to have curbed corporate policies such as these
which could have adversely affected the nations of the region. They may
even, in fact, have encouraged policies on the part of US companies
which have favourably affected these nations, in order to restrain anti-
American forces and attitudes latent in all of them.

Restraint by the US government on American companies in the
Caribbean reflects concern for stability and the *status quo*. But it also
reflects the existence of US economic interests that require restraining.
Investment, trade, tourism, and all other economic processes which have
external manifestations link the Caribbean inexorably with the United
States. With the possible exception of the French territories, it is impossible to find a country or territory within the area whose main economic
links are not with the United States. Plantation agriculture, the original
commercial motivation for European interest in these territories, has
become increasingly financed from the United States rather than from
Europe. Extraction of oil, iron ore, bauxite, and other minerals is almost
entirely through American companies, with European interests sometimes
even selling out to them, as in the case of the long-term British-based

oil producer in Trinidad, Trinidad Leaseholds, which sold out to Texaco in 1956. Industrialization, arising from deliberate efforts on the part of almost all of these small countries to diversify their economic activities into import-substituting manufacturing, has been financed in large part from the United States, and the factories are equipped with American machinery and run by American administrative and supervisory personnel. To travel, for example, from the airport at San Salvador into the city itself one takes the road along which the factories participating in the industrialization of El Salvador have almost all been built. The factory names present a succession of US household words in the field of the manufacture of consumer goods. Such a situation is repeated time and time again in country after country.

US participation in the organization and financing of productive activities thus leaves no doubt about the nature of the economic involvement. But even this high degree of participation in the manufacturing sector of the economy is outstripped by US domination of the activity which is of increasing importance for most of the Caribbean nations—tourism. Tourism in the Caribbean was initially centred on Cuba and was financed by US capital for the benefit of US visitors. It provided the types of facilities which the Americans could not get at home, as well as a climatically attractive winter tourist alternative to Southern Florida. The kind of tourism pursued, especially in Havana, was undoubtedly one reason for the later extreme reaction of Cuba against the United States. With its termination by communist Cuba, the increasingly affluent US middle class has sought opportunities for taking advantage of the Caribbean's climatic and other natural attractions from one end of the region to the other. Puerto Rico and Jamaica, already enjoying some degree of participation in the US tourist industry before Cuba's defection, have secured the lion's share of the capital and of the companies seeking to provide alternative facilities. But even without the stimulus to development elsewhere caused by the closure of Cuba to tourism, there would have been a spill-over into these and other islands. The increasing demand for such facilities has been stimulated by the growing number of Americans with sufficient discretionary income available, and by the speedier and lower-cost transport of the jet-plane age. It seems unlikely that the tourist boom for the Caribbean has reached its zenith, for both these factors continue to operate and even intensify. There are still beaches both in the Caribbean islands themselves and, to a larger extent, along some of the peripheral coasts, where new facilities can be financed to provide America's winter playgound. Such activity provides, of course, an even more significant visual manifestation of Americanism in the Caribbean than other forms of enterprise. It ensures not only the acceptance and ready circulation of the US dollar as a currency supplementing the local one, but also that increasing numbers of people are brought into immediate contact with the representatives of the 'colossus of the north'. The Caribbean's climatic and other physical advantages for tourism add a powerful weapon to the armoury of US economic imperialism. They make its economies even more dependent on the United States, particularly from the point of view of the substantial amounts of local labour required in the industry, such that any policy decisions which inhibit American tourists will cause significant local unemployment, with a consequential adverse effect on the popularity of the government of the day. Thus the growth of tourism makes for 'friendship' between the United States and the governments of Caribbean nations. The prospects for diversifying the tourist trade away from its predominant American base are, moreover, relatively remote. Discretionary incomes in Western Europe are lower; the distances involved in travelling from Europe are much greater, and there exist 'intervening opportunities' around the Mediterranean. All these factors will, for the foreseeable future, keep the Caribbean tourist industry almost wholly dependent on the United States.

Thus today most geopolitical considerations affecting the Caribbean nations involve the United States, whose almost total dominance in and control over the region for a variety of reasons have, it is hoped, been clearly demonstrated. Even bearing this in mind, it would, nevertheless, be wrong to exclude all consideration of Caribbean relationships with non-great-power and non-European nations. Such relationships with the rest of the 'third world' seem likely to be of increasing importance in the last decades of the present century. First and foremost amongst those relationships are those with the rest of Latin America—particularly its most powerful states. The Guianas, Venezuela, and Colombia, in that they share long land frontiers with Brazil, have, of course, long had to be aware of Brazilian expansionism. They remain suspicious of her territorial claims to parts of virtually uninhabited Amazonia, which Brazil sees as part of her 'manifest destiny' to come to occupy and use. But Venezuela and Colombia, together with all the Spanish-speaking areas of the rest of the Caribbean, already consider themselves as much Latin American as the rest of South America. They are part of the 'inter-American system' and participate in Latin American organizations. Within the inter-American system, however, their small voices are usually effectively moulded to supporting the US position—a situation which sometimes upsets the larger Latin American powers which thereby always find themselves in a minority. Perhaps this is one reason why there was a lack of enthusiam for proposals that new Caribbean nation-states—in the main, formerly colonies of Britain—should be admitted to the OAS and other organizations. They were viewed as 'lobby-fodder' for the United States. There was the further fear that their recent colonial status would confer on some of them real economic advantages over the existing membership. Such advantages are probably more imagined than real, but there is an element of realism in their fears because of continued preferential trading arrangements that sometimes remain from the colonial period. Undeniable also is the ability of the recent ex-colonies to attract foreign (mainly metropolitan) capital more easily than the countries of Latin America with which the metropolitan powers are less familiar and about which there are often suspicions of instability and corruption. Such a situation becomes doubly dangerous when such capital could be used to establish industries which would then take advantage of a preferential Latin American trading-area arrangement to export goods to the rest of the continent. Prospects for Trinidad's indus-trialization have sometimes been presented in these terms—the local advantages she has for industrialization (low-cost energy, a good infra-structure, political stability, an adequate financial system, etc.), coupled with preferential entry for her goods to a Latin American market, would certainly enable her to compete effectively with even the bigger Latin American countries. However, these issues focus on the practical problems that have to be solved before the non-Spanish territories of the Caribbean area are fully welcomed into a Latin American system; the desirability in principle of such integration has become increasingly accepted by all parties concerned. The United States is certainly in favour of such a development, as has been demonstrated in the diplomatic and mediation efforts she has made in the dispute between Guyana and Venezuela and continues to make in that between Guatemala and British Honduras.

In another respect, however, both long-time and recently independent nations of the Caribbean area do have suspicions of the large Latin American nations which arise out of their own political and economic weaknesses of small size and small populations. These suspicions can be rationalized into a fear of economic imperialism; a fear which is most apparent in the relationships of Mexico with the small Central American countries to the south. To the countries between Guatemala and Costa Rica, Mexico hardly appears as a 'fellow-suffering developing nation', but rather as a second 'colossus of the north' whose industrial power exceeds that of all the central American nations put together, and whose industry, already more than large enough to supply the limited Mexican market, is increasingly seeking market openings in 'soft' areas. Central America—and some of the other smaller Caribbean island nations—appear to offer the softest and most 'natural' of the markets for Mexico's surplus production: a prospect which the Caribbean nations relish perhaps even less than the continued inflow of manufactured goods from North America.

With the rest of the world the Caribbean nations' contacts are tenuous, often not even extending to formal diplomatic relationships, though some of the nations do have important contacts through economic interests in common with other countries producing the same primary products. Thus, for example, several of the Central American countries and Columbia are signatories of the international coffee agreement, and Venezuela is a founder and leading member of the Organization of Petroleum Exporting Countries (OPEC), which brings her into close contact with the other major petroleum-producing countries mainly in the Middle East. Finally, all the countries share membership of the United Nations and its specialized agencies, and to some degree make common cause with developing nations elsewhere in the world, particularly over issues of economic and commercial relationships with the industrialized nations. Within the third world, however, the Caribbean nations are treated with some reserve because of their lack of revolutionary zeal and their normally unswerving support for the views of the United States on political issues. This support for the United States, as we have seen inevitably arising out of geopolitical relationships, seems likely to inhibit any attempts by the Caribbean nations to enhance their standing in the third world. In particular, it dampens the potential for closer contact with those countries of Africa and Asia which, in earlier centuries, supplied the colonial Caribbean with much of its population.

This analysis of the geopolitical relationships of the Caribbean with the outside world has tried to take account of the effects of political changes within the region—changes such as the recent achievement of independence by most of the former European colonies. In concluding, however, it is perhaps worth speculating on the possibility of a change in relationships with the rest of the world which might arise from further change within the area itself. Not that one wants to give the impression that there is a high propensity for change: the hegemony which has been established by the United States seems unlikely to be upset. Even the presence of Cuba, with her nationally declared aim of exporting revolution and her development as a centre for subversion in the area, seems insufficient to stimulate other than minor upsets in the absence of adequate support for Cuba's aims from outside the region. Such support is not forthcoming from the Soviet Union, while China is, for the moment at least, incapable of supplying it. A somewhat more important element for change within the region emerges from hopes, and sometimes efforts, to achieve a higher degree of unity between the large number of small political units. However, not even the external stimulus and help of Britain in the immediate post-colonial period could persuade the former British territories to form a West Indian Federation, and the individual colonies have each gone their own way. Since then it has been difficult to discern any progress at all towards any form of unity, even between islands with the same language and similar cultural background. Greater political and economic strength in dealing with the outside world, arising from greater internal cohesion amongst the member states, seems to be getting ever more remote. Difficulties have arisen even for the Central American Common Market, which had previously appeared to be so successful. Since its formation some ten years ago, it has established not only a series of integrated institutions, such as a development bank, but also part at least of the political consensus required for the implementation of economic measures which treat the area concerned as a whole, rather than as a series of separate nation-states. Economic integration in that part of the Caribbean perhaps points the way in which the region's many small nations can begin to assert themselves positively in their relationships with the outside world. Otherwise they will remain merely the pawns in a game played in the Caribbean by the outside world as part of a wider struggle for power.

3 The Ex-Colonial Society in Jamaica

DOUGLAS HALL

THE Caribbean area offers large scope for comparative studies in colonial history. It also offers supporting evidence for those who indulge in comparative stereotyping of imperial policies and achievements. Some people think, for instance, of Cuba: full of voluble, excitable Latins, always torn by some deep controversy, and often by gunfire, the breeding-ground of dictators and of revolutionaries; and of Jamaica: less than a hundred miles south, full of black and coloured people whose native excitability and ignorance have been curbed and remedied by British government, British trade, parliamentary democracy, and the rule of law; to produce, over the centuries, a comparatively stable, dependable, political society, educated to conduct business on the right side of the fence. Evidence of these sorts of assessment abounds.

This chapter attempts to examine some of the deeper subtleties of the consequences of imperial control, and to show how the metropolitan-colonial relationship itself, as distinct from any individual acts of imperial exploitation or oppression, can be debilitating to the colonial society. In order to do this some historical background is necessary.

In Jamaica, under British rule, we have never had indigenous populations and settlers eyeing each other with jealousy, mistrust, and scorn. We have been an entirely imported society.[1] There were, for a long time, masters and slaves, and society was cut into its clear divisions of those who owned and those who were owned. But while plantation slavery divided, it also bound the free and the unfree in a terrible, sadistic intimacy. Planters lashed their slaves; but they also played with them.

The English did not introduce slavery to the Caribbean, but they learned to use it and they developed the use of it. They did this because they wanted to produce sugar and they needed a labour force. There were early attempts to provide, by forms of indenture, a labouring population of whites; but demand outran the limits of this supply and so the recourse to Africans began: not because they were black, or stronger, or less easily burned by the sun; but because they could be had in large numbers.

[1] By the time of the English conquest of the island from the Spaniards in 1655 the indigenous Arawak Indians had entirely disappeared.

Later, when African slavery was well begun, when the slave populations were sufficiently numerous, and the working whites diminished in number, the myth grew that Europeans could not labour in the tropical heat. The notion that certain occupations carry more prestige than others has always been accepted. The estate-owner, or manager, clearly was, and still is, considered to hold a more important position than the cane-cutter. But on the slave-estates it was also established that only negroes could be cane-cutters.

And so, for nearly two centuries, we were kept as a slave-worked plantation colony producing sugar and other tropical staples for export. With our small resources devoted to production for export we became dependent on imports. The siting of our important towns on the coastlines had nothing to do with aesthetic values or even with comfort. It reflected the dominant importance of the overseas connection. The ships brought governors, soldiers, imperial instructions, and essential supplies for the support of the plantation system; they took away the produce of the estates. Confined, for the most part, to the small transactions of unpaid slave-labourers whose chief efforts lay in estate production, the domestic sector scarcely grew and the economic preoccupation with exports and imports bred its social consequences. The eyes of those who conducted affairs were focused abroad where the markets lay. Moreover, because we were British and were tied by regulation, and then by association, primarily to the British market, our economic as well as our political welfare depended on conditions prevailing in the all-powerful metropolis. Even now, with political independence, we still look to 'the ship' with subservience. Because we live by exports we tend to ask questions about what people abroad will buy. Because of our dependence on imports we tend to look abroad for the necessities and the comforts we want. In short, we have not been taught by experience to begin with questions about our own needs and our own means of supplying them. We have learned to be first curious about the needs and the products of others.

In the Caribbean slave colonies people belonged to one or other of three main classes: the few whites, the growing number of free coloured people,[2] and the mass of slaves. Each class contained its own hierarchy, and within each class there was some room for social mobility; but between classes the lines were firmly drawn. Whites were free, but none of them was coloured. The free coloureds were neither slave nor white. The slaves were the unfree property of the others. And in this society, obviously, the attributes of the élite were whiteness, wealth, and education,

[2] Originating as children of white masters and slave women.

in that order. The greatest wealth belonged to the whites, a higher education was available only to the wealthy who could afford to go abroad to get it.

The abolition of slavery ostensibly removed the legal supports of these divisions. After 1 August 1838 all were equal citizens—according to the law, but not according to the general social view or in the eyes of those who were the makers and the administrators of the law. Still, it was now theoretically possible for a man to make his way up the ladder. In practice, the climb was hard and long; and for the majority, even of those who wished to attempt it, it was impossible. Slavery, as a legal institution had gone; but the society shaped by slavery remained with its criteria of whiteness, wealth, and education. And these criteria were upheld by British opinion of the proper structure of society; and by the myth that whites could not labour in the tropics.

In the social climb whiteness could be achieved only by long-term planning and parental strategy. But in the nineteenth century, as the fortunes of sugar-planting declined, fewer whites came out and many went back home in disappointment and bankruptcy. Improving the colour, by marriage or rather by concubinage, became less easy. Wealth was harder to achieve. So too, therefore, was education. The social climbers consequently became frustrated; and because it became harder to go up, they became even more determined that they should not slide down. The aspiring middle class felt the ladder becoming slippery when they were only half-way up. They therefore firmly drew a line beneath them to prove that they were not half-way down. Masters and slaves were no more. They had been succeeded by the 'we's' and the 'they's'.

Very few seemed to be aware of the growing irrelevance of whiteness, wealth, and education as measures of excellence in populations overwhelmingly composed of blacks, in islands in which the historical basis of wealth was in decline, and in communities in which village dames and catechists offered their largely irrelevant lessons to the uninterested.

In Jamaica, in October 1865, a group of small peasant farmers objected to a legal conviction following a charge of trespass laid against them by an estate owner. The event sparked off an accumulation of grievance and there was a riot. The riot was immediately defined, by the Governor, and by local people of influence, and by some of the black and coloured, as a 'Negro rebellion'. It was violently put down and the elected Jamaican Legislative Assembly, after 200 years of existence, abolished itself in favour of a form of Crown Colony Government. This act reflected both the prejudices of the Governor and the uneasiness of the established élite who feared the growth of popular influence in the electoral process.

Crown Colony government brought its administrative establishment of British officials. The responsible officers of government were no longer locally recruited. Metropolitan control, always distantly acknowledged, now became a clear and visual presence. Benevolent paternalism succeeded local oligarchy. They both have this in common: that those who govern say to those who are governed, 'listen and I'll tell you what is good for you'. The difference is that whereas benevolent paternalism is by definition benevolent, oligarchic government is not.

Crown Colony government, with successive modifications, lasted for seventy-eight years. In a way, it was surprising that it stayed so long. The old Assembly had yielded, in part because of growing demands for more popular representation in government. Crown Colony government did not answer that demand. The appearance of white British Colonial Service personnel magnified the frustrations of local people already slipping on their way up the social and occupational ladders. With their white skins, comparatively high salaries and perquisites, and their presumably better education, the administrators seemed to support a continuing relevance of the old criteria.

Commenting on the performance of Crown Colony Government, the report of the Moyne Commission, following further riots in 1938, contained the indictment: 'The efforts of Your Majesty's Government and of the Colonial Governments concerned have failed to make for radical reform.'[3] Clear, but irrelevant. The purposes of Crown Colony government had been to introduce order and economy in the administration, to further the economic prospects of the colony as an exporter of agricultural staples, and to advance the general social welfare of what was described as the 'labouring' population. These objectives, surely, were intended not to achieve, but to prevent, radical reform. The Moyne Commission report concluded that what was needed was money to enable spending on economic development and social welfare. But even after 1945, when the Colonial Development and Welfare organization began to operate, the emphasis was on welfare rather than on development; and it certainly had nothing to do with *change*, which is, presumably, the aim of any radical reform. The cake would be bigger, it was hoped; but the recipe was not to be much altered, and although it was intended that the slices should be more generous, they were to be cut in the accustomed proportions.

In 1944, after the riots of the late 1930s and the emergence of political

[3] GB, West India Royal Commission, 1938-9, *Report*, Cmd 6607 (1945).

parties based on militant trade union membership,[4] Crown Colony Government in Jamaica ended. A new constitution reintroduced representative government. There was to be a nominated Legislative Council, but a House of forty-eight Representatives was to be elected by universal adult suffrage.

Similar developments were taking place in the other British Caribbean colonies, and in 1945 moves openly began towards the creation of a self-governing dominion of the Federation of the West Indies. The British government supported the idea of federation, and they had long done so, chiefly for reasons of administrative tidiness, efficiency, and economy. In the Caribbean, large agricultural producers had for some time recognized the advantages of co-operation in bargaining for export prices and quotas and various producers' associations were already in existence. In addition, the intellectual middle classes, stirred by the events of the late 1930s and the early 1940s, had begun to feel a national fervour. For the first time, Caribbean writers and artists were producing works using the idiom and the imagery of their islands. By no means all the artists were of middle-class origin, but their Caribbean readers were; and their influence on this limited readership was increased when it was learned that the London critics had bestowed their praise. The move towards federation had some local administrative, economic, and intellectual support; but it did not have mass support. The people were not administrators, or large-scale producers, or readers of books and frequenters of art galleries. Of course, federations do not have to be built on popular support. But if they are not they must be imposed, and the imposition must be determined.

The Federal Government of the West Indies was created in April 1958. It was neither popularly supported, in the wide sense, nor forcibly imposed. Moreover, in writing the federal constitution our draftsmen had spent long hours studying the constitutions of the Canadian, the American, and the Australian federations. They had not given much

---

[4] In 1938–9, following widespread riots, Alexander Bustamante formed the Bustamante Industrial Trade Union (BITU) and Norman Manley formed the People's National Party (PNP), with dominion status for Jamaica as its objective. In 1943, consequent on a split between the two leaders, Bustamante formed the Jamaica Labour Party (JLP). Thereafter BITU support for the PNP dwindled. In the 1944 elections under the newly introduced universal adult suffrage the JLP swept the polls. In 1949 Manley brought together, into a Trade Union Congress, workers' organizations other than the BITU, but in the elections of that year the JLP again won the majority of seats, though the total number of votes cast for the PNP was slightly larger. In 1952 Manley registered the National Workers' Union. Since then the essential feature of party political organization has been the opposition of the two massive JLP/BITU and PNP/NWU. In the 1955 and 1959 elections the PNP were elected; in 1962 and 1966 the JLP were returned to power. See articles by Bradley and Phelps in *Soc. & Econ. Stud.*, Dec. 1960.

time to creative thinking based on Caribbean circumstances and needs. And in any case, if they had turned up with some strange constitutional scheme, how would the Mother of Parliaments have received it? Yet it seems a pity that so little attention was given to the writings of some who, like Simón Bolívar, were nearer home and had also said some very relevant things.

The Federal Government began to disintegrate in 1961, when Jamaica, and then Trinidad early in 1962, withdrew from it. Clearly, we held less in common than we thought. We had all been plantation colonies; but as such we had each looked separately to Britain. Inter-colonial communication was small. We had each corresponded with London rather than with one another. In addition, our peoples' politicians, recently come to office, were nervous of deserting their home grounds and close contact with their constituents in favour of election to a distant federal parliament. The fact that the Federal Government had little control over revenue, and small power, increased their reluctance. That was no place for the ambitious, nor did it tempt the able. Very few of our politicians or administrators of recognized ability went willingly to the federal capital.

In August 1962 Jamaica became an independent self-governing dominion in the British Commonwealth. Free of imperial controls, free of federal restraints, we would now 'go it alone'. But where? and in what style?

During its course of nearly 200 years the slave-holding society had clearly established its forms and its criteria. In the years since the emancipation there had been economic decline and social and political confusion. The influence of the old élite of white, prosperous planters, had declined; but no other group had clearly superseded them in the hierarchy. The great changes had come in too quick succession to allow new consolidation. The social upheaval of the abolition of slavery had been followed ten years later by economic decline when after the Sugar Duties Act of 1846[5] the estates faced the competition of foreign producers in an open British market. Twenty-years after that, before either the large social and economic questions had been resolved, and largely because they had not been, there had come radical political change with the institution of Crown Colony Government.

Almost immediately afterwards, in the last quarter of the nineteenth century, there had come further economic disturbance. The invasion of the British market by European subsidized beet-sugars had brought

---

[5] By which the preference given to British colonial sugar entering Britain was gradually removed over the next eight years.

further distress to the sugar planters;[6] and at the same time, from un-related and quite fortuitous beginnings, the peasant farmers had greatly benefited by the opening up and rapid growth of a trade in bananas with the United States.[7] The incompatibilities of successful peasant farming and successful sugar-estate farming began to make themselves clear.

In the twentieth century, the effects of two world wars and long economic depression had emphasized both the dangers of dependence on the export trade and the importance of domestic food production. But too great a concentration on the latter, in a small island with limited agricultural and industrial resources, would obviously lead to a reduction of living standards for the middle and upper classes in particular.

And so, as we approached 1962, neither the way ahead nor the manner of going was clear. Yet another major disaster had only recently occurred in the sad short progress of the federal attempt. Yet there seemed reason for hope. Not because we were on our own; but because during the past generation and a half the old, hampering, criteria of whiteness, wealth and education had been seriously undermined and the way seemed open for creative thinking and vigorous enterprise in the making of a new society. Black Jamaicans had learned from Marcus Garvey in the 1920s that their inferior position in society was not ordained by God. Politically, and in his economic enterprises, Garvey behaved with a naïveté that was sometimes astounding. But he was profound in his conviction of the fundamental equality of men, no matter what their colour. His great lesson, if it can be summed up briefly, was that the giving and receiving of respect had nothing to do with black, or brown, or white, but with character and behaviour. Jamaican workers, and this meant black Jamaicans, had also learned from Alexander Bustamante and others in the 1930s that they should claim more than the meagre share previously allotted to them. The supremacy of whiteness had come under heavy fire.

The abolition of property qualifications for electoral candidates and for the electorate, in the 1940s, gave opportunity to the poor man to make his way in politics. Wealth could be achieved through office. No longer was office reserved for the comparatively wealthy. Unfortunately, there is not any obviously greater merit in seeking office in order to obtain wealth than there is in using wealth to gain office. But the point is that the views of wealth and of office had changed. They were no longer the prerogative of the established élite. They were open to all who could

---

[6] See R.W. Beachey, *The British West Indies Sugar Industry in the Late 19th Century* (Oxford, 1957).

[7] See Hall, *Ideas and Illustrations in Economic History* (New York, 1964), ch. 4 & 5.

contrive, whether black or brown or white. This is not to say that the contrivance was easy.

The place of education, too, had changed. It was becoming more widely available. Elected governments always build schools because construction work gives employment, employment gives votes, and elementary schooling enables voters to read propaganda and to mark ballot papers correctly. These are not, of course, the *only* reasons; but they are not insignificant ones. In the past, although only the rich could afford education, not all the rich were educated. But those who were enjoyed an additional prestige because their education had been received abroad, in the schools and universities of Britain, Europe, and America, and because they were in the minority. In the minds of most Jamaicans, BA spelled 'culture'. Education was a decorative thing. This had been simply a reflection of an earlier British view. But by the 1950s we had begun to hear a good deal more about functional education—training for jobs and training for good citizenship. It is, however, easier to describe a job than to define good citizenship. It is therefore more difficult to say what educational content is relevant to the latter purpose. Be that as it may, it was abundantly clear, even in the 1950s, that the education of Jamaicans was practically empty of relevance to Jamaican needs. In our schools we were brought up on English literature, English history, English geography, and mathematical quizzes about the times trains took to travel from London to Glasgow if they ran at x or y miles an hour. In the process of learning, where the facts were irrelevant and the imagery foreign, we counted on memory rather than on understanding. More dangerous still, we came to assume that the only information worth acquiring was about people, places, ideas, and things abroad. It was not difficult to swallow this assumption. Our long subservience to 'the ship' had prepared us for it. Our monuments, our folk-lore, our history, and our social institutions were left to the often amateur curiosity of a few expatriate intellectuals who presumably already knew all that was worth knowing and so had time to dabble in the luxury of the inconsequential.

I do not mean to deny the competence or the sincerity of some of these people, or the importance which we now attach to the work they began. I simply state the Jamaican view of what they were doing; and indicate one reason why, as we prepared for independence, we failed to seize the opportunity for change. Since we knew and cared little about what we were, we could scarcely attempt to say what we should like to be or how to achieve it.

The framers of our political constitution for independence had, like their federal predecessors, displayed great energy and little, if any, creativity. With very minor deviations we readily assumed the garb of Westminster, and our members of the new parliament, bewigged or frock-coated, took their opposite seats as Her Majesty's Government and Her Majesty's Loyal Opposition. Eight years later we still have our two political parties, well balanced one against the other, and only occasionally disturbed by rumours of a third. We have our Speaker, our Cabinet, our front-benchers, our backbenchers, our Hansard, and all the trappings. We are sometimes priased for the stability of our two-party system; the envy, it is assumed, of other Commonwealth Caribbean nations in whose governments one party clearly dominates; and, of course, the democratic example to the wayward Cubans. The façade is impressive. Let us look behind it.

Jamaica contains just over 4,400 square miles, and a population rapidly approaching 2 m. Just over half the land is productive farm, forest, and pasture. About 40 per cent is unproductive, either permanent waste or undeveloped. About 5 per cent is urban area.[8] The most densely populated area is the capital, Kingston, and the surrounding urban and suburban lowlands of the parish of St Andrew. Here, in particular, but throughout the island generally, there is large unemployment and under-employment. The effect of this on party political behaviour is clear.

Population & Employment in Jamaica, April 1960

Parishes	Approx. area (sq. miles)	Population (nearest 000)	Density per sq. mile	Total labour force*	Unemployed	Percentage labour force unemployed
Kingston	8	123,400	15,425	58,100	10,800	19
St Andrew	166	296,000	1,783	136,200	22,200	16
Rest of country	4,070	1,190,000	292	454,100	49,000	11

* Presumably economically active population.

Sources: Jamaica, Ann. Abstract Statist, 1967, no. 26, tables 1 (p. 2) & 10 (p. 9); Jamaica, Central Planning Unit, Five-Year Independence Plan, 1963–8 (1963), p.36.

Vote for me and you might get a job. Vote for my opponent and, if I win, you probably won't. Harass my opponent in his electoral campaign and get a hand-out for a meal. The parties have no need for philosophies other than the simple creed of bribery. Indeed, as some well-meaning politicians have discovered, to have a policy and a programme can be

[8] See John Macpherson, Caribbean Lands (London, 1967), p. 42.

disastrous. The strongest position is one of non-commitment to anything but to the party. Ideologies and principles are dangerous; flexibility and room for manœuvre are all-important. In saying this about Jamaican political behaviour let me also say that I see the same conditions elsewhere; and although there are different illnesses behind the similar symptoms, I suggest one ailment in common: the beginning of the breakdown of parliamentary democracy as we are accustomed to think of it in terms of party-political organization. Perhaps, then, in Jamaica the trouble is that we have come into possession of an obsolescent system. Whatever the cause, it appears that the system of government which we have inherited from Britain is inappropriate; perhaps to the needs of the mid-twentieth century and certainly to the circumstances of Jamaica.

The most damaging consequence of powerful colonialism such as Britain exercised is the encouragement it gives to imitation and the deterrence to creativity. Authority lies in the metropolis. Colonial action is subject to that authority. It is always safer, therefore, to ask first if what we plan to do would be approved. Thus colonials learn that there is a higher judgement than their own. When colonials need help and advice, they tend first to turn to the metropolis. And because advice from the source of authority carries great weight, colonials learn that expert opinion lies outside their boundaries. In consequence, colonialism breeds a tendency to deference rather than confidence; and since the metropolis is most likely to approve attitudes and institutions which are similar to, or at least not incompatible with its own, colonialism breeds a tendency to imitation rather than creativity. Our institutions and our literature offer abundant examples of this lack of self-confidence. So does our present behaviour.

A clear illustration lies in our great propensity to ask for 'expert' opinion from overseas. If we want to fatten our pigs we send for an expert. If we want to change the school curriculum we send for an expert. If we want to build a dam we send for an expert. There can be no objection in principle to the use of experts; but there seem to be certain very important guide-lines to the proper choice and use of them. To begin with, in the employment of 'experts' it is wise to examine very carefully the mouth of the gift-horse. Free experts are often more free than expert. Secondly, it is nearly always better to send a good local man in search of information and advice than to invite someone in to give it. The visiting expert is usually a stranger to the country and its people; and if he is really any good, usually ends up having learned far more than he taught. Thirdly, the proper way to use an expert is to tell him the problem and ask his advice; the improper way is to invite him to state the problem for you

D

95761

in the first place. Finally, and perhaps most important of all, half-a-dozen individual experts, no matter how well-qualified and how helpful each may be in his particular job, are very likely to be less useful than a team of lesser geniuses who work in collaboration. At least the team may be expected to produce one policy and one design rather than six conflicting ones.

The uncertainties and insecurities are substantial in the state of the economy which offers little cause for confidence. Economists write of 'the race between development and discontent' and underline the essential difficulty:

Unemployment is clearly the major social and economic problem in Jamaica. The levels of unemployment and underemployment are high and are in part a result of the rapid growth of population. Unemployment is particularly high in the case of women and young persons, and there are serious difficulties facing school-leavers in regard to obtaining employment.[9]

Their concern can only be magnified when they consider the fact that the Jamaican population is largely a young one.

Population: Age-groups (to nearest ooo), 1965 (est.)

Age in years	No. (ooo)	Per cent
0–4	317	17·5
5–14	514	28·4
15–24	315	17·4
25–34	188	10·4
35–44	149	8·2
45–54	140	7·7
55–64	106	5·9
65 +	80	4·4
Total	1,809	100·0

Source: Ann. Abstract Statist. 1968, p. 14

Primarily, we remain an agricultural country in which the best agricultural land is occupied by the estates. The estates are, in general, efficiently managed; but efficiency does not equal economy. Our estates suffer from smallness of size, which limits economies of scale in their operation; and from the high cost of labour. Our precarious position in the markets for the produce of the estates is clearly indicated by the frequency with which we send people abroad in search of preferences, guaranteed prices, and

[9] Five Year Independence Plan, 1963–8, p. 11, 36.

quotas. But even if we did reduce costs by further substituting machinery for labour we should simply add to massive unemployment. In short, the society at large would pay for the sugar industry's gains. The time has come, it would seem, to begin the planning of a strategic withdrawal from sugar production. But we are a little mesmerized by the long drumming into our heads of the importance of the welfare of the sugar industry to the welfare of the country at large.

Because the estates are comparatively efficient and well provided, the government's agricultural policies have been directed rather to the development of peasant agriculture and small-farming. The amount and variety of aid given in the form of grants, credits, marketing facilities, and agricultural extension, has enormously increased and has not been unproductive. But unfortunately, there are two large motives behind the programmes: one is to increase agricultural skills and productivity; the other is to stem the flow of people from the rural areas into Kingston. Farmers can get money, urban dwellers cannot. A good deal of so-called agricultural assistance is in fact a form of subsidy to those who stay out of town and, in the long run, lends to a further fragmentation of small-farm units which is contrary to the expressed aims of agricultural policy.

The answer, it may be, lies in the reduction of population and of the rate of population growth.[10] The first, at least, seemed clear to those who emigrated or who wish to emigrate. But we have discovered that in those countries we have learned about as places of great wealth and opportunity though our labour may be welcomed we, as people of colour, are not. More effective than emigration would be birth-control. But some are opposed in principle, and in any case education in the use of devices takes time and money, both of which are short. It is not easy now to persuade people that they are multiplying too rapidly when for nearly 300 years they have been told that they were not multiplying fast enough. The estate owners, supported by the Colonial Office, were all in favour of large populations and cheap labour, until the trade unions appeared. Only recently have they discovered the greater uses of machinery.

There is no doubt that the structure of the Jamaican economy is now more attractive than it was fifteen years ago, or that the national production and income have increased. The range of exports has widened from the old dependence on agricultural staples to include minerals and mineral products and manufactured goods. Partly as a result of the discovery of

---

[10] 1960 census: 1·6 m. 1967: 1·9 m. (est). Average annual rate of population growth (1960–7): 2·3. After migration to Britain had been reduced to a trickle, the growth-rate went up by almost half.

bauxite and the development of that industry the value of domestic exports rapidly increased from £J17·3 m. in 1952 to £J62·1 m. in 1962.[11] Another indicator of growth is the national income per capita, which increased from £J15·1 in 1938 to £J136·7 in 1962. But, and here lies the heart of the matter, the economists also point out that 'although these figures are indicative of the progress made, they do not show the distribution of the income'.[12] There are the expected inequalities of wage-rates between various occupations, most strikingly between agriculture and mining; but even more productive of discontent is the distinction between those who are gainfully employed and the growing number of those who are not.

Average Weekly Earnings (£J) of Workers in Selected Industries

	Agri-culture	Mining	Manu-facture	Construction		Utilities		Com-merce	Trans-port & comm.	Selected services
				Pte.	Govt.	Pte.	Govt.			
Mar. 1963	3·7	18·3	6·6	8·7	2·3	17·8	3·0	10·2	7·2	5·4
Mar. 1964	3·7	20·0	6·9	8·3	2·7	17·2	3·3	11·1	7·6	5·9

Source: *Ann. Abstract Statist.*, 1967, no. 26, p. 115, table 137.

The bauxite industry, an extreme illustration, uses little labour. It is heavily mechanized, calls for a few skilled workers rather than a mass of labour, and labour costs are but a small proportion of total costs. The industry can afford to pay high wage-rates and in consequence there have been created around the mining and smelting operations pockets of workers whose incomes are high above those earned by people in the surrounding agricultural areas. This creates pressures on the general wage structure which, though they would lead to a very desirable end, are in our present (and foreseeable) circumstances embarrassing. Following the example of Puerto Rico and recommendations made by economists, we began, in the early 1950s, to encourage the setting up of light manufacturing industries. The main advantages to be derived were the provision of employment, the introduction of new skills, and a basic diversification of the economy. The government provided various incentives to attract investors. But we live in a very competitive world in which small, unimportant, high-cost producers cannot thrive. Because our trade unions are highly organized, wage-rates are high. Therefore, wherever possible, manufacturers introduce machinery. We gain by the skills and the consequent diversification of production; but the essential matter,

---

[11] Until Sept. 1969 £J = £1 sterling.   [12] *Five Year Independence Plan*, pp. 20–1.

unemployment, is hardly affected.[13] The incidence of unemployment does not diminish; and since our political parties are so firmly based on rival trade unions, government policies of wage restraint are politically dangerous and the possibilities of establishing labour-intensive rather than capital-intensive enterprises are weakened.

The impressive overall growth of the 1950s has not been sustained. Gross domestic product at current prices has declined from an average annual growth-rate of 7·9 per cent during 1963–6, to 5·0 per cent in 1967; and allowances must be made for the influence of rising prices on that calculation.[14] Rapid population growth, the impossibility of creating new employment at an equal rate (not to mention absorbing the backlog of present unemployment) and the clear imbalance between the agricultural and the mining and manufacturing sectors, provide the economists' nightmares. The 1968 budget provides for still greater financial assistance to agriculture, the lagging sector upon whose improvement, it is said, depends any 'real progress in solving the problem of unemployment'.[15] But the solution cannot lie in loans to farmers. A basic reconsideration of the systems of land tenure and of land use, with determination to plan for radical change, seem to be the obvious first steps toward solid achievement.

The island's third largest 'export' industry is tourism, which has rapidly expanded during the past fifteen years and now brings in about £29 m. a year. The problems raised by tourism are social rather than economic. As a dollar earner the trade is encouraged by the economists. But its influences are socially deplorable. The blame lies not with the tourists but with us. Because of our poverty and because of our basic lack of self-respect and self-confidence, we treat the tourist as a rich man to be robbed or as a god to be propitiated. We offer small goods and services for high prices, we beg for alms, we demand tips, we tell him how much we need him, and we try our best to show him what happy dancing souls the 'natives' are. Some of these features are common to tourism everywhere; but we are distinguished by a lack of confidence in our own house and an absence of real pride in our possessions, which we are satisfied to display chiefly as 'curiosities'. This is not surprising. Our colonial experience never led us to believe that we had anything of much value except sugar, bananas, and the tropical climate in which they thrive. But it is

[13] Twenty-three new industries established in 1962, involving a total investment of £3½ m, were expected to provide jobs for only 1,460 persons (Jamaica Govt., *Five-Year Independence Plan, 1963–8*, p.16).

[14] Jamaica, Central Planning Unit, *Econ. Survey of Jamaica, 1967*, p. 14.

[15] *West Indies Chronicle*, May 1968 (The West India Committee, London), p. 221, article 'Budget boost for Jamaica's economy'.

doubly unfortunate, since it encourages the tourist, at best, to offer high praise to our beaches and faint praise to us.

From these accounts the essential political and social challenges emerge. Have we the courage to attempt to create some new constitutional form which while protecting the rights of the individual citizen, and ensuring safety from the assumption of any dictatorial authority, would eliminate the obvious dangers of the present system of government? Ideally, the party political system assumes the existence of competing parties with competing policies offered to a discerning electorate. It assumes the right of any one party to win support away from another by the reasonable means of alternative proposal and successful argument. In Jamaica, party politics have been marked rather by physical assault, insult, and bribery; there is little tolerance shown by either side to the voter who is not clearly committed; and the one who is, is likely to be beaten rather than wooed by the opposing faction. Because of massive unemployment and the close relationship between rival political parties and their supporting trade unions, armies of support rather than bodies of opinion have tended to develop. There is obvious danger in this, and it is well recognized by the politicians themselves. Unfortunately, they too are in large measure slaves to circumstance, and so their response has been to arm and strengthen the police. The confrontation is more dangerous than we openly admit.

Obviously, there are political as well as economic reasons for concern about the rapid rate of population growth. And this raises the large social problem, for the mere reduction of population size cannot answer everything. The greatest need is for confidence, and this is hard to instil in a poor society, in which the standards of value are obscure, in which life is a scramble, and in which every move by every other man is suspect because the race is rough.

On some of the street walls in Kingston and the larger towns there are roughly painted signs which read: 'Birth-control is a scheme to get rid of black people.' Colour distinctions are still with us. But increasingly in Jamaica reference to colour, except in very straightforward descriptive use, is a reference not to shade of skin but to pattern of behaviour. 'White people' are those who have chosen to adopt or to continue in a European rather than a local way of life and thinking. In this sense some 'blacks' are very 'white'.

But it is no longer necessary to be 'white', either in colour or in behaviour, to get to the top. Once at the top, however, the temptation to adopt 'whiteness' is felt. This is not difficult to understand. Opportunity is, for most people, still very small. The majority remain, but with less patience, in their familiar world of poverty. The more enterprising manœuvre for position, and once they achieve it they do all they can to make their achievement both obvious and permanent. If ever they sink back, or even appear to do so, they might never recover lost ground. Somehow, their 'difference' must be established for all to see. Where opportunity is scarce, the search for patronage is keen. One way to demonstrate and to bolster superior position is by the exercise of patronage. Those who command it use patronage to win friends and influence people. Those who pretend to position pretend to have patronage also. In part, this also is a legacy of slavery and of colonial status. The slave, who had no rights, enjoyed privilege only at the allowance of his master. The colonial looked to his metropolitan governor and administrator for preference. But patronage, and its opposite, blackmail, thrive best in small societies, such as Jamaica, where anonymity is difficult to preserve. Jamaica will always be a small society. Population growth cannot alter that, for the 'smallness' of a society is a function of social propinquity and geographical size. In Jamaica, people live close together, and the divisions of social class are not now so clear as they used to be.

Familiarity need not bring contempt, but it will certainly wash away mystery, awe, and majesty. The judge looks less formidable in his wig and gown if we have often seen him in his shorts. There is consequently some compensating advantage in smallness. It can lead to straighter talking and to the substitution of earned respect for pomp and circumstance. But in Jamaica that will take time. In the days of slavery, in the traditional hierarchy of the estate personnel, in the system of Crown Colony government, communication ran, for the most part, in a one-way traffic, downwards. The high officials and the bosses issued the orders which were passed on to those who passed them on to others who carried them out. Labourers were expected to give labour, not opinion. This is no longer true. Trade unionism and adult suffrage have given importance to the voice of the labourer. But we are still accustomed to the assumption that important offices are always held by important men; and we are still reluctant to risk the challenge of authority. In the long years of our history that has been a dangerous exercise. Nowadays, moreover, even though we feel freer to offer criticism, we are little practised in the arts of discussion and inquiry. We deal rather in assertion and counter-assertion, in which the louder and the stronger frequently silence those who may be right.

We are not alone in this. There are others who, even less fortunate than we, have apparently abandoned the arts of discussion in favour of loud assertion. Less and less do we hear in international affairs, or even in the domestic affairs of older nations, the voices of those who really seek understanding.

And since we are a small, weak country in a world of larger and more powerful ones, we find it difficult to practise discussion. We are almost threatened into one or the other of the camps of assertion. If we ask too many questions we become suspect. And so the choice lies between inquiry at great cost or acceptance with the reward of patronage and protection. It is not strange that we seem to have chosen the latter course. The great opposing ideologies, each engaged in massive defence, do not like neutrality or middle-of-the-road attitudes. Each justifies itself and accuses the other. Where the great emphasis is on justification and defence, discussion wears thin and creativity is throttled.

Our chances of making a new society by processes of self-examination, by devising institutions more fitted to our needs and circumstances; and above all, by discovering some new and acceptable criteria of social achievement, are thus handicapped not only by our colonial heritage and our present domestic difficulties, but also by the international environment. This, none the less, stands as the greatest and most important of all the challenges that face us in the ex-colonial society, for these analytical and creative enterprises constitute the essence of the process known as 'decolonization'. Above all, the need is for confidence in ourselves, the courage to look where we will, and, taking stock from our own history and the relevant experiences of others, to build for ourselves in accordance with our newly-calculated needs, priorities, and resources.

Perhaps it should be made clear that to speak of the damage of colonialism and the inadequacies or irrelevancies of the colonial heritage is not necessarily to lay blame on the imperial power. Undoubtedly, certain specific policies and actions were culpable. But what I have been discussing here is the consequence of the relationship between metropolitan and colonial societies; and just as masters, as much as slaves, were affected by slavery, so it is not only ex-colonials who now have cause for stocktaking. In the long colonial relationship we came to know our masters very well. Masters sometimes indulge a curiosity about their servants; servants always study their masters. In the colonial relationship there was always the assumption of the inferiority of the colonial. That remains the greatest hazard to both the ex-colonial and the ex-imperial societies.

4 Foreign Influence in Guyana: the Struggle for Independence[1]

COLIN V. F. HENFREY

In discussing foreign influence in the context of Guyana, one faces an immediate problem: how is it to be defined? Given that the country's conception and growth are inherently colonial—both in the general sense of the economic and social structure and the more specific one of a traditional orientation towards one metropolitan power—where is one to draw the line between internal propensities and external influence? Or even between influence and intervention? Disagreement over this problem tends to reduce discussions of the topic to rhetorical recriminations between two camps with opposed preconceptions.[2] It can also be seen as the basis of the deep and continuing rift in practical Guyanese politics.

The best way to examine this rift without getting trapped in the rhetoric is to trace its historical growth. Its immediate background is as follows. When the former British colony became an independent state in May 1966, the government consisted of a coalition between two of the three major parties, the People's National Congress (PNC) and the United Force (UF); whilst the former describes itself as socialist, the latter had a narrow-based, mainly middle-class following and an explicitly marked capitalist ideology. This unlikely partnership sprang from their mutual opposition to the militantly socialist People's Progressive Party (PPP), which had dominated the politics of the pre-independence period and had still gained the largest number of seats in the previous (1964) election. In the election of December 1968, however, the PNC gained an overall if widely questioned majority which enabled it to abandon its coalition with the UF.

[1] For the sake of consistency, the spelling 'Guyana', adopted since independence, is used throughout, even when referring to the former British Guiana. Works cited in an abbreviated form in footnotes are listed in full on p. 81.
[2] Unfortunately the literature divides mainly along these lines. Examples of this on either side are Philip Reno, *The Ordeal of British Guiana* (New York, 1964) and Cheddi Jagan (1966) (see bibliography), as opposed to Michael Swan, *British Guiana* (London, 1957) and Peter Simms (1966).The only impartial and reasonably documented full length studies are Raymond Smith (1962) and Peter Newman (1964), on both of which I have largely drawn in this section. Unless otherwise stated, facts and figures given are based on these two works.

Meanwhile the government, whilst describing itself as neutral, had stated its interest in membership of the OAS (though the border dispute with Venezuela temporarily ruled this out) and had an economic policy which relied correspondingly on almost exclusively western aid, investment, and trade. It was clearly this position which, from 1964 onwards, ensured the political and economic Anglo-American support previously so long denied to the PPP government; and equally clearly, without this support the PNC could hardly have consolidated its power as it did in the 1968 elections, whether or not it did so legitimately. The joint Anglo-American and PNC justification for their mutual partiality is that the consequent *status quo* is more conducive to progress and stability, both hemispheric and Guyanese, than was that of the past; and that it offers better prospects for Guyanese democracy. The country's connections with the west have in no way affected her sovereignty, either internally or as regards foreign affairs. The PPP reply to this, ideologically at least, is now basically Marxist–Leninist, with overtones of Castro and Fanon: Guyana's formal independence is a meaningless contrivance, based on a government which, far from being democratic, is a product of electoral corruption and was conceived and materially sustained by the Anglo-American imperialism to which it is therefore subservient. This is a historical condition to be remedied not by piecemeal reform, but by revolution, however one chooses to interpret that word; PPP interpretations are somewhat vague and varied, though at leadership level they usually focus on the nationalization of basic resources and closer relations with the communist world.

Whilst either of these standard apologias is fairly easily sustained, current appearances rather favour the Anglo-American and PNC one. For the first time in some twenty years Guyana has at least the look of social and political stability and steady economic growth; and in 1968 this combination apparently appealed more to the country's electorate than did the PPP's relative abstractions. Outwardly, without pausing to examine its origins and ambiguities, the *status quo* appeared to be both widely accepted and durable. However, an objective analysis of it must start with a basic inquiry: did the past really offer Guyana the prospect of an independence corresponding more closely to the once nationally supported perspectives of the PPP? If so, what altered this prospect? And are those perspectives still relevant—are the implications of the *status quo* other than they appear to be, as the opposition asserts?

The question of options for a Guyanese nationalism was first posed, with dramatic rapidity, when in 1953 Britain conceded the colony a radically new constitution based on universal suffrage and an elective majority over officials and nominees in the Legislative Assembly. This produced a decisive victory for the PPP, newly founded as a socialist movement committed to seeking a rapid independence entailing an outright rejection of the colonial *status quo*, both economic and social. Jointly led by Cheddi Jagan, son of an Indian sugar worker, and Forbes Burnham, an African[3] lawyer, its basis was multiracial; by combining the votes of the mainly African urban and Indian rural proletariats, it annihilated the power of the small middle class which was politically dominant under the previously limited property-based franchise. Neither the overt racialism nor the political factionalism which dominated later events were apparent at the time. Instead, Guyana seemed united in almost unqualified support of the newly and hence broadly defined, but basic PPP dialectic: that of militant opposition to both the form and content of the country's colonial status. The unexpected unanimity of this electoral response suggested that the PPP had taken a realistic stand. All that seemed to be required was a strategy for its translation into concrete political terms. Yet ultimately it came to nothing. It was another thirteen years before independence was attained, and by then the changes involved were so few and the country was so bitterly divided that the independence ceremonies were heavily boycotted.

What accounts for the paradox of this total disparity between the complexion of 1953 and that of independent Guyana? Obviously its very existence reflects a PPP failure to evolve an adequate strategy; but this begs the question. Had their programme been at all feasible, the momentum they created would surely have brought either them or some comparable grouping at least closer to its realization. Why did even this not occur? Is the present just a return to the inevitable, as the conventional case implies? Or were the goals of 1953 potentially attainable but prevented from being realized by external factors?

I suggest that this is the best starting point for measuring 'foreign influence'. But first a note on the general background.

BRITISH GUYANA: THE COLONIAL BACKGROUND

If Guyana's present position does appear inevitable, this is due primarily to its continuity with the past, one rooted from its very beginnings in the expansion of capitalism as an international system. By the late 1940s a century and a half of British rule had simply institutionalized the main *raison d'être* of the original Anglo-Dutch settlers: minimum expenditure and maximum return. The notion of colonial administration as a more

---

[3] The traditionally preferred term in Guyana for people of African descent.

complex phenomenon was effectively post-second world war. It was not until after the recommendations of the 1938 Royal Commission that a government department of social welfare so much as existed. Previously the sugar estates were the only source of security, and a comment by Raymond Smith (p. 153) is an indication of the limited philosophy behind it: 'Because of the necessity for conserving the labour supply for the sugar industry, the provision of medical attention for the coastal population has always been regarded as a reasonable form of expenditure.' Even by the 1950s British attitudes had hardly changed. In 1954, for instance, monthly old-age pensions were raised to $5·50 (urban) and $4·50 (rural) for those with monthly incomes of under $6·50 and $5·50 respectively (figures throughout are given in US dollars). And yet in precisely the same year the Robertson Commission, inquiring into political unrest, found amongst the Guyanese 'a common—almost arrogant—presumption that from some fathomless source all things desirable should as of right be provided'.[4]

Certainly Guyana was less poverty-stricken than many British colonies: for instance, the average household net income in 1953 was $204. Structurally, however, it was a classic case both of underdevelopment, and of that term indicating not so much a total lack of development as a high degree of development of a very particular kind. The relevant facts speak for themselves. In an economy devoted mainly to primary production, over half the agricultural and almost all the mineral sectors were controlled by four expatriate corporations and one relatively small local sugar company. Between them, these accounted for an increasing proportion of exports, some 80 per cent by the late 1950s. Well over 50 per cent of the total still consisted of sugar and its by-products; these were almost wholly controlled by Booker Bros, McConnell and Co., whose London-based operations extended to almost every sector of the local economy. Bauxite and manganese were a further 25 per cent. Bauxite was mined by two companies, the Demerara Bauxite Co., a subsidiary of Aluminium Ltd (in which the US Alcoa has substantial interests), and the US Reynolds Metal Co. Manganese was mined exclusively by a US concern, Great Lakes Carbon Ltd.

The result was an economy almost devoid of diversification or infrastructural development. For want of local capital formation, industry was negligible, comprising only 3·2 per cent of the annual GDP and meeting only 14 per cent[5] of the local demand for consumer goods. The position was similar in agriculture. While the sugar interests' traditional means of

4 Cmnd 9274, p. 16.
5 Reno, p. 75.

ensuring a cheap labour pool by withholding uncultivated land and opposing investments in the interior were less rigidly applied by the 1950s, they were far from totally abandoned. Even in 1952 recommendations for land reclamation, subsequently accepted as being economically sound, were widely alleged to have been rejected on account of the opposition of the sugar interests for precisely this reason: a view which Smith accepts as likely. The overall result was a narrow, inflexible pattern of production whose only non-colonial sector, in the economic sense, was the rice grown by smallholders. Supplying the national market and also 10 per cent of exports, it was the one major item whose profits were both localized and widely distributed. Other products were minimal, coming mainly from the interior—timber, gold and diamonds, balata (wild rubber), and cattle. Despite their romantic frontier image, even these were offshoots of the wider economic system and proof of its all-encompassing grasp. Bookers, for example, monopolized balata production and also held investments in the Rupununi cattle ranches. The former kept hundreds of indigenous Amerindians in a permanent state of debt; the latter had driven thousands more off the land on which they depended and, thanks to the ranchers' influence, reform programmes were constantly shelved.[6]

Infrastructural weakness was a natural correlate of this monoculture and foreign control. Communications with the interior were almost non-existent, despite its agricultural potential. The only effective road system, running right along the coast and linking the plantations with Georgetown, kept the mass of the population within the sugar economy's orbit. The only railway, eighty miles long and run at a substantial loss, was directly parallel to it. Colonial development and welfare corporation schemes introduced in the late 1940s had in no way altered the picture, consisting mainly of welfare measures which, whatever their limited merits, were essentially non-productive. Booker Bros matched these measures with improvements in workers' welfare, but neither these nor reinvestment altered the sugar industry's role as the linch-pin of a colonial economy; rather they reinforced it, by providing houses for workers on the plantations, for example, rather than furnishing the workers with the means to afford their own. And since taxes were mainly indirect, they produced hardly any surplus for infrastructural expansion, a deficiency exacerbated by the bauxite companies' device of selling their ore to their parent company at an artificially low price to reduce their tax assessments. And this had further ramifications: Newman states, for example, that when asked to survey the possibility of developing the

6 Colin Henfrey, *The Gentle People* (London, 1964), pp. 267–8.

hydro-electric potential of the interior, they effectively shelved the issue, since it might have committed them to processing ore locally.[7]

To describe this structure as underdeveloped is an over-simplification. Rather it was a highly developed system of stagnation, tailored to foreign interests and therefore not susceptible, from an objective Guyanese viewpoint, to substantial real growth. Such growth as there was in the 1950s, occurring within this traditional structure, which was effectively supported by would-be liberal measures like the Commonwealth Sugar Agreement, reduced rather than hastened the prospect of fundamental change. The socio-economic data illustrate what this stagnation meant on the popular level. Unemployment averaged 11–18 per cent, according to the season and criteria used, and the urban rate was always higher. A 1956 survey, for instance, revealed it as fluctuating between 16·4 and 18 per cent, according to the cane season, while the Georgetown figure was 22·8 per cent. Real per-capita incomes actually fell in the late 1950s, despite the prevalent development schemes, marked wage rises in limited sectors, and a mathematically respectable if socially meaningless rate of growth. Wage improvements were much less significant than the figures at first suggest. The bauxite payroll was a drop in the companies' budgets, and affected only a tiny fraction of the working population. And set against inflation, an increasing average family size, and redundancy through mechanization, Bookers' much-quoted rises were a limited improvement of the real per capita income of a decreasing number of families in a rapidly growing population.[8] Given that they were balanced by a spectacular increase in productivity (42 per cent in the 1953–60 period), they represented no real change in the exploitative structure of the sugar industry, whose dominance of the economy was in effect increasing. The rate of population growth, which rose from just over $2\frac{1}{2}$ to almost $3\frac{1}{2}$ per cent per annum during the 1950s, made this general stagnation all the more ominous. Clearly the so-called development which was being implemented—most of whose items would have been part of the normal expenditure of any but a colonial society[9]—offered

[7] 'The Economic Future of British Guiana', *Soc. & Econ. Stud.*, Sept. 1960, p. 286.

[8] In the 1953–60 period prices rose by 12 per cent; of a plantation labour force of 26,300 some 5,800 became redundant; while the average wage rose from $325 to $603 p.a. and the population by 23·5 per cent. Thus the real increase for those employed was nearly two thirds. But some of this was presumably due to increased hours per employee rather than rate increases (Newman, who gives these figures, 1964, pp. 60–71, omits to mention this). And it must also be set off against an increasing family size and the fact that the proportion of the population standing to benefit fell by well over a third.

[9] The actual proportion of what was described as the 'development budget' which was spent on 'economic development' (the budget's own categories) was well under 25 per cent in the programmes of the 1950s.

no way out of the impasse. It may have removed its harsher symbols—the infant mortality rate of approximately 10 per cent per annum, and the ranges, modelled on slave huts, occupied by sugar workers, both still conspicuous in the late 1940s—but structurally it was just a retrenchment, a piecemeal updating of what remained, in terms of production and distribution, a wholly colonial economy. It could only be modernized, in the sense of producing a pattern of growth from which Guyanese would benefit, by basic structural changes: by moves towards national control, in the national interest, of the major resources, principally bauxite and sugar; and by substantial low-interest aid from any and every available source. Only this could produce the capital formation and localized planning initiative essential to diversification and infrastructural expansion.

By the early 1950s, then, when the prospect of independence was acknowledged by the British, it could have been rendered effective only by a government aware of these pre-conditions. The alternative was a continuation of the traditional stagnation implicit in the rigid economic structure and artificial social divisions, occupational and ethnic, which the past had created—divisions which frustration would deepen if the structure remained unchanged. Obviously, expatriate concerns and the local middle class, which was largely an outgrowth of them, would oppose such policies. But the balance of power was altering. These two groups were soon to lose their overt hold on the power structure. There were new metropolitan attitudes and Guyana herself was not unendowed; the educational level was high (80 per cent literacy), the potential economic resources were there and, above all, 1953 was to show that the foundations had been laid for the national awareness which any real change demanded.

DECOLONIZATION: THE CONTAINMENT OF NATIONALISM

Not unnaturally, in a pre-Suez climate, the British saw Guyana's future in a more conservative light. The trend that they anticipated is suggested by the constitutions imposed before that of 1953. Their eventual effect was gradually to extend the legislative power of the middle class by retaining an exclusive property franchise and increasing the proportion of elective, as against nominated, seats in the Legislative Council. By 1947, whilst the franchise limits remained, these seats were a majority, subject to the Governor's veto. This constitutional nurturing suggests that this particular class, as one formed in a British image, was seen as the ideal leadership for eventual independence. However, its representatives failed to measure up to this role, identifying consistently with the colonial *status quo* rather than even modest change. The 1947 legislature produced no significant groupings or coherent programmes; the only original proposals—those made by Jagan, the only radical elected, for fiscal, wage, and electoral reforms—were rejected wholesale. Evidently, given the pressures for change, this traditional group was too obsolescent even to contain, let alone direct them.

This was confirmed in the next elections, held in 1953 with universal suffrage and a fully elective lower chamber in a bicameral legislature. The hitherto dominant protagonists of the small middle class were swept aside. The PPP, newly formed under Jagan's and Burnham's leadership as the first grass-roots political party, won eighteen out of the twenty-four seats. Apart from the Governor's veto and a mainly nominated upper chamber, they were virtually without opposition, a result unexpected even by them.

The explanation apparently lay in the nature of the party, unprecedented in several ways. First in its interracial quality. This issue is a crucial one, in that any analysis of the fate of Guyanese nationalism hinges very much on the question of whether it was due simply to the nationalists' failure to contend with racialism, as is generally alleged, if not assumed;[10] or whether the racialism was itself mainly provoked by external circumstances. Obviously both Burnham and Jagan were charismatic figures for their respective ethnic groups; but this was natural and constructive, since these were first and foremost occupational and regional groups with different roles in colonial history. It was this which distinguished them, rather than ethnic awareness as such. While the Africans were mainly urban, the Indian descendants of indentured labourers had tended to remain on the land. Overtly racial feeling was evident in only a few specific areas. First, in the small middle class: constituted mainly on the basis of the British principle (still implemented wholesale in public office at the time) that brown was at least better than black, this group had, by definition, a vested interest in race. Vaguely similar sentiments were common among higher caste Indians; but this was a traditional prejudice, amongst a dwindling minority, against darkness rather than race. At

---

[10] e.g. by Swan (1957) and Bradley (1961); both, however, brief and in this respect superficial observers. Whilst Smith's (1962, ch. 5) analysis of the Guyanese social structure, much the most detailed available, has the opposite implications. He argues that the emphasis on racial categories was essentially British and regularly reinforced by the exaggerated gleanings of hurried official commissions. And though Glasgow (1970) presents a fairly informed case for ethnic and cultural pluralism as a political determinant, he never evaluates sufficiently the extent to which it may have been activated by political events, rather than vice-versa.

grass-roots level tension was principally confined to two spheres and these were both institutional and specifically colonial. First, in the tendency of sugar plantation management to encourage racial identity as a barrier to class interests, something that genuine unionization would make much more difficult. And second in the position of Africans, despite their subordination within the bureaucracy, as minor officials *vis-à-vis* Indians: this because the Indians were relatively recent immigrants, with in consequence a lower rate of recruitment to national institutions. This gulf was a widely felt and at moments deep one: it meant, for example, that when in 1948 a number of sugar-workers on strike were shot by police, the latter were African and the workers mainly Indian. Certainly, then, the PPP leaders had an acute responsibility for avoiding the temptation of appealing to racial loyalties in a way which might prevent them from working across these traditional lines. But the party's composition and thorough-going opposition to their colonial context were already major steps toward this.

The party's second striking feature was its coherent organization both at local and national levels. Modelled on that of the British Labour Party, this had been the keystone of the PPP's rapid growth and compared favourably with the authoritarian element in the subsequent politics of much of the rest of the Caribbean. At the same time its programme was free of any sectarian pressures. Though vague on many specific issues— and this was only natural, given the lack of precedents and the speed at which it had grown—it was basically socialist and geared to rapid independence.

Clearly, the election results called for a prompt, mutual adjustment. A recognition by the PPP that, despite short-term irritants, a politically sophisticated, rather than merely rebellious, strategy was the only possible route to full power; and British acceptance of the fact that the Guyanese had voted for independence and socialism with a unanimity producing a virtual one-party system. But neither side made this adjustment. The British Governor nominated an upper chamber whose members came largely from Booker Bros, the church, and the traditional conservative groups heavily defeated in the elections. The PPP, for its part, soon launched a series of radical measures, whose provocative style tended to offer a charter for conservative reaction. With tactful presentation and an objective audience, they could have been recognized as the basis of a constructive and even surprisingly mild programme. Predictably, though, the upper chamber simply rejected them outright. The PPP, not unnaturally, concluded that the would-be democracy of the new constitution was wholly hypocritical. However, for want of a pre-planned

E

strategy for this fairly foreseeable outcome, they had little but their rhetoric to fall back on.

There were two main bones of contention: the secularization of schools, still controlled by the church, though financed by the government; and a Labour Relations Bill requiring recognition of unions on the strength of workers' polls to be held at the discretion of the Minister of Labour. Secularization was obviously aimed at the schools' highly conservative expatriate atmosphere;[11] the labour bill mainly at the Man-Power Citizens' Association (MPCA), the more moderate sugar union and the only one recognized by the sugar industry, whose unrepresentative character was suggested not only by PPP leaders but also by sugar workers' strikes in support of the bill. Both measures were vehemently attacked, in the upper chamber and also in the various institutions from which most of its members came; in pulpit, press, and Chamber of Commerce they were branded as communist and totalitarian, terms soon applied indiscriminately to the PPP's every move. The Governor, naturally sympathetic to his own nominees, was apparently convinced by their opinions. Five months after the elections, with the labour bill still pending, the constitution was suddenly suspended without any attempt at conciliation. The immediate justification offered was the involvement of PPP leaders—as elected union officials—with the sugar strikes, during which arson occurred; the aim, as announced by the British government, was 'to prevent communist subversion of the government and a dangerous crisis both in public order and in economic affairs'.[12]

Subsequent recriminations have blurred the background to this decision. Clearly the sugar interests played a very considerable part. Their publications, together with those controlled by other commercial concerns—the sum of the country's daily press—had stridently opposed the PPP; shortly before the elections, they had even paid the MPCA to distribute leaflets alleging PPP subservience to the Kremlin.[13] Traditionally inflexible and still hesitant over union reform, they were clearly nervous of the PPP's plan to effect it; their nominated representatives in the legislature's upper chamber were, by tradition and definition, close

---

[11] Even by the later 1950s only 21 of 319 schools were government run, though all were government financed; nearly all the rest being church run. This meant, for example, that compulsory religious instruction in Christianity alone was imposed on a population less than 50 per cent Christian; that Hindus could not easily get employment as teachers; and that the whole tenor of education remained absurdly English oriented. It was also widely and specifically anti-PPP.

[12] Cmd 8980, p. 16.

[13] Cmd 9274, p. 39.

to the Governor's ear. In the circumstances, their conventional plea that they played no part in politics was scarcely credible. However, they were not without allies. Ecclesiastical pressure was also very influential. There were unsubstantiated (though the British implied that they believed them) allegations of a PPP plot to destroy the Georgetown palace of the Archbishop of the West Indies;[14] and both Anglican and Catholic priests were still mainly expatriate and openly opposed to the PPP in principle as well as over control of the schools. Finally, Jagan alleged that the US government had also contributed to the suspension. While it is not possible to verify this, US policy in the following year in Guatemala lends the charge some credence and certainly the British report on the suspension was steeped in McCarthyism.[15]

However, the decisive factor was probably a less tangible one: the apparent inability of British official and vested interests to adjust to the reality of what democracy had produced. Admittedly, the PPP did not go out of their way to help them; but it would have been hard to do so, given that the British apparently never recovered from the shock of the elections, a measure of which can perhaps be gauged from the statement by the Waddington Commission which had drawn up the new constitution, that no strong party was yet likely to emerge.[16] What they seem to have expected was one of two alternative bases for a moderate balance of power very different from the virtual one-party system which the elections were to produce. Either the traditional middle class, consisting mainly of independents, would win an effective majority; or else the new nationalists, should they gain power, would adopt a *realpolitik* of co-operation with the British and the middle-class minority. Either would have meant only gradual progress to a far more measured independence than that originally demanded by the PPP. But the latter had long since made it clear that they planned to press within legal limits—which they never effectively exceeded,[17] despite their verbal indiscretions—for a further constitution in which legislation would be independent of the veto of nominees. In appointing an upper chamber whose membership was an anomaly—an attempt to enforce precisely the balance which the electorate had rejected—the British immediately hardened the PPP's stand by challenging them, in effect, to forgo democracy or be damned.

[14] Ibid., p. 60, esp. paras. 175 & 178.
[15] Cmd 9274, p. 84.
[16] Col. 280, p. 17.
[17] A fact implicitly admitted even by Harold Macmillan, speaking from the Conservative front bench on 23 Oct. 1953 in favour of the suspension, when he said: 'none of these separate accusations [against the PPP leaders] could be held sufficient in itself to justify the serious course which Her Majesty's Government have had to adopt' (HC Deb., vol. 518, col. 2269).

Obviously it is easier now, in the light of post-colonial history, to see that a virtual one-party system was a social reality and not just an offshoot of Stalinism, as the British apparently thought;[18] but their blunt reaction deepened the conflict implicit in their lack of foresight over the possible outcome of the elections. The situation was unworkable, and it was the British who made it so, not merely by offering a conditional democracy—this much was foreseeable from the nature of the constitution—but by translating the conditions, once the elections had taken place, into a veto on any change of the dimensions clearly demanded in the PPP's electoral platform. To charge them with non-co-operation, in such circumstances, was meaningless.

The mild absurdity of what followed tends to support this interpretation. PPP leaders were detained, all political meetings were banned, and the US and British West Indian authorities refused Jagan and Burnham the transit visas which they required in order to fly to England. Even the British Labour Party forbade local groups to give them a platform once they finally arrived.[19] The explanatory White Paper (Cmd 8980) was grossly one-sided, complaining of the PPP's stance on issues such as the unions and schools without so much as considering the patent inadequacies in these spheres. Even the PPP's version of the Labour Party's organization was described, apparently without humorous intention, as an elaborate cell system designed for violent subversion. The minor allegations were especially indicative of the climate of the suspension.[20] A group led by the Jagans had planned to set fire to Georgetown. The Boy Scouts and Girl Guides had been subverted and 'communist literature' had been imported—some of which, as it later transpired, was actually anti-communist. Since most of these charges were virtually undocumented (including the arson charge against the Jagans, the history of which is symptomatic of the bizarre tenuousness of the whole British case),[21] they read as they were widely interpreted—as a thinly disguised reaction to the mere existence of an unexpectedly widely-backed radical party.

Despite the original nervous response from the local administration, an honest assessment of the facts might still have opened communications

[18] Cmd 8980, pp. 10–11 and espec. para. 41.
[19] Jagan (1966), pp. 149 & 153.
[20] Cmd 8980, paras. 8, 15–21, 30–1, 36, & 38.
[21] Attributed to 'reliable sources' (ibid., para. 3), it was reaffirmed by the Robertson Commission although, on their own admission, they made no attempt to question the informers, one of whom had acted on second-hand and the other on third-hand information (Cmd 9274, p. 84). In the circumstances it is hardly surprising that Jagan, who demanded to be brought to trial as a means of clearing his name, remained unprosecuted. (See his *What Happened in British Guiana*, London, n.d., foreword by Jennie Lee).

between the nationalists and the British. As it was, this immediate White Paper and even the subsequent Robertson Commission, which had much more time to deliberate, exchanged any pretence to neutrality for a considered commitment to both local and international reaction. Though stemming from the horizons of the moment—largely those of the cold war—this failure of the imagination was to shape Guyana's future. It was a straight slap in the face, not only for the nationalists but also for such liberalism as might have existed in the middle class, Booker Bros, and the church, and, at a later date, in the State Department. And meanwhile it was institutionalized in the form of an interim government which was wholly nominated and consisted of much the same figures as had served in the former upper chamber.

The negativism of the British position was emphasized in the maintenance of this government for a further four years. During this period the socio-economic development for which political unity had furnished a sound basis virtually remained at a standstill. Its main features were the two-year and five-year development programmes introduced by the Governor and the Colonial Office in 1954 and 1956 respectively; both conformed rigidly to traditional economic patterns, avoiding productive diversification in favour of service and welfare spending. Even from a quantitive viewpoint, the changes promised were minimal—there was immediate underspending even on the limited budget of roughly $11 m. per annum. But qualitatively they were nil. The emphasis on welfare rather than expansion, apparently designed for the short-term goal of reducing political pressure, tended to raise expectations without significantly enlarging the national capacity to fulfil them. Like the actual suspension, the programmes could hardly have been better designed to suggest that the British envisaged independence as little more than a modified form of colonial status.

The effect of the suspension on the PPP was traumatic. Gradually its leaders seemed to adopt the roles in which the British had cast them, oscillating between the acceptance of paternalistic measures and a verbal rebelliousness with little positive counterpart in policy recommendations. The British made the most of this contradiction. Official pronouncements adopted a theme of distinguishing 'moderates' from 'extremists' within the ranks of the PPP.[22] The apparent aim was to split the movement which they had previously hoped to balance, along the overt dividing line of urban and rural militants—the implied mark of 'extremism' being connection with the sugar strikes. As in 1953, the exact proportion of calculation to naïveté in this gesture—the fuse to a lastingly factional

[22] Cmd 9274, pp. 35-8 (esp. para. 106).

and increasingly violent future—is hard to judge. Not so its outcome. The PPP had gone a long way toward combining the country's two main occupational and ethnic groups, which colonial history had set apart; but their unity was a new one, dependent on concrete goals. Rapid independence, in facilitating these, should have confirmed it: but frustration was only likely to fragment it, perhaps irretrievably. And apparently the British decided to encourage this and even specifically point the way. If so, they were highly successful.

The immediate tip of this iceberg, which the British did anticipate, to judge by the actual naming of the 'moderates' and 'extremists', lay in individual ambition and personality differences between the two Jagans and Burnham. In 1955 Burnham left the party with a minority following. There was no concrete ideological difference between the two resulting factions, both of which continued to call themselves the PPP, until Burnham's adopted the label of People's National Congress (PNC). Significantly, the latter's main protest was culled straight from the Robertson Commission—the Jagan wing was too 'extremist', a synonym for the communism long imputed to the PPP by the conservative local press, which contributed heavily to the party's international image. Certainly Jagan was given to describing himself as a Marxist, whilst distinguishing this specifically from membership of the Communist Party. If indiscreet tactically, however, such statements were misleading rather than significant; as Simms (p. 70) points out, contrary to the myths preponderant in Guyanese and international circles, neither Jagan nor his wife Janet had been a member of any communist party, nor is Janet Jagan a member of the Rosenberg family (convicted in the United States for spying). Ironically, the one leader of the 1953 PPP to whom Simms (himself a strong Burnhamite) attributes some evidence of youthful communist party membership is none other than Burnham (p. 82). Jagan's actual policies—as opposed to occasional statements, spiced perhaps with the pleasurable sensation of pulling the British lion's tail—were very far from doctrinaire; and it is rather doubtful whether any of the PPP leaders, with the single exception of Janet Jagan, were deeply acquainted with Marxism as more than one of the many sources of their essentially eclectic goals. Certainly there was little basis for describing the party, as opposed to members of it, as committed to Marxism, whatever that might mean in the context; and on the electoral level it was a complete non-issue, except as the main slogan wielded against the PPP ever since 1953, both locally and internationally. As regards their socialism, the real difference between Jagan and Burnham was one of consistency, background, and method: notably of Burnham's greater ability, apparently well perceived by the British, to gauge and accept the unwritten colonial dictum that compromise was the price of power.

The British made little attempt to disguise this. Almost immediately after the split, a new constitution was introduced with a unicameral legislature which was 50 per cent elective. The PPP won nine seats against the PNC's three and were given an executive role limited by the Governor's reserve powers. Had they modified their style and maintained their revolutionary programme, they might have recreated the dynamism of 1953. Yet in each respect they did the reverse; and interestingly, the policy of this second period of limited power is the one political error which Jagan now seems willing to admit. Had he restated his position and demanded independence within a given period, revolutionary nationalism might have survived, if only through the PPP's resignation. But their mettle had apparently weakened. Seemingly mesmerized by the stalemate contrived by the British, they virtually adopted the latters' terms for an acceptable policy, including a traditionally limited concept of development. Whilst a few minor measures were passed, they never reformulated a programme of basic long-term goals to reiterate that radical change was a precondition of real growth. There was no further talk of fiscal reform, the opening of the interior, import substitution, or the nationalization of productive resources.

This regression suggests that Guyanese colonialism had left a marked psychological imprint. The pattern is conjectural but too pervasive to be ignored, especially as the British apparently fathomed and played on it carefully. Throughout the decolonization period, would-be nationalist politics never quite became that in practice: Guyanese leaders alternated between rebellion and dependency on imperial authority, rather than rejecting it in a revolutionary sense. Specifically, they never decided at what point they were going to abandon the constitutional framework imposed and manipulated by the British; still less how they were going to do so. Despite their opposition to the British, they failed to cut loose, even non-violently, from the mythical morality—mythical in that its authors only observed it at their convenience—of the colonial rules of behaviour. That they sounded at first like an opposition was constitutionally inevitable; but their continuing to do suggests a neglect of the implications of their overriding charter (in terms of their own dialectic) of massive popular support. Thus they had no political answer to the assertion of gunboat power. In a curious, self-fulfilling way they behaved politically as if involved inexorably in the end of something, not its beginning. And they continued to do so: in Jagan's case purely verbal rebellion and in Burnham's compromise replaced radical nationalism with almost fatalistic ease. Whilst continuing to rebuke the British, they took to modelling their policies (Jagan in government and Burnham in opposition) strictly on British initiatives. And similarly they succumbed to British encouragement to restructure their loyalties along factional, colonial lines. As Glasgow (p. 116) points out, they did in a sense concern themselves so exclusively with opposition to imperialism that they failed to produce concrete political alternatives or positive substitutes for the social divisions bequeathed by it. Revolutionary historians of their own colonial dilemma, they became political victims of it. Even Jagan's and others' eventual commitment to Marxism–Leninism—its inflexibility, rather than the fact of it, as Glasgow suggests (p. 140)—has an imported and hence colonial flavour to it.

The extent to which these inconsistencies exposed what was left of nationalism to further external manipulation became increasingly evident after the introduction in 1961 of a new constitution with a fully elective legislature; this, quite explicitly, as a prelude to full independence.[23] Already the consequences of the 1955 split and of mounting US concern over post-revolutionary Cuba, with whom the PPP maintained contact, were beginning to emerge. First there was the increasingly racial basis of party alignments. The PNC was being influenced by the colour-minded middle class with which it had reached a rapprochement by absorbing the United Democratic Party, a minor conservative group left over from the early 1950s; and the PPP had at best failed to take race into account, in legislating primarily for the rural, i.e. Indian, sectors of the economy. Nevertheless, it was still the persistent lack of deeper distinctions, social or ideological, which threatened to elevate race to a dominant political role. Another new factor was the emergence of the militantly right-wing UF party, with support from the United States (see below), the still mainly expatriate church, and the British Conservative Party.[24] Concentrated in Georgetown, mainly in the Chamber of Commerce and upper strata of the civil service, it was led by Peter d'Aguiar, a millionaire liquor producer of Portuguese origin. Its content was a combination of nineteenth-century liberal economics, Moral Rearmament fervour and vigilante election techniques loaded with anti-communist slogans aimed at the PPP.[25] The most significant omen of all was increasing US influence, in

[23] Cmnd 998, p. 13, para. 59, where it is anticipated that in the next conference 'there should be no question of substance for discussion save that of independence'.

[24] Bradley (1961), p. 21.

[25] Apropos of which an extract from the UF's official history, discussing the 1961 elections, is unwittingly entertaining: 'The UF fought a consistently anti-Communist campaign, but it was hampered by the fact that Jagan had not publicly committed himself to Communism' (cited in Simms, p. 150).

which the British apparently acquiesced. D'Aguiar's pugilistic electioneering, aided by his control of a major newspaper, was largely the creation of the representatives of the US Anti-Communist Crusade, equipped with mobile film units and supplies of right-wing literature. And by now the established TUC was also US dominated. Its grass-roots sympathies were originally PNC, but its leadership was UF, and the International Affairs Unit of the AFL–CIO had been wooing it since the mid-1950s, together with the American Institute for Free Labour Development, chaired by J. P. Grace of W. R. Grace & Co., a multi-million-dollar investor in Latin America.[26] Whilst overt US hostility to the PPP government was still confined to these and other relatively extremist fringes,[27] later events suggest that their views were not unheeded in higher, supposedly more liberal, circles.

Finally, there was the worsening of the economic situation, rooted in the maintenance of Guyana's colonial background, through the undermining of the PPP and the enforced implementation of the British model of development. Apart from the *a priori* inadequacy of the 1956–60 programme, it was repeatedly under-subscribed and most of the funds which were raised compounded inherent economic weakness with heavy debt-servicing charges, deriving mainly from British loans with a 6 per cent interest rate. By 1959 Guyana's total public debt stood at $49 m., of which some 80 per cent had been raised in Britain. And in the same year debt charges outstripped the expenditure on economic development with which they had steadily been catching up.[28] The deficit was largely due to the local fiscal system, which with its deference to company and middle- and higher-level private incomes, was unable to produce the scheduled surplus. Other loans were very few, direct grants from Britain were small ($2·6 m. per annum), and they were virtually negligible from the other governments—the US and Canadian—benefiting from taxes paid to them by their national investors in Guyana. Meanwhile, the Colonial Office vetoed low-rate Cuban loans on the grounds that they came within its own constitutional sphere of foreign policy.[29] Also the expatriate banks, primarily Barclays DCO and the Royal Bank of Canada, invested their local holdings abroad, setting a trend followed

[26] Jagan (1966), pp. 297–302 (where the details are documented from US sources).

[27] e.g. Congressman Rousselot of California, on hearing of the PPP victory in the 1961 elections, demanded 'immediate, dramatic and aggressive action to forestall the establishment of Communism' (cited by Reno, 133), a sentiment shared on the same occasion by the better-known Senator Dodds (*NYT*, 4 Aug. 1961).

[28] The figures are: 1957, economic development $5·3 m., debt charges $4·7 m., 1958, $5·8 m. and $4·9 m.; 1959, $5·6 m. and 5·7 m.

[29] Jagan (1966), p. 235.

increasingly by the Guyanese middle class, as was later indicated by the need for exchange-control measures. And while Jagan's case for foreign aid tended to be prejudiced by the fragmentary nature of his proposals, this itself was largely dictated by the base-line established under the interim government and the continuing shortage of funds. Consequently annual growth was running at a sluggish 3 per cent (less than the population increase) while unemployment remained high, exacerbated by the sugar redundancies. For want of the necessary funds, the 1960-4 development programme offered no escape from this downward spiral. In real terms, there was little change either in the rates, sources, or targets of investment, which was still to come partly from local resources, but primarily from British loans.

Despite this gloomy outlook, the elections of 1961 repeated those of 1957, leaving the PPP in command with 19 mainly rural seats to the PNC's 11, nearly all urban, and the UF's 4. The PPP programme remained the same. While it restated in general terms a commitment to socialism and aid from every possible source, it avoided major issues like nationalization, union reform, or changes in economic priorities. And typically Jagan now embarked on one of the aid-bargaining trips which had become an ironically regular landmark on the road to independence. It was totally unsuccessful. Admittedly in the United States, where, despite the recent launching of the Alliance for Progress, he incurred a virtual refusal,[30] he prejudiced his own case by confessing under public pressure to having Marxist sympathies—a tactlessly improvident answer which, since he had formulated his hat-in-hand role of the moment, could and should have been avoided. But it seems to have conditioned European as well as US reactions, confirming that Guyana's fate was passing into US hands. West Germany, France, and Italy all rejected Jagan's requests; Britain maintained her traditional policy of barring all communist offers,[31] made only a token response herself, and declined to reduce her interest rate,[32] despite the already prevailing excess of debt charges over expenditure on economic development and the latter's overall inadequacy, which even the British enquiry of the following year would acknowledge. Subsequent events must be seen in the light of this damning lack of the Western sympathy on which Britain had kept Guyana dependent.

The result was waning confidence and a flight of capital. By January 1962, despite an exchange-control system, it was already evident that, in addition to a heavy deficit on current expenditure, annual development

---

[30] Cmnd 998, pp. 11–13.
[31] Jagan (1966), pp. 234–5, where full details are given.
[32] Col. 354, para. 39.

funds were falling still further behind schedule.[33] The budget of February 1962 attempted to redress the balance. It included taxes on property, capital gains and advertising, and a compulsory savings bill for incomes above a specified rate. Clearly the effect of these measures—which were very much in line with Alliance for Progress recommendations and approved by the international press as a radical move towards reinvestment—would fall mainly on commercial concerns and the better-off. The reaction therefore indicates just how far external influence had shifted the local balance of power, carrying the professedly socialist PNC with it. A whirlwind attack by the press, led by d'Aguiar's *Chronicle*, helped to accentuate the increasingly vociferous opposition from the UF and PNC, the Georgetown Chamber of Commerce and the US-influenced and UF-led TUC, which had recently incorporated the highly conservative civil service unions. This alliance produced some unusual combinations, such as the TUC's demand for the withdrawal of increased company and advertising taxes[34] and an all-embracing attack on the budget by d'Aguiar's *Sunday Chronicle* (4 Feb. 1962): headline 'Tax Avalanche will Crush Working Class', leader 'Budget is Marxist'. As arranged in the Chamber of Commerce, many Georgetown businesses closed down and paid their workers to strike, whilst the two opposition leaders, supported by right-wing union officials, joined forces at the head of illegal demonstrations.[35] Boosted by the number of urban unemployed—which could only have been reduced by development programmes radically different from those imposed by the British—they were prodigiously effective. Disturbances, largely incited by d'Aguiar, developed rapidly into riots and within a short while the centre of Georgetown was burning. With the PPP now standing to lose, the stance of the British, still responsible for dealing with emergencies, was precisely the reverse of that adopted in 1953. Although both PPP ministers and the Commissioner of Police had asked the Governor for troops on the previous evening, he declined to send for them until it was already too late.[36] By the time they did restore order, the damage stood at over $6 m., with five people dead and eighty injured.

The riots were a turning point. They introduced a political ethos which persisted for several years, until its ends had been achieved. Violence had become an effective weapon, virtually sanctioned by the British military

[33] The figures are: 1960 (overall) development estimates $13·7 m., expenditure $8·8 m.; 1961, 13·3 m. and 12·0 m.; 1962, 17·6 m. and 10·4 m. The current expenditure deficit was over $8 m. (ibid., p. 61).

[34] *Guardian*, 17 Feb. 1962.

[35] Col. 354, pp. 29–31, 33 & 35.

[36] Ibid., pp. 41–2.

hesitation and the clearly adopted implication[37] that the crisis constituted proof of the country's unreadiness for the rapid independence which had previously been promised. And its character was significant. Selective attacks on Indian stores already gave it a racial flavour: and its non-ideological basis on the part of the PNC suggested how extraneous, yet deeply manipulable, their split with the PPP remained. At the constitutional conference later in 1962, the opposition, clearly aware of this subtly changed balance of power, countered PPP reminders of Britain's commitment to a prompt independence with demands for fresh elections and a wholly new constitution based on proportional representation. This paid rapid dividends: in the resulting deadlock the British dismissed the conference and subsequent PPP offers to the PNC for a coalition failed to produce any results.[38]

The PPP continued to govern, despite economic and social tensions. The former were only alleviated by the opposition's acceptance of several of the budget measures to which they had objected so violently; and the latter were intensified when, in 1963, the PPP reintroduced their Labour Relations Bill for the recognition of unions on the basis of workers' polls directed by the Ministry of Labour. A long-standing item in PPP policy, this had been a major point of dispute in the 1953 crisis. Ostensibly the bill was a liberal measure to counter the alleged symbiosis, which certainly existed to varying degrees, as the previous year had shown, between the employers and the leaders of recognized unions. The retort of the opposition, supported by union leaders, notably those with UF connections, was that the bill was totalitarian and politically motivated. The latter was undoubtedly true, but the bill would have been hard to misuse, and in any case the unions themselves had always been highly politicized. Given that their leadership was so implicated in violence and openly involved (and latently still more so) with external interference, it was hardly surprising that the PPP should have sought a means to challenge it.[39] Two major spheres were involved. In Georgetown the Guyanese TUC, based principally on urban workers' unions, had traditionally been led by middle-class professionals; after a brief radical phase in the early 1950s its leadership had now reverted, largely

---

[37] Cmnd 1870, p. 6.

[38] Simms (1966), pp. 165–6.

[39] In view of which one observer suggests, not unreasonably, that possibly something far more decisive than the bill was required, a Ghanaian type of affiliation between the unions and ruling party often being necessary for stable post-colonial development. This was corroborated by the PPP government's experience, though it could hardly have come about without healing the 1955 split (B.A.N. Collins, 'The Civil Service of British Guiana in the General Strike of 1963', *Carib. Q.*, 10/2 (1964), p. 12).

under US pressure, as described on p. 67, to a highly conservative and anti-PPP position under its president, Richard Ishmael, who had been a militant UF supporter primarily responsible for the TUC's part in the previous year's disturbances.[40] A similar pattern had developed in the sugar industry, where the only recognized union, the conservative MPCA, a member of the TUC and also led by Ishmael, was opposed by the Guyana Agricultural Workers' Union (GAWU); the latter was closely identified with the PPP. The PPP's allegation that the MPCA was a company union with only minority support—one of the main arguments behind the Labour Relations Bill—was in part justified, if somewhat over-simplified. The MPCA had apparently received money from the Sugar Producers' Association,[41] which offered to recognize the GAWU only on very limited terms, including the obvious deterrent that a worker could still only resign from the MPCA through management,[42] on the grounds that dues were otherwise automatically deducted from wages. And in fact most of the sugar workers probably belonged to both unions, regarding the MPCA as a proven, if limited bargaining force—this in part precisely because of management's anxiety about the GAWU—and the GAWU as a possible source of basic reforms in the sugar industry. In practice the moral recriminations from both sides on the whole issue were little more than a mutual façade, given the unions' inherently political nature. Each side inevitably saw them as a means to incompatible goals—on the one hand a conservatism ranging from Bookers' belief in the role of expatriate private enterprise to an uninhibited UF-cum-CIA aim (see below) of overcoming the PPP by any means available; on the other a radicalism ranging from socialist goals—to which means could also have been secondary, though this was far from demonstrated—to a simple determination that the unions should not be used as an instrument of foreign-backed subversion. By 1963 a virtual deadlock had been reached: direct UF-PNC control of the urban union sector and a *de facto* PPP hold on the agricultural workers through the militant GAWU. The translation of any external concern into direct influence might therefore be a decisive factor in the political balance of power.

Reaction to the bill was based on the previous year's experience. Demonstrations in Georgetown, again outwardly fostered by the local business sector and conservative union leaders, developed into a general strike. Violence recurred and again it was racial, partly because most of

[40] Col. 354, paras 23–5.
[41] Cmnd 9274, pp. 59–60.
[42] Communication with Booker Bros., Aug. 1968.

the members of the GAWU, which refused to join the strike, happened to be Indian. PPP overtures were rebuffed by the union leaders, and as Robert Willis, General Secretary of the London Typographical Society and acting mediator, put it: 'The strike was wholly political. Jagan was giving in to every thing the strikers wanted, but as soon as he did so, they erected new demands.'[43] Eventually the strike was ended by the labour bill's repeal, the implication of which was clear—namely that the government could simply be held to ransom. The strike had lasted eighty days and crippled the economy. Apparently the strikers' resources could last as long as politically necessary—in strike pay alone the bill was nearly $1 m.[44] Since this was out of all proportion to the TUC's resources, one immediate question was: where did it come from?

Jagan's answer, the CIA, seemed too much of a cliché to merit attention. However, in view of Willis's statement, reported demands by the State Department for the removal of the PPP began to lend it a certain credence. On 29 June 1963 it was stated in *The Times* that Dean Rusk had urged Lord Home and Colonial Secretary, Duncan Sandys, to suspend the constitution. Then on 10 July the *New York Times* reported that President Kennedy had been assured that the British were no longer contemplating independence for Guyana: it added that Dean Rusk had suggested the imposition of proportional representation. Questioned on these reports by Jennie Lee in the House of Commons, Sandys simply replied that he was unaware of them and also, therefore, of any need to 'warn' the State Department.[45] Subsequently Drew Pearson, in a syndicated article published on 22 March 1964, went so far as to claim that the 1963 strike had been fomented and financed by a combination of the CIA and British intelligence bent on forestalling independence under Jagan.[46] Despite this, there was no further comment until three years later, when the *Sunday Times*, on 16 April 1967 gave a detailed analysis of the CIA operation, based on information from the ex-president of the union used, on his own admission, as a front by the Agency. Throughout the strike this union had been passing on CIA funds to Guyana through the representative there of Public Service International, an international trades union secretariat to which it was affiliated, itself a member of the International Confederation of Free Trade Unions. And a week later the *Sunday Times* added that according to 'a senior British security officer' this was done with the complicity of the British Prime Minister, Colonial Secretary, and head of security. These reports were not denied by any

[43] ST, 16 Apr. 1968.
[44] *The Times*, 5 July 1963.
[45] HC Deb., 17 July 1963, col. 529.
[46] Cited in Jagan (1966), p. 303.

of those implicated, nor by any official body; and their details were consistent with those of Britain's ambivalence throughout the strike crisis, now virtually tantamount to a direct opposition to the PPP government.[47] What was significant, however, was not the evidence itself—the operation was a logical outcome of Anglo-American policy—so much as the astonishment it provoked. It was an indication of the vital credibility which the British government had always enjoyed in its handling of Guyana. Even Newman (p. 94 n.), a far from gullible observer, had taken the original allegation of CIA involvement in the 1962 troubles as 'the most bizarre explanation yet seen'.

In October 1963 the constitutional conference was reconvened. Despite the long-standing undertaking (see n. 23) that the only outstanding issue was the date of independence, Sandys again changed his mind on this issue, since Burnham and d'Aguiar were still pressing for fresh elections and the proportional representation reportedly suggested by Dean Rusk. Eventually all the parties agreed, in view of the persistent deadlock, that the Colonial Secretary should impose a binding settlement. How Jagan ever consented to this in the light of his past experience is the crowning paradox of his career. Again the curious surrender at the most critical juncture to none other than imperial authority. No doubt he acted in despair at circumstances which had left him without a vestige of real power; but why, again, did he not resign whilst he still had substantial backing? Sandys's solution was a duplicate of the UF–Dean Rusk proposals: new elections; a new constitution, entailing the most extreme form of proportional representation (according to Jagan, recently described by Iain MacLeod, the previous Colonial Secretary, as a 'rotten and abominable' system and long before officially rejected[48] as inevitably comprising a device to remove the PPP); and, presumably in case the PPP managed to survive this, an indefinite postponement of independence. Burnham, apparently confident of the outcome of the elections, professed indignation at the postponement. Jagan castigated all three decisions. D'Aguiar, somewhat superfluously, expressed unqualified approval.[49]

This was yet another drastic change in the formal British position. It was not just a 'fiddled constitution' to overthrow the PPP, as Harold Wilson described it in the House of Commons on 17 June 1964, before

---

[47] Two of its features were the Governor's refusal of Jagan's request that alleged CIA employees Doherty and McCabe be deported as constituting threats to national security (*Guardian*, 17 Apr. & 29 May 1963); and the British rejection, reportedly under US pressure, of a suggested UN mission to inquire into the strike (ibid., 6 Nov. 1963).

[48] Jagan (1966), p. 327; Cmnd 9274, p. 30.

[49] *Guardian*, 2 Nov. 1963.

he sanctioned it. In precisely implementing the opposition's programme, it finally vindicated their part in the violence of the previous two years. The apologia was a thin one. The constitution purported to aim at obviating racism and encouraging new leadership. In fact it was almost guaranteed to cement the existing leadership; the lack of a constituency system meant that people were bound to turn to familiar political figures. As for its effect on the racialism already so highly coincident with acts of British policy, it rapidly inflated it. Early in 1964 the pattern of the previous year was reversed when the majority of sugar workers struck to reassert the GAWU's claim for official recognition. Violence again began in Georgetown, where the recognized TUC was brought out to demonstrate against the strike. This time there could be no mistake about its basically racial pattern. Retaliations spread through the country on exclusively racial and increasingly violent lines: bombings, murder, and arson were commonplace. There was even widespread talk of partition as the only solution to the racial conflict which had by now developed typically from a gloss on the focal issue—the economic frustration and political factionalism engendered over the past ten years almost wholly by outside pressure—into an all-consuming prime mover.

With the economy almost crippled, the country went to the polls again in December 1964 under the Sandys constitution. Even Britain's timing of this was directed against the PPP, whose term of office could have run for a further period which would have brought substantial numbers of new Indian voters into the electorate. The results were predictable, corresponding almost precisely—and thus precisely contradicting the alleged aim of the constitution—to the country's ethnic ratios: the PPP gained the most votes but fell short of the absolute majority necessitated by the new constitution. With a record 96 per cent poll, this confirmed that racial anxieties were now a universal as well as an exclusive force. Despite their higher proportion of votes, the PPP offered Burnham a coalition, which would have given him the premiership and equal party representation on a ministerial level. He had good reason for refusing. When he did so, the Governor asked him to form a government of his own, which he achieved predictably through a coalition with the UF. He still maintained, as he always had, that his position was socialist. However, he omitted to explain how he managed to reconcile this with a coalition with a party which he himself had characterized as standing exclusively for 'big business'.[50]

Clearly this coalition was the modified basis of the long-standing British model for an independent Guyana. By this time, however, the

[50] *Guardian*, 14 Dec. 1964.

evidence suggests that they were acting primarily on behalf of the State Department, rather than in their own right. Guyana had run the full gamut of postwar Conservative rule, from its pre-Suez days to the post-MacLeod phase, in which dependencies were acknowledged as little more than an embarrassment. Economically problematic and politically bewildering, this small but strategically important case was clearly no exception. The 1964 constitution and its electoral results were the foreseeable culmination of a decade-long policy, but one which the British might well have abandoned but for its new and wider significance. When it was finally implemented by a Labour government, it was a largely vicarious gesture, tailored, as it had been financed, to fit the US definition of western hemispheric order.

INDEPENDENCE: THE CONTRADICTIONS OF THE INTER-AMERICAN SYSTEM

Fitting this definition so closely, the PNC–UF coalition promptly rode high on the foreign aid and moral support available to it. Comment was muffled by the detention of several PPP leaders: and violence declined at a rate which was generally construed as a measure of the government's stability, rather than one of the extent to which violence might have depended on an opposition with external support. The Labour government in Britain, formerly so critical of Tory policy on Guyana, did nothing to alter it. The coalition and the 'fiddled constitution' were approved as the basis of the independence granted in 1966, when the country became 'Guyana', despite nation-wide and peaceful PPP protests.

In the short term this was predictable as the framework of an independence which had come to be limited to the client sovereignty of a divided community. What, then, in longer terms, of the Guyana which had seemed possible only thirteen years before—one which aspired to an authentic and united independence? Was the nationalists' brief success just a historical cul-de-sac, or does it still have some political relevance?

At present, despite some changes of style and, to a lesser extent, of content, the country's clientship role, with the single complex exception of the bauxite economy, seems increasingly dominant: the profusion of protests to the contrary—usually governmental and uncritically adopted abroad—is in part a response to the crisis symptoms for which that traditional scapegoat, the PPP, can no longer be blamed. Nor is this continued lack of independence surprising. Since Guyana is small but strategically important, replete with colonial liabilities and yet free of the more glaring social contrasts of other South American countries, the

F

incentives for manipulation are high and the problems involved are relatively few. The accession of a government supported by the western powers did inevitably produce a face-lift. British, Canadian, and above all US aid and investment soared. Since the 1964 election the latter's per capita rate, previously negligible, has been exceeded only by that to Panama:[51] and for all its openly political intent—expressed succinctly by one quite impartial observer as the 'sinking of Jagan'[52]—it did stimulate higher exports of primary products and the initial resources for some import substitution. Politically too the balance continued to alter in favour of the moderates. PPP leadership grew diffident: Jagan resorted increasingly to a Marxist fundamentalism still devoid of strategic adaptation to the Guyanese specifications, while the youth wing of the party under Moses Bhagwan adopted a verbally Guevarist line. Neither of these was likely to appeal to the party's traditional following; Bhagwan's group dwindled after he left the country to study, and in any case violence in Guyana, unless highly strategic and subsidized, as previously, is now bound to lose political direction in a purely racial morass. Any disruptive policy would have to concentrate carefully on the contradictions in Burnham's position. And initially these were only latent; rather, outward stability and formal economic growth gave his regime a certain prestige. By the time the UF left the 1964 coalition, in response to mounting allegations of PNC partiality in the registration of voters for the 1968 elections, enough opposition members had crossed the floor of the National Assembly to give the PNC an independent majority. Even before the first election in a sovereign Guyana, the ghost of 1953 and authentic independence was for the moment apparently laid.

Not, however, without deep scars. From 1966 onwards authoritarian rule and eventually corruption deepened dramatically, whilst social divisions remained. And despite some success in other fields, notably the diplomatic and to some extent the economic, all this occurred in forms directly traceable, both in principle and detail, to the Anglo-American handling of late colonial politics. This was most evident in the maintenance of the old colonial tradition of constitutional manipulation, though in ways distinctly less discreet than those developed by the British. As the 1968 elections approached and the PNC talked increasingly of their need for an absolute majority, constitutional amendments flowed. Amongst other things it was now ruled that political parties need no longer list their candidates; they could be appointed by party leaders after the elections, so that the winner would in effect appoint not just his

51 *NYT*, 22 Dec. 1968.
52 *The Times*, 10 Feb. 1968.

cabinet but his legislature as well. Another bill transferred control of the registration of voters from the all-party commission previously specified to the hands of the government alone; and a third extended the franchise not only to Guyanese permanently resident overseas, but also to anyone born in the country, anyone whose father was born there, and the wives of all these categories, regardless of nationality.[53] As their registration was organized by PNC-picked diplomats and party members in New York and London, it was widely assumed that it would be as partial as was already alleged of registration in Guyana; and that with these innovations the government would be unbeatable. Nevertheless, they were taking no chances. A few weeks before the elections seventeen PPP members were arrested and held on vague charges.[54] And when the international press did produce evidence of massive anomalies in the overseas registration,[55] local papers were forbidden to publish it. The staff of the only one which did mention it were arrested on criminal charges.[56] Despite all this, the elections went ahead. The constitutional provision for a neutral electoral commission was ignored and with the whole electoral machinery firmly in government hands ballot papers were finally counted, after being taken there by the openly pro-PNC police, in six heavily guarded centres, instead of the electoral districts as formerly.[57] Though observers could not detect any outward trend away from the PPP, the official results gave the PNC 30 parliamentary seats to the PPP's 19 and the UF's four, with the major proportion of their lead resulting from the dubious 'overseas vote', which was 23 per cent of the total vote cast and 94 per cent PNC. Moreover in Guyana PPP voters, put by the party at several thousand, were stated to have arrived at the polls to find that their votes had already been cast by unauthorised 'proxy voters'. Given free elections, there is little to suggest that the results would have differed greatly from those of 1964. Scandalized overseas reactions failed to assess the degree of continuity between this and the way in which power had long since functioned in Guyana under British supervision and added US influence. The one new aspect was the scale

---

[53] *NYT*, 27 Oct., 13 & 16 Dec. 1968.
[54] *Le Monde*, 8 Jan. 1969.
[55] For a summary of the sources see *ST*, 15 Dec., 1968. An Opinion Research Centre sample of 1,000 names and addresses from the official registration list produced the following results: proven errors (non-existent addresses etc.) 72 per cent; queries (e.g. not available after four calls) 14 per cent; correct 15 per cent. Granada TV samples in London and Manchester produced similar results. The poll among overseas voters, however, was over 50 per cent of the official list; and this despite numerous complaints from legitimate voters, mainly PPP members, of not receiving ballot forms.
[56] *NYT*, 13 Dec. 1968.
[57] *Guardian & NYT*, 16 Dec. 1968.

and overtness of what occurred. It was apparently assumed that as long as elections were held their actual form would soon be forgotten, at least abroad. Burnham's open derision for the opposition's protests were symptomatic: they were 'petty details', he said, merely 'the bleatings of the losers'.[58]

In effect he was right, since they went unheeded. An apparently guaranteed, though not in essence unprecedented, form of political control had emerged; and the PPP's conservatism, an increasingly old-world blend of Marxist–Leninist language and strict parliamentarianism, offered no positive opposition. Rather the remaining weaknesses of a quasi-democratic structure, geared in origin and essence to the maintenance in power of a minority regime, were carefully eliminated. Further constitutional and legal amendments made the contesting of electoral corruption through parliamentary or legal action technically almost impossible: notable among them were the repeal of the obligation to publish proxy voter lists and the imposition of a heavy advance deposit against costs on legal actions over registration or alleged electoral fraud. And in 1970, when local government elections were due, the system was put to the test again, this time with proxy voting as the main bone of contention. Traditionally proxy votes were conceded only to those physically unable to cast their own—invalids, etc. But by 1970 the qualifications for a proxy vote had broadened so far that any voter could obtain one (or be persuaded to) if voting in person was 'impracticable' for him because of his occupation 'or for other good cause'.[59] As a result, since then the obligation to cede one's vote has become a common precondition of any, especially public, employment. Despite the legal and other less formal barriers to protest, there is available evidence that by the time of the local elections (June and December 1970) 'proxy' votes, including extorted and invented ones, were some 15–20 per cent of the total and the keystone of the system.[60] In the face of this, plus eye-witness accounts of police removals of ballot boxes and the intimidation of opposition agents and voters, both opposition parties withdrew after the first few contests, held

[58] *The Times*, 16, 17, 19 & 20 Dec. 1968.

[59] Representation of the People (Adaptation & Modification of Laws) Act, 1968, 31.

[60] Since the previous obligation to publish proxy voting lists had by now been repealed, the only statistical source for this, as opposed to numerous random testimonies, consists of the figures gathered by opposition agents at polling booths in the five districts fought in June. In these 16·7 per cent of the 65,000 votes were proxy and a fair proportion were disputed by the persons in whose names they were cast. (The figures varied from 13·7 per cent for the Greater Georgetown District to 37·0 per cent in Bartica: the sample was 100 per cent and the documentation appears reasonable). Also the electoral list had grown more in the four years between 1964 and 1968 than in the previous eleven: the figure for some government-controlled districts being over 100 per cent, for some opposition ones less than 5 per cent (each vote of which would of course weigh, under proportional representation).

in June in advance of the others. Even the miniature, ephemeral opposition parties of every Guyanese election with no connection with the big ones and only a handful of candidates complained of exactly the same treatment. Not unnaturally, every single local authority is now PNC-controlled, many without opposition. The country's outward political culture is, it seems, coming into line with its now virtually dictatorial political structure. It is not wholly flippant to suggest that Guyana has joined the category of inter-American democracies not entirely immune to the danger of their elections being won by over 100 per cent of the votes.

This process has been described in detail because it demonstrates not only the persistent principles of power in Guyana but also their direct origins in recent 'foreign influence' and their compatibility with the perfectly respectable image which the regime still enjoys. Indeed, one might argue on the PNC's behalf that it can hardly retreat from these principles, even given the will to do so; that having been forged from without by constitutional manipulation, artificial social conflict, and ultimately by absolutism in the form of imperial authority, it may simply have to sustain and perhaps even intensify such mechanisms of control in order to remain in power. And however diplomatic in outward appearance, these were precisely the mechanisms on which British policy depended for thirteen formative years. Whilst democracy and social cohesion were the stated criteria for mapping a course towards independence, both were visibly dispensable for British and US authorities alike when they conflicted with their interests. In the circumstances it is hard to imagine any clear-seeing Guyanese emerging from the period with a vision of democracy and constitutional forms in general as anything more in practice than the manipulable means to self-legitimizing power; or unaware that factionalism had been made a far more reliable rallying point than any quest for cohesion.

Up to and including the elections of 1968, when it might have been argued that the new regime was simply consolidating its power, it was still possible that, despite its origins, the PNC would seek a more genuinely popular basis by confronting the contradictions of Guyanese society. And there are indications—notably in the declaration in February 1970 of a 'Co-operative Republic' to involve the masses in development and eradicate a 'colonial mentality'—that the issue was so defined. Other economic moves also point, if modestly, to the same horizons, notably Guyanese influence on Caribbean regional integration and the government's demands for a controlling interest in Demba, the main bauxite concern, and subsequently for its nationalization. In overall practice, though, the regime is riding rather than resolving the contradictions which helped create it. For all its credibility—the first phase of the 1970 elections, for instance, was internationally reported simply as 'a landslide PNC victory'[61]—it appears to have forgone any hope of conciliation and basic change on the socio-economic, as well as at the electoral, level. As elsewhere in the Caribbean, increased wealth in the middle sectors is far more evident than any reduction of poverty in the mud-ridden coastal villages and 'tenement' (wooden range) slums of Georgetown. This is borne out statistically by the real stagnation at low wage levels—the government minimum of $2·10 per day is now one of the lowest in the Caribbean—compared with the growth at high levels. In such circumstances the spectacular national growth figures (still mainly accounted for by the sugar and bauxite industries) merely suggest that social reform is as far away as ever: as does the persistence of the traditionally high unemployment[62] synonymous with the continuation of an almost exclusively primary-producing economy. Foreign debt also continues to soar, having by 1968 quadrupled in the previous twelve years,[63] eroding foreign-exchange earnings and resources for reinvestment; this too is inseparable from the past, in its derivation from the dependence on foreign—and exclusively western—aid and investment capital. And despite the implied admission, in the anti-colonial mentality ideology of the 'Co-operative Republic', that this commitment was counter-productive, foreign capital continues to play a major part in the economy: an unprecedented proportion of capital receipts for 1971 are scheduled to come from foreign loans.[64] As to the Co-operative programme's role in the social framework

[61] *The Times* 1 July 1970. And since credibility is the issue, it is worth noting that this report was reproduced in Embert Hendrickson, 'New directions in a republican Guyana', *The World Today*, Jan. 1971, p. 39. This without any assessment of the allegations over the conduct of the elections, although they are cited.

[62] Internat. Financ. News Survey, 1 Sept. 1970, where it is stated that according to the Minister of Finance the 1969 growth in GDP was 9 per cent; those of sugar and bauxite being 14 and 20 per cent respectively. No official figures on unemployment are published and assesments remain difficult: however, it is generally admitted that if reductions have occurred, they have at best been minor. At the PNC Congress in April 1970, for instance, it was put by Hubert Jack, Minister without Portfolio, at 'between 15 and 20 per cent' ('Policy for the New Coop. Republic', 13th PNC Ann. Congress, Georgetown, 1970, p. 89).

[63] *FT*, 30 Oct. 1970. In 1969–70 this rate of increase continued. And by this time 70 per cent of the total national debt was foreign. (*Estimates . . . . for the year 1971* (Georgetown, 1970) p. 6).

[64] The figures have increased steadily since 1968: for capital receipts as a whole, they are as follows: 1968: external grants $2·9 m., internal loans $2·4 m., external loans $8·0 m.; 1971 (est.): $0·06 m., $5·5 m., and $24·0 m. respectively (*Est . . . for the year 1971*). And the government's public statements continually mirror this contradiction, depending on whether they are for local or foreign consumption. (Cf., for example, Burnham's references to socialism and the evils of foreign capital in *Policy for the New Coop. Republic*, pp. 7–11 and the emphasis on 'private enterprise in a developing community' in Min. of Information, *Guyana in Brief* (1970).)

of the ten-year development programme launched in 1970, its scale and actual social effects remain to be seen. Despite its international acclaim, Guyanese themselves seem sceptical; inevitably so about 'self-help' (on which such emphasis is placed) to finance basic services, when corruption is alleged to be rife[65] and luxury expenditure is so ostentatious among ministers; and about co-operatives, when they are as yet few and are widely believed, sometimes demonstrably, to bring disproportionate benefit to precisely the same ministerial sector.

Socially and politically, the price of Guyana's having been moulded into an acceptable shape is still evident. The almost total persistence of the ethnically separate communities to which refugees fled seven years ago casts doubt on the claim that 'self-help' has reduced racial mistrust. A recommendation by the International Commission of Jurists for ethnically balanced recruitment into the traditionally African defence and security forces appears to have been largely ignored, although the government committed itself to taking its advice; and the conventional apology that Indians make reluctant recruits does little to reduce the divisive effect of these forces' ever-increasing presence, with road-blocks and searches as an everyday procedure. Not surprisingly in the circumstances, PNC assertions in the 1970 election campaign, that the price of opposition victory would be a return to racial violence, were taken as threats rather than warnings. It is widely and deeply felt, and not just among Indians, that the government is a racial, not a national, interest group; and its leaders—except verbally and in part it seems for export—have done little to reduce this feeling. The reason for this probably is that having had power thrust on them in a context of consciously racial alignments, they are politically unable to dispense with their racial overtones. Should they try to do so, at least one explicitly racial grouping—the Association for Cultural Relations with Independent Africa, which dates from the violence of the early 1960s, when its leader Sidney King advocated racial partition—could well threaten overnight such popular hold as the PNC has. (Significantly, as proof of their strength and a relevant factor in the government's radical stance over bauxite, this group is particularly influential in the bauxite workers' union.)

Given that political alignments are themselves now so racial, increasing authoritarianism in the conduct of government adds to the tension. In addition to the strict security laws allowing for detention without trial ever since 1966 and deteriorating relations between government and

[65] The auditors' report on government expenditure for 1967 was unable to account for some $10 m., for example. And recently several high-ranking and non-political figures in Guyana, including local churchmen, have denounced the prevalence of corruption (*Guardian*, 23 Feb. 1970).

unions, due partly to pending labour legislation severer than the PPP's,[66] Parliament is now as constrained as in the period of imperial nominees and vetos: the house is rarely convened on days allocated to members' motions, and standing orders are suspended at convenience to rush through government bills almost without opposition, let alone public comment. The political interpretation of this and the otherwise impractical degree of electoral steam-rolling is that the PNC may be aiming at a one-party system. This too has respectable third world precedents: but not in contexts like Guyana's. Burnham already rejected a broad, nation-building, one-party structure when in 1964 he spurned the coalition offered by the PPP in favour of one with the UF, in keeping with his personal and with British preferences and contrary to those of his party's left wing. Should it now be imposed, as seems possible, it would institutionalize, not bridge, the political divisions imposed by the uniquely colonial format of Guyana's 'independence'.

Ironically any such formal move, in its final suppression of the dialectic still faintly sustained by the opposition, would be even closer than the present situation to Britain's retreat in the 1950s to direct imperial rule. That the PPP have failed to update or advance this dialectic is after all no reflection on its basic validity; and despite their inflexibility, they still lend weight as an opposition to the persistent contradictions underlying the present regime and so help to force concessions from it, notably over bauxite and more widely on a verbal level. For the moment it is on this latter level, in the highly disparate images which the regime must cultivate for its different audiences, that these contradictions remain most apparent: an internal image of radical reform, yet based necessarily on a thinly-veiled suggestion of force; externally one of *ad hoc* change based on reconciliation. Obviously these inconsistencies[67] will be increasingly hard to sustain, as internal expectations come into conflict with externally-derived constraints. As yet, however, the ultimate price of an independent Guyana's dependency remains to be seen.

[66] In its current form the National Security Act still allows, among numerous other items, for arrests and detention without charges being brought, a clause alleged by the opposition to have been regularly used for political harassment. The Trades Disputes Bill, still pending, would give either side in a dispute the right to call on the government to arbitrate compulsorily. Meanwhile troops have on various occasions been called in to confront strikers, as the sugar militants maintain their strength and the urban unions turn away from their leadership. In the first nine months of 1970 there were 115 strikes, 72 of them in the sugar industry. (*Guyana Graphic* (Georgetown), 9 Dec. 1970).

[67] Cf. note 65 for an illustration of this with regard to economic policy, the most striking one in the social sphere being with respect to the largely unimplemented recommendations of the Inquiry of the International Commission of Jurists; unimplemented despite the fact that Burnham personally requested the inquiry in order to allay alleged British anxieties at the prospect of granting independence to 'a government by Mr Burnham and the Negroes' (*NYT*, 7 Mar. 1964, cited by Glasgow (1970), p. 131).

REFERENCES

Bradley, C. P. The Party System in British Guiana and the General Election of 1961. *Caribbean Studies*, Oct. 1961.

Cmd 8980, 1953. GB, Colonial Office, *British Guiana; suspension of the constitution*.

Cmd 9274, 1954: British Guiana Constitutional Commission [Chairman: Sir James Robertson], *Report*.

Cmnd 998, 1960: British Guiana Constitutional Conference, *Report*.

Cmnd 1870, 1962: British Guiana Independence Conference, London, October 1962, *Report*.

Col. 280, 1951: GB, Colonial Office, Constitutional Commission, 1950–1 [Chairman: Sir Eubule J. Waddington], *Report*.

Col. 354, 1962: GB, Colonial Office, Commission of Inquiry into Disturbances in British Guiana in February 1962, *Report*.

Glasgow, R. A. *Guyana; race and politics among Africans and East Indians*. The Hague, 1970.

Jagan, Cheddi. *The West on trial*. London, 1966.

Newman, Peter. *British Guiana: problems of cohesion in an immigrant society*, London, 1964.

Simms, Peter. *Trouble in Guyana: people, personalities, and politics*. London, 1966.

Smith, Raymond. *British Guiana*. London, RIIA, 1962.

5 The French Antilles and their Status as Overseas Departments

GUY LASSERRE and ALBERT MABILEAU

THE law of 19 March 1946 conferred the status of overseas departments (*départements d'outre-mer*, known as DOM) on France's four 'old colonies' in the tropics, Guadeloupe, Martinique, French Guiana (Guyane), and La Réunion. It was at the request of the General Councils of the territories themselves that the Constituent Assembly, immediately after the second world war, unanimously voted for this measure of assimilation. From then on the inhabitants of these territories were no longer 'colonials' but as wholly French as those of the metropolitan departments. The colonial problem seemed to have been finally settled by this measure of integration, which crowned the process of decolonization begun in 1848 with the abolition of slavery in the French colonies and with the grant of suffrage to freed Negroes.

It is undeniable that assimilation gave rise to a remarkable economic impetus in the islands and to some improvement of the social conditions of the workers. Nevertheless, for a dozen years this policy of change to departmental status has been contested, sometimes with violence, and it is evident that it has not been able to settle all the economic and social problems of the former French colonies. This chapter will only discuss the French Antilles and will begin by considering their distinctiveness from France; we will then deal with the evolution of their political status before analysing aspects and causes of the current malaise.

I. THE CHARACTERISTICS OF THE FRENCH ANTILLES

The French Antilles consist of Guadeloupe and Martinique, but although they belong to France and are currently closely integrated with her through their departmental status, it should not be overlooked that they are very different from France and have their own specific problems arising from a tropical geographical situation and from over three centuries of colonial history.

1. Overpopulation

Martinique and Guadeloupe, which are separated from each other by the British island of Dominica, belong to the Lesser Antilles. These are tiny islands: Martinique covers 425 and Guadeloupe 583 square miles. Martinique would fit into an area 20·5 miles square and Guadeloupe into one 24 miles square.

The cultivable land is greatly restricted by the mountainous nature of the country and also by the climate. Situated between 14° and 16° north latitude, the Antilles have a hot and humid climate, but the rainfall, which is too abundant on the high slopes of the volcanic massif, is inadequate in the lower regions which cannot break up the Atlantic clouds, and even more so on the leeward coastlines sheltered from the trade winds. Thus it is its diversity that best characterizes the geographical personality of the French Antilles: the rocky, sun-scorched hills of the Caravelle, south Martinique, the Ile des Saintes, and St Barthélemy, the monotonous limestone plateau of Grande Terre, the evergreen equatorial forest of the Pitons du Carbet or the slopes of the Soufrière, the wind-swept and remote summits of the highest mountain ranges.

Human settlement has reinforced this natural diversity in the variety of physical types because of the heterogeneity of the population and the differences in land occupancy and cultivation.

The settlement of the French Antilles is intimately related to the development of tropical sugar plantations. The labour force of the great domains, known as *habitations*, was drawn from Africa and poured into the sugar islands by slave ships. The rapid disappearance of the original inhabitants, the Arawaks and Caribs, who were few in number, the installation of whites, who were rapidly outnumbered by black slaves, the interbreeding between whites and blacks, all resulted from the plantation system.

The Antilleans still distinguish between various groups within the population: the 'Blancs-France', the 'Blancs-Pays', Syrians, Negroes, 'Indians', and half-castes or 'coloureds' in the strict sense of the word. Each of these groups is in turn subdivided on the basis of criteria which are not only anthropological but also sociological. The Negro lawyer or doctor does not belong to the same group as the plantation 'Nég' because he does not come from the same social class. The 'Blancs-France' are either birds of passage or recent settlers: officials, technicians, soldiers, etc. Another stratum of whites is that of the 'Blancs-Pays', called 'Békés' in Martinique. These are Creoles, i.e. local-born whites of families who have been in the Antilles for several generations. They all speak the Creole patois and have property in the islands. In Martinique they are in possession of most of the land. Within this group are the 'Petits-Blancs', whose situation in the social scale is a good deal lower. In Guadeloupe this white population of modest rank is mainly represented in the 'petites dépendances' (Désirade, St Barthélemy) and the region of Grands-Fonds in Grande Terre, where the 'Blancs-Matignon' or poor whites live.

The Syrians are to Guadeloupe what the Chinese are to La Réunion, but there are very few of them in Martinique. They specialize in trade. As for the Indians, they are the descendants of workers recruited in India after the abolition of slavery in 1848. They were mainly introduced during the thirty years from 1855 to 1885. Most of the population of the Antilles consists of Negroes and coloureds, but each island has a different skin tone. Martinique is more hybrid than Guadeloupe. The 'petites dépendances', which are too small and too dry to permit of plantation agriculture, have a very light coloured population, especially St Barthélemy, where an almost pure white element constitutes nearly 90 per cent of the population. The history of settlement is thus indissolubly bound up with the occupation and exploitation of the land.

The population of the Antilles has a very vigorous growth-rate and its rate of increase gives much cause for concern and makes the problem of unemployment more and more serious. In 1954 the two islands had a total population of 468,250 persons; at the 1961 census they had 573,918; in October 1967, 633,000; of these 320,000 live in Martinique and 313,000 in Guadeloupe. The population has doubled in some twenty-five years. Population density per square kilometre is very high: 175 per sq. km. in Guadeloupe and 290 in Martinique. Density per hectare of cultivable land is five or six times higher in the island overseas departments than in metropolitan France.

The growth-rates of the population are extremely high: 2·4 per cent in Martinique and 2·9 per cent in Guadeloupe, as against 0·7 per cent in metropolitan France. This results from the fact that crude birth-rates are very high while crude death-rates are rapidly falling thanks to an improvement in public health conditions and in living standards and the continuing rejuvenation of the population. Between the two wars the natural population increase was about 4,500 a year in the French Antilles: 2,000 in Guadeloupe and 2,500 in Martinique. At present it is 16,500 a year, 8,000 in Martinique and 8,500 in Guadeloupe. This has had two main consequences. The first is the youth of the population. While in metropolitan France only 33 per cent of the population consists in persons under twenty years old, in 1966 the percentages were 52·6 in Martinique and 53·1 in Guadeloupe. It is the youth of this population which explains why death-rates are lower in the French Antilles than in metropolitan France.

The second result is the importance of dependants which adults of working age have to support. In France in 1961, 100 adults had to support 99 persons (64 young people and 35 elderly). In the Antilles the burden is much heavier and consists mainly of young people. In Martinique 100 adults were responsible for 144 persons (126 young and 18 old); in Guadeloupe they were responsible for 148 persons (131 young and 17 old). Every plan for social and economic development must first take into account these truly alarming demographic facts.

2. Economy and Employment

The economy of the French Antilles is characterized by intensive specialization in agricultural products and by the high share of services—over 60 per cent—in the GDP, while the share of agriculture has greatly diminished as is shown in the following table:

GDP by sector (per cent)

Sector	Guadeloupe			Martinique		
	1961	1965	1968	1961	1965	1968
Primary (agric.)	33	25	15	28	22	12
Secondary (bldg, public works, industry)	11	14	15	14	16	17
Tertiary (trade, rents services, educ. & health)	} 56	} 61	57	} 58	} 62	58
Administration			13			13
GDP	100	100	100	100	100	100

Sources: Comm. Centrale des DOM, V^e plan 1966–70, rapport général, p. 82 & Inst. d'Émission des DOM (IEDOM), Rapport d'activité; exercice 1969 (1970), p. 17.

The major part of the population is engaged in some or other branch of agricultural activity: in 1961 37 per cent of the Martiniquans and 46 per cent of the Guadeloupans, and in both islands 62 per cent of the population was rural, as against 38 per cent which was urban. It is impossible to realize the economic and social problems of the French Antilles if one does not see them in their true context; they are essentially part of that group of tropical countries in which the peasant economy is at subsistence level and is of prime importance in the overall picture. However, alongside of this are the great sugar plantations established by Europeans; they have the lion's share of the land, and it is because of them that the sugar islands have had the reputation of being rich and prosperous. The marked decline in agriculture between 1965 and 1968 has been mainly due to four hurricanes, to high wages and production costs, and to urban migration, especially of young people. Both islands lack raw materials for industry and have to import fuel from Curaçao and Trinidad to produce electricity; they are basically agricultural in outlook, depending on overseas trade—overwhelmingly with metropolitan France—for exports and imports. They have preserved a colonial-type economy and their sugar-island background and lack of natural resources have been responsible for this. A striking feature of the economy is the size of the sector devoted to the production of food for domestic consumption, but even so foodstuffs swell the imports of consumer goods required by the highly salaried employees in the public sector; these employees, who constitute only 10 per cent of the employed population, share about half the total of all salaries.[1]

The major agricultural products are sugar-cane and bananas in Guadeloupe, bananas, sugar-cane, and pineapples in Martinique. In the northern part of Martinique bananas have been particularly important because they can be grown on smallholdings and need no mechanization, and because cane was associated with slavery and has the disadvantage of requiring processing in factories belonging to *Békés*. Thus bananas totalled some 60 per cent of Martinique's exports, as against 30 per cent for Guadeloupe, until the plantations were severely damaged by hurricanes. The crop was in any case vulnerable to fluctuations in demand and there was no prospect for any increase in production since France is the sole customer. Other outlets are closed because bananas are produced more cheaply elsewhere.[2]

Sugar is still the basic staple of the economy. On average it accounted for half the value of exports from the islands (in 1969 for 115 m. francs out of a total of 412 m.).[3] Again, except for some 30 per cent of the total for Guadeloupe, France is overwhelmingly the main customer. For 1955–68 Guadeloupe produced some 195,000 tons and Martinique 85,000, but because of hurricane damage, production fell in November 1969 to 165,000 and 32,000 tons respectively, and the islands have not been able to fulfil the EEC quota allocated to them. Replanting and reorganization is being undertaken with French help, which includes the provision of

---

[1] *Le Monde*, 6 Jan. 1970.
[2] *Ibid.*, 6 Jan. 1970.
[3] IEDOM, *Rapport . . .* 1969, p. 42.

mechanical equipment and the introduction of new methods of cutting the cane.[4]

The production of fresh and tinned pineapples has been a notable feature of the economy of Martinique, accounting for 10 per cent of the total of exports; in 1968 three factories produced 18,000 tins. However, since the islands became subject to EEC regulations for fruit and vegetables, Martinique has suffered from a fall in demand for tinned pineapples; half of the French market is supplied by the Ivory Coast and the overseas territories.[5] Another export is rum (108 m. hl. in 1969). Attempts to cultivate coffee and cacao have been almost abandoned, but there has been a limited success in producing fresh vegetables for export in Martinique (2,000 tons in 1969).[6]

Industrial production remains slight, despite considerable investment during recent years. In Guadeloupe it accounted for only 4 per cent of GDP in 1965 and 6 per cent in 1968, the figures for Martinique being 5 and 6 per cent respectively (excluding industries of agricultural origin such as sugar mills, distilleries, and pineapple-canning factories).[7] The colonial heritage, shortage of raw materials, and the very limited local market for industrial produce all account for this, but so too does departmental status. For this has imposed on the islands a high level of salaries and social costs which deter private investment. They are financed by the metropolitan government, but such aid is non-productive. The metropolitan share of public expenditure has been steadily mounting: in 1969 it amounted to 834 m. francs compared with 551 m. francs generated locally, representing an increase of 9 per cent in Guadeloupe and of 13 per cent in Martinique.[8] In the four years 1961–5 public expenditure more than doubled, and in 1969 had gone up by 12 per cent. It is these incoming public funds which encourage the serious adverse balance of trade, whereas in 1964 Guadeloupe's exports slightly exceeded imports and those of Martinique balanced.

As for tourism, on which so many hopes were founded, its contribution is still small. While the number of tourists has increased from 9,000 in 1961 to c. 50,000 in 1969, this is a negligible figure compared with the whole Caribbean (c. 3 m. in 1969).[9]

It is thus not surprising that unemployment and underemployment

4 Guadeloupe Préfecture, *La Guadeloupe économique*, Sept. 1967 (mimeo); *Le Monde*, 23–24 Nov. 1969.
5 *Le Monde*, 6 Jan. 1970.
6 IEDOM, *Rapport 1969*, p. 32.
7 Ibid., p. 33.
8 Ibid., p. 74.
9 Ibid., p. 36.

are serious problems. In the course of the fourth Plan, which ran from 1961 to 1965, only 24,000 jobs were created. A distinct falling-off in numbers employed in agriculture reflects progress in mechanization and the disinclination of young people to work on the land; the new jobs were created in the services and public departments. The fifth Plan (1966–70) envisaged creating rather more than 12,000 new jobs in each island, whereas it was estimated that demand would be some 22,000 in Martinique and 25,000 in Guadeloupe.[10] For the duration of the sixth Plan it was established that a minimum of 30,000 jobs would be necessary for each island, but industry has only a few dozen vacancies a year. According to a census of the potentially active population conducted by INSEE, in Martinique there were only 85,000 jobs for 180,000 persons and in Guadeloupe the same number of jobs for 110,000 persons.[11] The situation is especially alarming among young people. The fall in employment figures reflects the entry into an already saturated market of the postwar population bulge. The situation is one which can only deteriorate, for no increase in the number of jobs can keep step with the current population expansion. The only remedy is emigration, almost all directed to metropolitan France, which since 1963 has been organized by a Bureau known as BUMIDOM. In 1969 some 2,500 persons from each island migrated to France; the figure envisaged by the fifth Plan was 3,000, and is currently about 8,000 per year. French Guiana, which is very underpopulated and is now the site of the National Centre for Space Studies, might attract immigrants from Martinique and Guadeloupe, but at present they would rather go to Paris than Cayenne.

Even this brief analysis of the economic and demographic organization of the French Antilles is sufficient to show how profoundly they differ from metropolitan France. Their problems spring from their geographical location, their historical past, over-population, and in part from their departmental status. The tertiary sector occupies the preponderant place in the economy, paid for by public funds transferred from France, which also finances the cost of administration. Indeed, most of the islands' activities—industry, trade, tourism, and cultural life—are run from France. For some this overlapping of interests is an argument in favour of departmental status, but for others, who are eager to change the present economic and social structure, it is a powerful argument against the present status since it makes their dependence on France so absolute. Hence the interest of the analysis of the development of the political status of the French Antilles which follows.

[10] Comm. centrale des DOM, *Ve plan 1966–70*, p. 565.
[11] *Le Monde*, 7 Jan. 1970.

II. THE EVOLUTION OF THE STATUS OF THE ANTILLES

Since 1635 the 'Isles d'Amérique' have been French dependencies. During these three centuries relations between the Antilles and France have oscillated between two contradictory political formulas. Autonomy was the incessant demand of the local councils and the white people of consequence, who believed that this would enable them to assert a local particularism and put a brake on metropolitan tutelage. Assimilation was the principal objective of the metropolitan administration and of the Negroes, the one bowing to the traditional centralization of the French political and administrative system, the others seeking to be brought into line with the metropolitan power and an end to the economic and social domination of the whites. This contradiction has largely obscured the evolution of the status of the Antilles from the time of the colonial regime to the current modified departmental status.

1. The Old Colonies

Under the monarchy the Antilles were ruled by a Governor appointed by the king, with the help of a Council, consisting of white grandees who were nobles of French origin. The Council was the supreme power and often refused to bend to the royal will; its constant preoccupation to preserve the autonomy of the islands was combined with a determination to maintain the servitude of the coloured population. With the Revolution of 1789 the great issue became the abolition of slavery which, with the propagation of revolutionary ideas, dominated the political life of the Antilles and conditioned their status. Paris leaned to the side of autonomy in creating General Councils in 1827, finally proclaiming the abolition of slavery by the Schoelcher decree of 27 April 1848.

This was a decisive turning point. Not only was political equality bestowed on all the inhabitants of the islands, but a democratic regime was installed in France. The new colonial regime, settled until 1946 by a senate decree of 1854, was based on a democratic ideology and institutions. It had autonomist tendencies in spite of developing ever stronger ties with Paris.

The basic instrument of government remained the Governor. Directly representing the Minister for Colonies, he appeared to be the agent of the colonial power. His powers were indeed regal. He was aided by a consultative Privy Council consisting of the heads of the administrative services and men of consequence nominated by the metropolitan government. Nevertheless, the position of the Governor was an uneasy one. He could not permit himself to engage in open conflict with the local élites who

G

disposed of the political fiefdoms solidly entrenched in the islands and certainly all-powerful in Paris. There was also the General Council. It was the representative of the colony and exercised the autonomy bestowed on it; its budgetary powers and control of customs dues made it exceedingly powerful. It was the centre of local political life and its presence prevented the setting up of any system of direct administration. It was, however, far more preoccupied by political problems than by sound administration. The General Council upheld a tradition of independence *vis-à-vis* the metropolitan authorities.

Nevertheless the desire for self-government was never absolute. The term was associated with the old colonial regime, and the word 'colony' evoked memories of slavery. On the other hand the fiscal and financial autonomy of the islands, which was the most cogent indication of their autonomy, lost some of its charm when there was a crisis and a fall in prices; it would then have been preferable for the country's status not to have prevented the granting of metropolitan subsidies. Finally, for the new coloured élite France had a growing attraction: democracy, liberty, progress, lay across the sea with all the enchantment lent by distance. This is why the trend was reversed during the years preceding the second world war. This latter event broke the ties with France and simultaneously re-established government by whites; it further loaded the scales of opinion in favour of integration. The Fourth Republic was rapidly to institutionalize this development.

2. The Change to Departmental Status

The status of the Antilles was transformed in a new political context: the socialist and communist parties of the Antilles demanded assimilation, and the tripartite left-wing coalition government in Paris voted the law of 19 March 1946, which transformed the former colonies into departments and enshrined the assimilation formula with a view to abolishing distinctions from the metropolitan power and to associating the inhabitants in the running of their own affairs. Guadeloupe and Martinique became overseas departments. But French policy, above all in colonial affairs, was often content to state principles, leaving their application to the whim of circumstance, thereby destroying any continuity. As Marius Moutet, an expert in colonial problems, said so cogently during the parliamentary debates on the 1946 law: 'Will the populations of these former colonies always be governed by Paris or will they govern themselves? This is the problem: centralism or decentralization, subjection or autonomy.'[12] The

---

[12] Cf. Descamps de Bragelongne, 'Le problème du statut des départements d'outre-mer: Guadeloupe et Martinique', *R. jurid. et écon. du Sud-Ouest* (sér. jurid.), 1964, p. 78.

application of the new status was to lean towards the first solution but at the same time to bring about its first partial setback.

The new departments are totally assimilated with France in the political organization of the Republic. The Antilles are represented in parliament. The 1946 constitution put the legislative regime of the overseas departments on the same basis as that of France. The normal administrative system was introduced in the Antilles, and this means that local administrative services are each dependent on the relevant minister. The unity in conception and treatment resulting from the sole jurisdiction of the Minister for Colonies disappeared. The files were dispersed in various ministerial branches more anxious to preserve their respective authority than to solve problems, while the local administrative organs became increasingly separated from one another, giving up what individual powers they had in order for all decisions to be taken in Paris. The horizontal dispersion of local services paradoxically reinforced the process of metropolitan centralization.

The classic French departmental structures were swiftly installed. A decree of 1947 gave each departmental Prefect the same prerogatives as his metropolitan colleagues. Like the former Governor, he is in addition responsible for the external defence and internal security of the island; he also has discretionary powers over prices and can regulate imports and exports. This extension of prefectoral powers was justified by distance and the necessity for some genuine local authority. But one must not be deceived: this authority does not give the Prefect any real weight *vis-à-vis* the ministries and government in Paris. In fact he keeps in step with the metropolitan Prefects because his temporary sojourn in the Antilles constitutes only one step—sometimes a perilous one—in his career. He is above all the agent of the Minister of the Interior in a department where the maintenance of order is far more difficult than elsewhere. His administrative functions thus take second place, and he has an essentially political role, which consists in ensuring the 'fidelity' of the island and he occasionally plays this role at the time of elections.

The General Council is the principal element for him to take into account. The metropolitan regime is strictly applied to this assembly; a decree of 1946 abolished the former financial autonomy of the councils. The General Council has thus completely lost any authoritative role in local politics, even its right to control the administrative services. The symbol of Antillean autonomy and decentralization, it has been the greatest loser from the policy of assimilation. It was hardly astonishing, therefore, that the establishment of the new administrative system met with systematic hostility from the Council, which claimed over and over again that 'it could no longer have confidence in M. le Préfet' and went on to support social demands which could only bring disorder, even though to do so often brought the risk of its own dissolution.

Nevertheless, assimilation stops short at the threshold of the social and economic structure, the domain in which differences with and opposition to Paris are most pronounced. In this respect the policy does not aim higher than an attempt to prop up the economy of the islands and to bring some sort of equilibrium to the social structure. The change-over to departmental status has favoured the installation of the great national economic services, which permit of state intervention and the progressive development of planning and long-term economic policy. This was the moving spirit behind the creation in 1948 of the Fonds d'Investissement des Départements d'Outre-Mer (FIDOM), which is financed by the state budget. But it was difficult to get the new system going, and its first social measures, conceived within the framework of assimilation, soon clashed and came dangerously near disturbing the balance of island society. Social security was introduced in 1947, but no system of family allowances was put into operation; wages were related to those operating in France, but in practice they could be fixed by the Prefect. Since 1950 the financial aid of the state, which for the most part forgoes the resources of taxation, has subsidized the local bodies and embarked on an expenditure on equipment without parallel in the metropolitan system, an indication of the limits and inadequacies of departmental status.

In fact, contrary to the hopes of those who supported the principles and ideology on which it was founded, the conversion of the French Antilles into departments has not been successful. Departmental status is totally ineffective, not to say in some cases a restraining mechanism, for the economic and social development of the islands. Whenever underdevelopment was the basic fact, departmental structures and procedures proved ineffective. This inadequacy was accentuated by the haphazard way in which the new status was applied. The revolution it implied has profoundly shaken the structures of administration but without really affecting traditional mentality and behaviour. Further, the political basis of power was eroded,[13] and this intensified with the progressive weakness of the metropolitan governments. Prefect and General Council clash, because one lacks responsibility and has no freedom of action, while the other has lost its jurisdiction and takes advantage of this by attributing

[13] Cf. the opinion of M. Mireau in *Marchés tropicaux*, 29 Jan. 1949: 'The new regime could easily cause a weakening of authority. A Governor's authority, less representative of the government than a Prefect's but nevertheless symbolizing the power of France itself, enjoyed a traditional prestige which was very important. . . . Authority will lose its strength when scattered between these different departments.'

all the difficulties to the administration, while at the same time the illusory promises of assimilation increase its disappointment. The government sometimes yields and recalls the Prefect; at other times it dissolves the General Council. But in the end there is always a return to the traditional system of a Prefect who 'governs with his majority'. Gradually people began to realize once again that, according to the celebrated saying of a Martiniquan politician of the Third Republic, an Antillean is 'a Frenchman in a continent which is not French'. The contagion of decolonization was the final blow, with the outbreak of the Algerian rebellion in 1954 and the Defferre *loi-cadre* for Africa in 1956, with which the French Antilleans felt in sympathy. That was the moment when assimilation lost its psychological attraction. By then the new departmental structures had already come under fire.

3. *Modified Departmental Status*

M. Conombo, Secretary of State of the Interior, announced to the General Council on 16 November 1954:

It is the wish of the government that the situation [of the DOM] should be the object of careful study, from all points of view, to discover the rate and terms whereby they could best profit from democratic and republican institutions which have been tried and proved in France. What is in question is an additional stage in the process of assimilation and no kind of retrograde step.

There was therefore no change in either basic principle or general purpose; this was still the assimilation of the French Antilles to the mother country at some unspecified date in the future. But means, methods, and basic structures had to be more realistic; it was these which had to be 'modified' to meet the situation in the islands.

Modification has taken place at three different levels. The first is that of political and administrative co-ordination of the DOM. The government was to have one member specifically responsible for the DOM. The co-ordination of administrative activity has been ensured since 1958 by a secretary-general of the DOM, who is consulted on all measures applicable to them and who presides over an interministerial council for the co-ordination of the DOM. The mechanism is repeated at the local level, where since 1960 the Prefect has been the 'co-ordinator of activities' of all the service heads. It seems that this reorganization has made it possible to re-establish a unity of conception in the administration of the islands which was largely overturned by the 1946 status.

But it is above all on the level of administrative organization that the reform is best known, on the basis of the decree of 26 April 1960 which increased the powers of local authorities. Besides his new co-ordinating activities, the Prefect is in full charge of all the administration of the island: he is kept informed of all the plans and activities of public enterprises, whether state or semi-public; he appoints local officials and can propose their recall to France since the 1960 ordinance, an arrangement much criticized because it was used to penalize subversive opinions held by the autonomists and the communists. Some measure of decentralization was added to this notable effort towards devolution, which resulted in increasing the powers of the General Council. Henceforth this was to be the instrument for the 'adaptation' of the islands to their particular situation: it is consulted on every draft law or decree issued with this in view, and even has the right to propose any special measure which seems desirable for its own department. It participates in the same way in economic and social policy by its role in the running of FIDOM.

In fact the new measures basically relate to the economic and social position of the Antilles. A decree of 1960 defines the machinery of FIDOM, whose investments in the local sector are decided by the General Council and the Prefect. A law of 1960 established a plan to improve the equipment and economic expansion of the DOM. All these measures have the objective of putting in hand the economic and social development of the countries by successive steps, of which the first landmarks were the agrarian law (1961), equalization of family allowances (1963), the alignment of wages with those of France (1965).

Modified departmental status decidedly marks a new stage in the status of the Antilles, if not in principle then at least in political and social reality. Considered from the point of view of the traditional options, the 1960 status—as it is currently termed—indicates some return to the machinery of autonomy and self-government. But this evolution is far more in line with efforts at regionalization and territorial improvement undertaken at the same time in France. The Antilles are treated as a special 'social and economic region'. This is translated into practice by means of a certain amount of administrative regionalization. But in the political sphere the dogma of departmentalism persists: regionalization stops where politics begin. Perhaps this lack of harmony explains the political malaise experienced in the Antilles at present.

III. THE POLITICAL MALAISE

In spite of the new reforms there is an undeniable political malaise in the islands. The frequency of strikes and disturbances, the incidental recurrence of outbreaks of violence and their inevitable repression bear unfortunate witness to this: riots at Fort-de-France (1959); arrest and trial of students accused of conspiracy (1963); new riots at Fort-de-France (1965); and explosions of violence at Basse-Terre and Pointe-à-Pitre (1967). It is nevertheless true that violence and repression have always been part of the political climate of the Antilles, and their persistence has not irremediably cut the ties between them and France. The extraordinary calm of the islands during the events of May–June 1968 which exploded in France is clear proof of this. That is to say that one must appreciate the real measure of this malaise before one can determine its place in Antillean opinion and its effect on French policies.

1. Reasons for Malaise

The underlying reason is certainly to be found in the impact on the Antilles of the contact between an underdeveloped society and the organization and techniques of an industrialized society. A consumer society, itself questioned in France where, however, it fits in with the prevailing social psychology, has directly clashed with the very basis of an underdeveloped society—if one views the development of the Antilles in the light of the standards prevailing in France itself. This conflict between two types of society affects the political structures as well as the psychological reactions of the Antilleans.

The reforms which have taken place since the end of the last war have been relatively swift and far-reaching, but they do not seem to have had any profound effect on local politics. In fact, political structures function without having the slightest effect. In colonial times, the local powers had both authority and prestige, something they no longer command today—even if the personality of General de Gaulle offered the islands an illustration of the power of France. Nothing has replaced this former legitimacy, despite the efforts made to provide the local élites with new responsibilities: the 96 per cent of the population who are non-white have a (formally) dominant position in island politics.[14] The traditional élites have lost the confidence of a population in full demographic development. The traditional political game has continued alongside the new structures. The beneficiaries of all kinds of privileges—privileges of race (whites and mulattos), economic privileges (the local bourgeoisie, civil servants) put the brake on development and encourage the inertia of the political and administrative élites. Things are kept in order by the maintenance of the traditional *status quo*, whilst the existing

[14] Cf. Arvin Murch, *The Policy of Assimilation in the French West Indian Departments Opposed to Independence* (1966). This thesis, submitted at Yale University, was discussed in *Outre-Mer français* (1968).

institutions seem to undergo some sort of surface change and local confidence fades dismally. Island politics have an innate futility which dooms every reform to failure; this has been responsible for the collapse of almost every plan for agrarian reform.

Despite all this, as has been seen, the economic and social development of the Antilles since the war has been considerable. The per capita income of the inhabitants of Guadeloupe and Martinique is treble that of their neighbours in the neighbouring British islands.[15] The new structures, which operate largely on metropolitan funds, have been much more successful in the economic field than in the political context. But it is also noteworthy that economic progress has not had the expected results. Bearing in mind that economic changes can only have long-term social effects, the social climate of the islands remains uncomfortably disturbed. Social inequalities are intensified by economic development. Certain sections of the working population, notably administrative civil servants and higher economic personnel, have a considerable advantage over their colleagues in France, while in contrast the average wage-earner lags far behind his French counterpart. This disparity is the more hotly resented in that it corresponds with racial differences: 78 per cent of the white population dominates the economic life of the islands.[16] To this must be added chronic and seasonal unemployment which migration to France and the start of industrial development has not succeeded in alleviating[17]— it is not without significance that outbreaks of violence usually begin with strikes and social clashes. Social inequalities inevitably express themselves in terms of political disorders and these, of course, are useful ammunition for the left-wing parties. They constitute a source of political unrest and bring to the forefront the problem of social and economic development of the islands.

However, this malaise goes deeper and its roots lie in the psychological make-up of the Antillean character. The history and particular characteristics of island society produce contradictions which come to the surface in times of crisis or change. The contact between underdevelopment and a consumer society thus causes psychological reactions which currently seem to be the basic reason for the existing malaise. One must at this point acknowledge the fact that local aspirations vary. Island society is simultaneously introvert and extrovert.[18] Everyone's gaze is constantly directed towards France. People adopt the mentality of

[15] See Murch.
[16] Ibid.
[17] See above, pp. 87–8.
[18] Cf. A. Mabileau, 'Gouvernement et administration dans les îles françaises d'outre-mer', Outre-Mer français, Numéro spéc. 'Colloque', p. 20–2.

those on public assistance, and they are also sensitive about anything that might be interpreted as heralding a policy of abandonment by France. But at the same time the islands wish to assert their 'local personality' and manifest their desire to be responsible for their own affairs, which would confer on them the dignity and equality of Frenchmen. These divergent reflexes are more marked among the autonomists than among the traditional élite, whose sense of dignity is blunted by the privileges they enjoy. Another psychological factor is international opinion. The myth of decolonization exerts a pressure favouring the loosening of ties with the metropolitan powers: it has affected the Antilles despite the care of the authorities to control news media. But one should note that this aspiration is counterbalanced by the experience of neighbouring islands; the recent independence of other Caribbean islands and even of Cuba was felt to be an object lesson in Guadeloupe and Martinique where the standard of living is much higher.

There is, in conclusion, one more factor that needs to be mentioned: the complex influence of island nationalism, or particularism. This is not basically directed against France as a whole, but against the white élite in the islands; there is also more than a trace of rivalry between the two islands themselves. It is not the classic nationalism of underdeveloped countries, for in some curious way it manages to include a genuine feeling of being French. This *romantisme de la France* is an accumulation of various things—a long-established attachment of local culture to French civilization, the prestige of France herself, and, in recent years, also the personal prestige of General de Gaulle. All these contradictions crop up in the political malaise and explain different nuances in public opinion in the Antilles.

2. Public Opinion in the Antilles

Between 1946 and 1956 opposition to the principle of assimilation was rather vague and ill-defined. The Communist Party criticized certain aspects of the idea of departmental status but on the whole maintained the basic concept of assimilation. The Socialist Party too supported the existing policies, but suggested a more decentralized status: centralization and the power of the 'technocrats' in Paris had increased after the islands had become departments.

The year 1956 marked a turning point in Antillean consciousness of the problems inherent in the status of the DOM. The Defferre *loi-cadre* launched French black Africa on the road of decolonization; destalinization and the events in Hungary caused a crisis in the French Communist Party. The deputy mayor of Fort-de-France, Aimé Césaire, broke with the French Communist Party, took up a position against departmental status, created the *Parti Progressiste Martiniquais* (PPM), and opted for a federal type of solution. To avoid being overtaken on the left by the PPM, the local communists also broke off from the French Communist Party (March 1958). From then onwards the Communist Parties of Guadeloupe and Martinique severely criticized departmental status and claimed autonomy for the Antilles. They demanded the setting up of a territorial assembly endowed with legislative powers and of an executive responsible to this assembly. These various demands led all political parties without exception to condemn France's integrationist policy and to recommend that the government 'modify' the existing departmental status to fit the special requirements of the islands, and to increase the decision-making powers of the General Councils.

On 4 May 1958 the *Revue guadeloupéene* organized a symposium on assimilation, which made a deep impression. There were two opposing viewpoints: on the one hand the supporters of the policy of 'modified departmental status' and on the other those of 'self-government' in a federal framework, or of 'internal autonomy'. Most of the political parties (*Indépendants, Union Nationale Radicale*, Socialists) came out in favour of the first point of view; they had a majority in the General Council and represented the opinions of both the local élite and of the majority of the population. The second point of view was promoted by the PPM, the local Communist Parties, the *Parti Socialiste Unifié*, and 'left' groups (the Association of Antillean Students in France, Catholic students of the *Jeunesse Étudiante Chrétienne*, etc.). The words 'self-government' or 'autonomy' in any case did not have the same political content for all the militants, but all wished to maintain union with France and demanded a legislative and executive power which would ensure the running of Antillean affairs by the Antilleans themselves.

The measures taken in 1960 to devolve and decentralize the administration by giving local authorities and elected members a greater part in local affairs did not put an end to the arguments about the status of the overseas departments. The defenders of modified assimilation do not fail to criticize the defects of the system, but they felt that the integration of the French Antilles into the French Union will mobilize national solidarity and in time give Martinique and Guadeloupe an economic and social standard more closely related to that of the metropolitan departments. *Match*, published at Pointe-à-Pitre, is the organ of the defenders of modified departmental status.

L'Étincelle (in Guadeloupe) and *Justice* (in Martinique), organs of the Communist Party, and above all *Progrès social*, organ of the Guadeloupe autonomist intellectuals, on the other hand, wage war on assimilation. The advent of Castrism in Cuba, the FLN victory in Algeria, the total independence of the French African states, the fascination exercised by the Chinese revolution on the young communists are all factors which have hardened the attitudes of the Antillean separatists. The legal opposition of the political parties has thus been outstripped by violent revolutionary action, which is met by arrests and deportation. The latest of these violent episodes were the serious riots of 26 and 27 May 1967 at Pointe-à-Pitre, riots which followed two months after those of Basse-Terre! It is possible that this uncontrolled burst of violence developed spontaneously at the time of a building strike and was led by workless youths who had never become integrated into the work force; it might also have been organized by autonomist political groups, in particular by GONG (the *Groupe d'Organisation National de la Guadeloupe*). The government acted on this latter supposition in arresting a large number of intellectuals (teachers, journalists, doctors) accused of undermining state security. But the State Security Court of France on 1 March 1968 gave a lenient verdict in the so-called 'Guadeloupe Nationalist' trial: there were thirteen acquittals and six of the accused received suspended sentences. This trial gave the maximum publicity to the autonomist cause. The future will show whether this has constituted an important step on the road leading to a revision of departmental status.

3. Current French Policy

There are those who have doubted the very existence of any French policy towards the Antilles. The memory of governmental ultra-conservatism under the Fourth Republic, the distance between the islands and metropolitan France, the natural inclination of local government representatives to avoid disturbing the precarious political and social equilibrium, all these have led to the notion that the great plan was to leave things as they were, while ready to make a few hasty concessions whenever the situation looked threatening.[19] But General de Gaulle's declarations during his visits to the Antilles, the speeches of his ministers, and the official communiqués have not given this impression, although one must, of course, make a distinction between the broad lines of this policy and the problems inherent in its application in distant islands where the social context is very different from that of France.

French policy in the Antilles is based on the assumption that the islands

[19] Cf. Aimé Césaire's pronouncement to the National Assembly on 26 April 1962: 'The history of the Antilles over the past few years has been the history of minimal measures when it has not been eye-wash pure and simple.'

are French and wish to be French, that France alone is competent to solve their problems. In 1964 came the final parting of the ways between the former African territories and the Antilles. The decolonization policy was right and natural in Africa, since these countries consisted of 'autonomous peoples forming large units'. In the Antilles things were quite different, with a mixture of African and European peoples within a framework of French civilization. In the Antilles 'departmental status seems to be the only solution to fit our times'. Within this framework, French policy basically relies on the social and economic development of the islands: 'practical decisions . . . must be taken for the development and social improvement of the people'. It is assumed that the political malaise will disappear with the raising of the standard of living and the bringing about of a new economic and social balance. Two additional points complete this policy. The first relates the Antilles to France's global policy: they are a 'French outpost in the American hemisphere';[20] this effectively defines their role *vis-à-vis* the influence of the United States and revolutionary initiatives or movements for regrouping in Central or South America. The second point is a warning to those who seek a solution in a new political status and in independence: since 1958 and the experience of Guinea, the attitude of the French government has been clear and unyielding: all French aid ceases with independence.

In conception, this policy at least has the merit of being clearly defined. But at the local level, these declarations of principle arouse response only in so far as they are applied in practice. The agency to implement this policy is naturally a new economic and social administration. The development agencies envisaged by modified departmental status have been set up; they are run by the traditional establishment, who have been endowed with new economic and social powers. However, the change of function which has fallen to the administration is not proceeding without difficulty. The same old conflicts remain between administration and policy, and the Prefect and his colleagues find it difficult to forget their political preoccupations to devote themselves to their new responsibilities. Nor are the administrators themselves always properly equipped for their new functions. A development policy can succeed only when shock tactics sweep away all obstacles. In this respect the conduct of the administrators is often inadequate; 'There are too many people in positions of responsibility, civil servants who are never brought to book for their mistakes.'[21] Some of the civil servants who were transferred from Africa

[20] Text of an electoral poster for the UNR during elections for the Legislative Assembly (*Le Monde*, 24–25 Dec. 1967).

[21] Cf. Report of a parliamentary mission from the Commission des Finances to the National Assembly, 1963.

after the independence of the former overseas territories have been quite unable to cope with the situation, and local officials seem inextricably involved in nepotism and the clannishness typical of island behaviour. Not even the emergence of a body of specialists—the economic secretariat of the DOM prefectures—has been sufficient to inject a fresh spirit and new methods into the traditional administration struggling to cope with a new policy.

But what really hinders the proper development of this new policy is the attitude of the local élites, who form a barrier against the infiltration of government policy into the island environment. Many social and economic improvements threaten their privileges, and naturally they prefer the maintenance of the *status quo*. The Europeans want to maintain their existing position (though there are exceptions to this, and notable efforts have been made in certain economic circles): the planters through mere conservatism or loss of confidence; the local companies to maintain their monopolies. The local bourgeoisie, except for a fringe won over to gradual social change, are happy with a situation which ensures their social superiority and some equality with the whites. The local politicians are imprisoned by their political reflexes and positions which that social change might threaten. The government's new policy cannot hope to be successful outside the purely material field without the full co-operation of the island élites.

The French Antilles have now held departmental status for over twenty years, and in the final assessment this may be judged as an original experiment which is almost, but not quite, a type of decolonization. But its outcome remains in doubt. This uncertainty arises partly from the lack of continuity, which is often the defect of French policy, and partly from the want of harmony between official principles and the implementation of a policy which demands empiricism at every point. French policy in the Antilles has not yet been taken to a successful conclusion. It would be dangerous to make departmental status a step on the road to independence. That would be catastrophic for the Antilles in a world in which poverty and underdevelopment prevails, nor would it correspond with the wishes of a population where rich and poor alike are attached to French culture[22] and whose reactions are always permeated by a *romantisme de la France*. But the *status quo* is just as dangerous, and some evolution is clearly indispensable. It is still an open question to what extent economic and social development will be able to free the French Antilles from the prospects of underdevelopment. Moreover, considerable changes in behaviour and attitudes both for France and for the islands are

[22] Cf. the results of Murch's investigations into the status of the French Antilles.

required. The plans for regional autonomy which were announced in Paris after the crisis of May 1968 might well provide a framework for future developments:[23] they could ease the centralizing process by which the islands are assimilated to metropolitan France and allow the population of the Antilles to take on constructive and realistic responsibilities within the administration of an individualized regional unit inside the French Community.

[23] Cf. the study of the Association for the Defence of the Interests of Guadeloupe, *Le Monde*, 11–12 Aug. 1968.

6 The Dutch Caribbean and its Metropolis

HARRY HOETINK

I. THE NETHERLANDS ANTILLES

THE small and arid island of Curaçao off the coast of present-day Venezuela was conquered by the Dutch in 1634. Aruba and Bonaire near
Curaçao, and St Eustatius, Saba, and the half of St Martin in the northern
group of the Lesser Antilles also came into Dutch possession in the
1630s. The conquests were motivated more by considerations of military
strategy in the Dutch War of Independence against Spain than by promises
of agricultural riches. The 'plantations' on the main island, Curaçao,
never became more than symbols of social prestige and conspicuous
consumption. Their owners were mostly retired civil servants or merchants, who not seldom had to risk bankruptcy in their efforts to keep
the 'Great House' intact.

Curaçao, then, was not a genuine 'plantation colony' at all; its importance lay in its commercial activities. It was a centre of the Caribbean slave
trade during most of the seventeenth century, when use was made of an
asiento granted by the Spanish king to Italian traders, who allowed the
Dutch to obtain slaves in West Africa and freely trade them throughout
the Caribbean. Fortifications of the Dutch West India Company on the
west coast of Africa facilitated this trade which, however, lost much of its
importance when—by the Treaty of Utrecht in 1713—Britain obtained
a general permission for the trade from Spain. In the eighteenth century
Curaçao enjoyed short periods of great prosperity as a market for weapons
and other necessities for all belligerent parties during the wars between
the French and the British and also during the North American War of
Independence. From St Eustatius the flag of the thirteen North American
States was officially saluted for the first time in 1776; the British answer
was an effective bombardment by Admiral Rodney in 1781 which
brought the island's 'Golden Age' to an end. A decade later the West
India Company was dissolved.

The nineteenth century brought a pronounced economic decline to
the Dutch islands. This was not caused by the abolition of slavery in 1863,
but rather by the new independence of the neighbouring former Spanish

colonies. This liberated them from Spanish mercantilistic policies, so that direct free trade with Europe and the United States became possible and much preferred to Dutch commercial mediation. But Curaçao's links with the mainland were not altogether cut. It is interesting to observe, for instance, how the Sephardic Jewish merchants in Curaçao—who had settled there soon after the Dutch conquest, some coming from the lost Dutch colony of Recife, others directly from Europe—were actively involved in the internal political and economic affairs of some newly independent Latin American nations. In the 1840s several younger sons of these Jewish families went to the Dominican Republic,[1] just as they had earlier gone to some of the British Antilles. They also went to the important commercial centre of St Thomas and to Cuba, Venezuela, and Central America. They remained part of a family network of commercial relations which extended into Western Europe, and were thus in an excellent position to act as brokers in the many negotiations of the young states for European-financed loans and trade arrangements. In the 1850s the Curaçao firm of Abraham Jessurun financed most of the Dominican wars against Haiti as well as the internal revolutions of Santo Domingo. The same house was instrumental in getting a loan for the Dominican Republic from an Amsterdam banking firm, large enough to have a representative of that firm act in the 1890s as special administrator of Santo Domingo's customs. (The Amsterdam house failed nevertheless and sold its rights to the San Domingo Improvement Company of New York; the start of US economic and financial preponderance in the Dominican Republic can be dated from this event.) The same Curaçao firm also had, towards the end of the century, control over part of the Venezuelan customs, as a guarantee for a substantial loan to that country. Yet in general terms Curaçao's economy declined in the last century and many members of the lower classes had to go cane-cutting and railroad-building in Cuba and elsewhere. A slight upsurge occurred in the 1870s, when the European iron steamships were prevented from calling at many mainland ports because of their increased size. The fine natural harbour of Willemstad, Curaçao, then temporarily functioned as a transit station, with sailing schooners transporting the goods to and from the neighbouring countries of Venezuela and Colombia.

The islands seemed doomed to a somewhat fitful but sure decline, when the outlook changed dramatically in the present century. One can

---

[1] H. Hoetink, 'Materiales para el estudio de la República Dominicana en la segunda mitad del siglo IXI: cambios en la estructura demográfica y en la distribución geográfica de la población', *Caribb. Stud.*, Oct. 1967, pp. 3–35.

truly speak of an economic 'miracle'.[2] In 1916 oil refineries were esta-
lished by the Royal Dutch Shell on Curaçao, and in 1924 by Standard
Oil of New Jersey on Aruba. The crude oil was imported from Venezuela
and—to a lesser extent—from Colombia. Suddenly the two islands
became underpopulated from an economic point of view. A stream of
immigrants began to flow from the other Dutch islands, from the British
West Indies, from Surinam and the Netherlands, from the Latin American
neighbouring countries, from Madeira, Eastern Europe, India, China, and
the Lebanon. In a few decades the population of Curaçao increased from
30,000 to 120,000, and in 1960 28 per cent of it was not born locally
and/or was not of Dutch nationality. Yet in that year a forceful economy
drive—necessitated by increasing international competition—had already
started; its goal was to maintain, through the introduction of automation,
the same production level with substantially less manpower. The contribution of the oil industry to the GNP dropped from 40 per cent in
1957 to a little over 20 per cent in 1966. An effort to increase the economic
significance of tourism resulted in the same period in an increase in its
share in GNP from 4 to 12 per cent, but the net national product increased
only from $218·4 to $228·7 m. in these years. The drastic automation
drive of the oil industry led to a substantial lay-off, first among the
foreigners, then also among the national labour force. The total number
of personnel in the oil industry was reduced from 12,000 in 1952 to a little
over 5,000 in 1966. The percentage unemployed of the total productive
labour force is currently estimated at about 20 per cent.

This labour force increases yearly by approximately 2,000 persons. In
order to create work for this group—without taking into account the
already existing unemployment—a minimal annual investment of $32·4
m. would be needed, which amounts to 15 per cent of national income.
It is clear that only outside capital can satisfy such a demand. The execution of present long-term plans, which aim at improvements in the infra-
structure (roads, airports, water distillation, harbour facilities) is mostly
financed by the Netherlands. The EEC also gives financial and technical
assistance, though less to the Antilles than to Surinam. It is still an open
question whether the Netherlands Antilles' association with the EEC
will, in practice, bring all the commercial advantages that had been hoped
for—though the regulated import of its oil products into the Common
Market is a clear benefit. The prospects for large-scale industrialization

---

[2] Cf. T. G. Matthews & others, *The Politics and Economics of the Caribbean: a contemporary
analysis of the Dutch, French and British Caribbean* (Univ. Puerto Rico, Inst. Caribb. Studies,
spec. study no. 3); Sir Harold Mitchell, *Caribbean Patterns: a Political and Economic Study* . . .
(Edinburgh, 1967); F. M. & S. Andic, *Government Finance and Planned Development: Fiscal
Surveys of Surinam and the Netherlands Antilles* (Puerto Rico, 1967).

H

are certainly not rosy. There is a scarcity of raw materials, fresh water is expensive—it has to be distilled out of sea water—the internal market is small, and the wage level high and hard to push down. As yet only Aruba can point to some successful projects, among which is a US $20 m. ammonia fertilizer plant, owned by a subsidiary of Standard Oil. Labour intensity in this type of industry is low, however. A recent project in Curaçao aimed at increasing the docking facilities up to 90,000 tons may prove successful. Tourism, the poor state's main hope, is the only viable alternative, and numerous hotels—many financed with US capital—have recently started operations in Curaçao, Aruba, Bonaire, and St Martin. This last island, together with Saba and St Eustatius, suffered indirectly from the oil industry's automation drive, which forced many former inhabitants of these tiny islands to return home. The same goes for Bonaire. Fortunately, the last few years have seen a remarkable decline in the Netherlands Antilles' birth-rate, which had maintained itself during the last decades at approximately 2·5 per cent, so that one may realistically expect it to have dropped to approximately 1 per cent by 1975. This decline seems partly due to a massive birth-control campaign, carried out with the silent approval of the churches, including the Roman Catholic Church.

From the eighteenth century onwards, the Dutch settlers in the islands can be divided socially into two groups or 'estates', which I have called the higher and lower Protestants, to distinguish them from the Sephardic Jews who lived separately.[3] The higher Protestants were high-ranking government employees, military officers, owners of 'plantations', and members of the liberal professions. They kept aloof from the lower Protestants, who were small tradesmen, artisans, and junior clerks. The higher Protestants intermarried, or married West European newcomers, and maintained their Dutch Reformed Church affiliation as a mark of social distinction. The lower Protestants looked to the South American mainland for marriage partners. This resulted in a certain 'latinization' of this group and the conversion to Catholicism of part of its members. The coloured and Negro groups also became Catholic, since neither Protestant nor Jew showed much enthusiasm for missionary activities amongst them. The higher Protestants saw themselves as the cultural and political representatives of Holland, and regarded the Netherlands Antilles as an extension of European Dutch society. They painted the shutters of their

[3] For the development of the social structure cf. Hoetink, *Het Patroon van de oude Curaçaose Samenleving* (with Engl. summary, Aruba/Tiel, 1966) & *The Two Variants in Caribbean Race Relations* (London, 1967); J. & D. Keur, *Windward Children* (Assen, 1960).

houses in the colours of Amsterdam's coat of arms, and, though they had
no documents to prove it, they stated before a Dutch Commission in
1789 that they had always enjoyed the same rights as the Amsterdam
burghers. Their conception of colonial society was a pseudo-homogeneous
one. They saw all other population groups as *Fremdkörper*, as alien bodies.
When referring to the Sephardic Jews, they insisted on speaking of the
'Portuguese nation'. While most Indians had fled the island when the
Dutch occupied it, they maintained the function of 'Officer for Indian
Affairs' when hardly an Indian was left. In short, they tried hard to
maintain, between themselves and all other groups, as many culturally
distinctive symbols as possible.

This is not to say that their relations with any of these groups, including
the coloured and Negro sections of the population, were worse than elsewhere in similar societies. Hardly any conflict ever arose with the Jewish
group, which lived apart by its own free choice. Relations with the slaves
and freedmen were decidedly mild: since Curaçao was a commercial
society rather than an agricultural one, large slave herds did not exist.
Most slaves were so to speak luxury goods, and worked as house and
personal servants. Manumission of slaves occurred frequently, if only
because commercial depressions led to economic austerity. The smallnesss
of the islands facilitated social control and generally prevented excessive
cruelty in the treatment of slaves. The one important slave uprising,
which occurred in 1795—and which was indeed cruelly crushed—appears
to have been inspired by the revolutionary events in Saint Domingue
(Haiti): coloured 'agents' from the French islands had come to Curaçao and
preached rebellion. But although master-slave relations were comparatively mild, there inevitably did develop a rigid code of behaviour with
clearly defined roles for whites and coloured, masters and slaves. These
patterns of behaviour hardly underwent any change at all upon the pro-
clamation of abolition in 1863. In any case this only affected a small
number of slaves, as most had been freed previously.

The smallness of island and population did foster a number of common
cultural characteristics, in spite of the social isolation aspired to by some
groups. The most remarkable of these common traits is perhaps Papiamento, a Creole language with strong Portuguese overtones. Unlike
similar languages elsewhere in the Caribbean, which are spoken only by
the lower classes, in Curaçao, Aruba, and Bonaire Papiamento became
the vernacular for *all* social groups. The reason for its general acceptance
was perhaps that it bridged the language gap which originally existed
between the Portuguese Jews and the Dutch Protestants. A number of
Dutch Protestant families had continued to speak Dutch among themselves

until the establishment of the oil refinery in this century. But then, in an interesting social process, they also took to Papiamento. As we have seen, that group of higher Protestants had always considered itself the cultural representative of the Netherlands. But when, as a result of industrialization, the number of European Dutch employees and civil servants increased considerably, the local higher Protestants discovered how much their creolized cultural variant differed from the cultural heritage of the European newcomers and how, to a certain degree, the latter considered themselves culturally superior. In reaction the few Curaçao families who still spoke Dutch among themselves began to adopt Papiamento as their own language—even though Dutch remained the official one. They even became the proponents of cultural nationalism —the word 'landskind' (child of the country) was invented in the 1920s— which broadened into a movement for political autonomy. The outcome was the adoption in 1954 of the Charter of the Kingdom, by which the Netherlands Antilles, as well as Surinam, achieved 'internal independence' within the sovereign and tripartite Kingdom of the Netherlands.

The internal political structure of the Netherlands Antilles is federative in character.[4] There are four 'island territories': Aruba, Curaçao, Bonaire, and the three northernmost islands—the 'Windward Islands'—together. Each of these territories has a certain degree of internal autonomy. Each has its own bureaucratic apparatus and its own governing bodies. These consist of a democratically elected Island Council and an Island Board made up of elected deputies presided over by a lieutenant-governor, who is appointed by the Crown on the nomination of the Netherlands Antilles government. The lieutenant-governor also acts as local head of the police force. Although the island territories are permitted to levy a number of specific taxes, the greater part of their income derives from federal taxes which are distributed by the federal government to the territories on the basis of a formula decreed by the federal parliament. The federal government (*Landsregering*), which has its seat in Willemstad, Curaçao, deals with all matters of national policy as defined by the broad limits imposed by the Charter. It has complete autonomy over fiscal policy and determines its own customs regulations. The formal head of the federal government is the Governor, appointed by the Crown. He is the representative of the Queen, and his formal political powers are comparable with those of the Queen in Holland. (Both Surinam and the Netherlands Antilles currently have native Governors.) Effective political power is in the hands of the *Landsregering*, which is controlled by the

---

[4] Cf. A.L. Gastmann, *The Politics of Surinam and the Netherlands Antilles* (Puerto Rico, 1967); also Matthews.

democratically elected federal parliament, the *Staten*. There are 22 seats in the *Staten*, of which 12 are reserved for representatives from Curaçao, 8 for those from Aruba, and 1 for each of the other island territories. Since the ratio between the populations of Curaçao and Aruba is approximately 12 : 5, it is clear that the latter island is over-represented (as are also the small island territories). This has resulted from threats by Aruban politicians to leave the Federation and establish a special and separate relationship with Holland, made during the negotiations over the Charter of the Kingdom. Ever since colonial times Aruba has felt that it has been subject to discriminatory treatment in comparison with the main island of Curaçao; now it is felt that a slightly disproportionate representation in the *Staten* might prevent this in the future.

There are no national political parties in the Netherlands Antilles embracing all islands. Hence the federal government is always formed on the basis of coalitions between parties from different islands. In recent years Aruba and the smaller islands have benefited from the serious political divisiveness in Curaçao, as a result of which Curaçao's largest party, the Democratic Party (DP) needed the support of parties from *all* other islands in order to get a working majority in the *Staten*. Aruba's favourable political position in the recent government coalitions has led to considerable efforts to boost the island's economy. During 1967 an important faction of the large Curaçao opposition party, the National People's Party (NVP), decided after the death of its charismatic founder and leader, Dr M. F. da Costa Gomez, to co-operate with the DP.

However, the politics of Curaçao were transformed by riots which occurred on 30 May 1969 as a result of a march of protest by employees of contractors for the Shell Oil Co., who were striking for higher wages. Rioting, arson, and plundering occurred in Willemstad, and there were gun battles between the rioters and Dutch marines, who were called in to help the police. Two labour leaders were killed and one was seriously injured, scores of rioters were arrested, and the damage was estimated at over $40 m.[5] The DP-oriented government which had won a slender majority in the 1966 elections resigned. New elections on 5 September gave three seats in the *Staten* to the *Frente Obrero y Liberación 30 di mei* (30th May Workers' Liberation Front), a radical party formed by some trade union leaders and strengthened by the support of several young intellectuals, loosely centred around the radical weekly *Vitó*. The DP lost its majority, but it proved difficult to form a new government since the parties were bound by pre-election pledges of non-co-operation.

[5] *Int. Herald Tribune*, 3 June 1969.

However, on 16 December Ernesto Petronia (Patriotic Party of Aruba) succeeded in forming a coalition with the DP and the *Frente Obrero*.[6] Further difficulties were created for this government by new strikes early in December 1969 with demands for higher salaries, and it was forced to resign in January 1971 when it failed to obtain the necessary majority for a proposal to raise income tax and impose other taxes to try to balance the budget.[7] At the time of writing the outlook remained uncertain; although there is some improvement in the economic situation because of a revival in the demand for Venezuelan oil which has a low sulphur content, and because low income-tax rates attract foreign companies and banks, the new activity offers little employment for the large pool of unskilled Negroes.

The system of political federalism combined with insular autonomy was clearly a viable answer to the prevailing parochialism of the islands. But it also has considerable disadvantages. It exerts heavy demands on the limited quantity of political talent and has caused an impressive increase in bureaucracy. More seriously it leaves open the possibility of a grave crisis within the system itself in cases where the political composition of an Island Council is the diametrical opposite of that of the federal government. This did occur a few years ago with Curaçao opposing the federation. In such a case each party in the conflict can obstruct the other's work. Thus while the whole system presupposes close co-operation between islands and federal government, yet does not make this type of political conflict impossible, one must conclude that the chance of a temporary breakdown has, so to speak, been built in.

In the Netherlands Antilles, in contrast to Surinam, no articulate voices favouring complete independence can as yet be heard; this must be seen as mainly due to the smallness and geographical dispersion of the islands, as well as their weak and one-sided economic structure. Moreover, with the worsening economic situation during the last decade, which makes considerable help from Holland and the EEC desirable, and the socio-political changes due to universal suffrage, the still dominant white Protestant group has seemed to look again to the Netherlands as its eventual haven of refuge and its psychological mother-country. The proximity to and economic dependence on Venezuela have created strong ties with that country, but no desire for political absorption by Venezuela can as yet be found outside the small 'latinized' population groups. The numerically most important part of the population feels more cultural and ethnic affinity with the other Caribbean islands than with the Latin American mainland, but the prospect of a political association with

[6] *Le Monde*, 16 Dec. 1969.   [7] Ibid., 3–4 Jan. 1971.

islands poorer than their own has never been regarded as attractive. The government of the Netherlands Antilles has shown an interest in Caribbean co-operation; it was instrumental in converting the metropolitan-inspired Caribbean Commission—a product of the second world war—into the more independent, but short-lived, Caribbean Organization.

In summarizing Curaçao's relations with the rest of the Caribbean, it is no exaggeration to state that the island has for long been one of the nerve-centres of the area. This was so in an economic sense because of its function as a depot for slaves, merchandise, and money; in a cultural sense because, especially during the last century, its private schools served pupils from all the neighbouring republics, and the publishing house of Agustín Bethencourt produced books and music for the whole region; and in a political sense because Curaçao was one of the principal havens of refuge for political exiles, from Haitian emperors to Venezuelan, Colombian, and Dominican presidents and generals. Yet, in the final resort, neither the Netherlands, nor the Dutch Antilles had other than purely mercantile interests in the Caribbean; merchants rather than politicians or, in earlier times, raiders rather than conquerors came to the area from Dutch lands or ships. Once, in the 1820s, under the inspiration of the 'Merchant King' William I, more daring projects for Dutch penetration of Latin America were designed; one thinks specifically of William's plan in 1827 to build a canal through Guatemala. But nothing came of it, and the king's dream of making Curaçao the main station on the route from the Atlantic to the Pacific did not materialize. Soon his attention, like that of his European citizens, was once more directed towards Holland's richer colonies in South-east Asia.[8]

II. SURINAM

Surinam, although part of the South American mainland, has always been more of an 'island' than Curaçao from the point of view of its relations with its immediate environment. The country, with at present some 320,000 inhabitants and a territory more than four times the size of Holland, has always been oriented towards the metropolitan power. Its contacts with neighbouring countries, including Brazil, have been scarce and insignificant, apart from the occasional border conflict, such as the one with Guyana which was making headlines in 1968.

Surinam was a real plantation colony with large, isolated plantations

[8] For commercial activities and plans of the Dutch in the Caribbean between 1780 and 1830 see Th. P. M. de Jong, *De Krimpende Horizon van de Hollandse Kooplieden: Hollands Welvaren in het Caribisch Zeegebied 1870–1830* (with Engl. summary) (Assen, 1966).

where the numerical proportion between slaves and masters was very different from that in Curaçao, and where the treatment of slaves was considerably more cruel.[9] Originally there was a white upper social group of Dutch origin in this colony, but most of its members left the country after the individual plantation owners were ruined by a crisis at the Amsterdam stock exchange in 1773. Their sugar and timber plantations then became the property of Dutch companies which sent administrators to their Surinam estates. Though this administrative personnel often entered into institutionalized sexual relationships with Surinamese women, they only stayed in the country for a limited time and could hardly be considered part of its 'real' population. This absence from Surinamese society since the last quarter of the eighteenth century of a Dutch white dominant layer is one of the main causes of the formation of a coloured ('Creole') élite. Together with a small group of Sephardic Jews, this Creole élite came to occupy many of the leading positions in the colonial bureaucracy at a time when in Curaçao these were being reserved for the white 'higher Protestants'. This has had certain important consequences. Thus in essays dealing with the marked differences in 'personality type' between the Netherlands Antillean and Surinamese Negroid élites, attention is often drawn to the supposedly greater keenness of the latter for education, and the greater value they attach to diplomas and academic titles as status symbols. This can be explained by the differences in occupational structure just mentioned, which result in the emergence of distinct 'reference groups' for the coloured population in the two societies: a bureaucratic élite in Surinam, but successful coloured merchants, protected by their Sephardic patrons, in Curaçao.

The economic importance of the Surinamese plantations decreased rapidly from the second half of the nineteenth century. The country's economic position worsened because of the opening of the Suez Canal which shortened the distance to competing South-east Asia. Market prices for several Surinamese products decreased, and the abolition of slavery in 1863 created a serious shortage of agricultural workers. Efforts to import indentured labourers started already in 1853, when Chinese and Madeirans were brought into the country. The largest group of immigrant labourers were the Indians from British India (often called East Indians to distinguish them from West Indians—who are Creoles of predominantly African origin—and (American) Indians) of which 35,000 arrived between

---

[9] For the development of the social structure see R. A. J. van Lier, *Samenleving in een Grensgebied* (The Hague,1949). On differences between race relations in Curaçao and Surinam, Hoetink, 'Diferencias en relacionces raciales entre Curazao y Surinam', *R. de ciencias sociales*, 1961.

1873 and 1916; in 1918 the government of India forbade further recruitment. Between 1890 and 1940 several thousands of Javanese were also indentured. All these efforts could not save the plantation system, and Surinam increasingly became a country where small farming predominated over large-scale agriculture.

The first thirty years of the present century were a period of economic stagnation; between 1925 and 1930 alone more than 2,000 persons left the country for the Netherlands Antilles to work there in the oil industry and the expanding public services. From the 1930s, however, bauxite mining expanded rapidly and came to occupy the position in the Surinamese economy which had formerly been reserved for sugar. In 1936 already the value of bauxite exports was 56·4 per cent of total exports, and by 1940 this percentage had increased to 83·5 per cent. From then on it kept fluctuating around this level. The strategic significance of this mineral led to the economic upsurge during the second world war. By 1950 total production had reached approximately 2 million tons, while the industry provided employment for some 3,000 men.

Since then, with the exception of the period 1962–4, when year-to-year totals were adversely affected by the US stockpiling programme, Surinam production has increased from $4\frac{1}{2}$ m. tons (1966) to over 5 m. (1967).[10] Exploitation is in the hands of two companies: the Surinam Aluminium Company (a subsidiary of Alcoa) and the (Dutch) Billiton Mining Company. However, in August 1970, under a new type of arrangement, the Surinam government signed a 50:50 ownership agreement with the Reynolds Metal Company whereby two independent companies, one formed by Surinam and the other by Reynolds, are to co-operate. It is envisaged that the Surinam company will later develop newly discovered bauxite deposits in west Surinam which are not part of this agreement.[11]

The year 1947 saw the beginning of efforts towards a planned economy with the foundation by the Dutch government of a Welfare Fund for Surinam which was to finance projects in the fields of agriculture and transportation. In 1954 a Ten-Year Plan was drawn up, which was followed by a National Development Plan; the emphasis was on the expansion and improvement of the economic and social infrastructure. These plans provided for the building of a hydro-electric plant at Affobaka on the Surinam river, about seventy miles from the capital. The electric power is used for the production of aluminium. Alcoa agreed to carry out

[10] Commonwealth Economic Cttee, *Non-Ferrous Metals* (1966); US Bureau of Mines, *Minerals Yearbook 1967*, vol. i–ii (1968), p. 229.
[11] *Christian Science Monitor*, 26 Aug. 1970.

this plan, which included building an aluminium plant and smelter with a capacity of 40,000 tons per annum, and accepted the condition that the hydro-electric plant would become the property of Surinam after seventy-five years. This illustrates the growing importance of US capital for the country's economic development. Surinam now domestically processes part of the ore traditionally exported and now exports bauxite (over 90 per cent to the United States), aluminum, and alumina; alumina exports soared from 59,000 metric tons in 1965 to 345,000 metric tons in 1966, while aluminum exports increased from 1,254 to 25,503 metric tons.[12]

But in spite of the injections of capital by the Netherlands government and the EEC,[13] Surinam is far from achieving economic independence and has an adverse trade balance; its imports for food consumption amount to twice the value of the agricultural commodities it exports (mainly rice, which is subject to adverse weather conditions and to fluctuations in price). This is partly because of the continuing emphasis on mono-production, and partly because of the population increase, which has meant that about half the population is under the age of 15. The government is hard pressed to find jobs for young people, and unemployment, officially given as under 10 per cent, is in fact estimated at about double and is increasing. There is also tension caused by the lack of social facilities for the unemployed and because of the increasingly inflationary situation generated by annual wage increases which foreign and local companies have been forced to concede.[14] Until the second world war most of the Asiatic inhabitants lived in rural districts, and Paramaribo was a predominantly Creole capital. From then on a migratory movement towards this only urban centre developed, especially of younger-generation Indians, who had come into contact with city life during their period of conscription. They showed economic ambition and a keen interest in schooling: in 1946 the first Indian received a degree from a Dutch university. In a surprisingly short time they penetrated many middle-class occupations—later even the professions—until then in the

[12] F. M. Andic, 'The Development Impact of the EEC on the French and Dutch Caribbean', *J. Common Market Stud.*, Sept. 1969.

[13] Of the total development aid of $64·6 m. in the 1968 Dutch budget, $36·8m. was earmarked for Surinam and the Netherlands Antilles. Surinam has also received assistance from the European Development Fund which, in 1968, allocated over $23 m. for hydro-agricultural improvement, school and port construction, water supply for Paramaribo, etc. This consists of a low-interest loan. But the Fund only exceptionally assists industrial projects and has therefore not assisted the bauxite industry. Although Surinam stands to gain from the EEC's expanding demand for aluminum, as an associate member she must also lower and finally eliminate import duties and quotas on her imports from the Community, with a corresponding erosion of public revenues (see ibid., pp. 46–7).

[14] *FT*, 11 July 1969.

hands mostly of Creoles, Europeans, and immigrants from the Near East. The percentage of Indians in Paramaribo increased from 11 in 1940 to 21 in 1950; in the same period the percentage of urbanized Creoles grew only from 62 to 69.

In general, the demographic growth of the Indian group has been greater than that of the Creole population. In the years 1922–5 48 out of every 100 live births were Creole, 32 Indians, and 16 Javanese; in 1951–3 these figures were respectively 42, 42, and 14.[15] From 1964 to 1969 the numerical strength of Creoles and Indians has approached parity, and in the latter year the population consisted of 35 per cent Creoles, 35 per cent Asians, 15 per cent Javanese, and 2 per cent each for Amerindians, Chinese, Jews, Lebanese, and Europeans.[16] The Javanese have a smaller rate of increase than the two main population groups and their relative numerical position is expected to weaken further, but from 1925 the two Asian groups of Indians and Javanese have *together* been in a numerical majority over the Creoles. In politics, however, they have so far acted separately, and thanks to an ingenious division of political districts, the Creole population group has been able to maintain a certain political dominance.

The Javanese group has not basically changed its original economic and social position, and rice growing in the Indonesian tradition is still its main occupation.[17] In contrast, both the demographic growth and the socio-economic advancement of the Indians are such that the preconditions for conflicts and tensions between them and the originally dominant Creole group are clearly present, the more so, since the change in the Indians' economic and social position did not go hand in hand with a complete absorption of Creole culture. Juridically, their exceptional legal status as immigrants was abolished in the 1920s, and from then on they enjoyed full rights of citizenship in Surinam. The economically successful among them showed great capacity for the absorption of Dutch education, but the process of their cultural assimilation was in no way unselective and general, nor was it a one-way traffic. The cultural heritage of the Asian groups was formally recognized in 1937, when Governor Kielstra— trained in the Netherlands East Indies' colonial administration and there-fore respectful of *adat* (common law)—submitted a draft bill to the *Staten* of Surinam, which gave legal recognition to marriages performed according to Hindu or Moslem rites. In spite of strong Creole opposition,

---

[15] On the Indians see J. D. Speckmann, *Marriage and Kinship among the Indians in Surinam* (Assen, 1965).

[16] *FT*, 11 July 1969.

[17] See A. de Waal Malefijt, *The Javanese of Surinam: Segment of a Plural Society* (Assen, 1963).

the law was put into practice in 1941, though polygamy was prohibited. While civil divorce procedures were introduced for Hindus, the Moslems retained their right of repudiation of the female partner. This legislation undoubtedly strengthened the Asians' awareness of cultural identity, as did new religious reform movements which gathered strength in the 1920s and 1930s. Thus the modernist Hindu reform movement of *Arya Samaj*, which reached Surinam via Guyana, and which gained support amongst an estimated 16 per cent of the Indian population, not only fostered an India-centered cultural revival but also strengthened the immigrant's ethnic awareness. Similarly a reform movement among the Moslem part of the Indians—approximately 20 per cent of the entire immigrant group—reached Surinam during the same period by way of Trinidad. This *Ahmadiyya* movement, like the *Arya Samaj*, tried to adapt the sacred teaching to a modern, universalistic society. The *Ahmadiyya* maintained frequent contacts with its main centre in Lahore, so that since 1947 the Moslems of Surinam have come to identify culturally with Pakistan.

The Creoles, for their part, had reserved the term 'Surinamese' for themselves, thereby indicating that in their image of society the others were still aliens. Small wonder that party formation, which got under way after the second world war, came to be predominantly based on ethnic affiliation. In 1945 the Creole *Staten* members and their friends created the National Party of Surinam (NPS), but after the introduction of universal suffrage in 1948, the leadership of the party shifted from upper-class Creoles and Jews to those of mainly Negro origin, and the Negro masses gave their support to this party.[18] Under the present electoral system, 27 of the 39 seats in the *Staten* are filled by means of district elections, while 12 are 'free' seats to be allocated on the basis of proportional representation. Until recently the NPS, led by Premier J. Pengel (who died in 1970), occupied 18 seats, the United Hindustani Party (VHP), including Hindus and Moslems, which was founded in 1949, had 11 seats. The Javanese have their own party. But despite the ethnic basis of Surinam's parties, government there—in contrast to Guyana—has not been monopolized by one ethnic group, as no party (or ethnic group) has been able to establish absolute dominance. Coalitions between the Creole and Asian parties have, therefore, been the rule.

In February 1969 the Johan Pengel NPS government was forced to resign after a series of strikes and demonstrations. Elections on 25 October produced for the first time a clear majority for the East Indians' party, the VHP, whose leader, Juggernath Lachmon, was then asked to form a

[18] Gastmann, p. 53.

new cabinet. Typically, he decided to have a Creole, Dr Jules Sedney, as the new Prime Minister, while other Creole intellectuals came to share the cabinet posts with East Indians, thus conserving the tradition of a government based on the support of both population groups. Lachmon himself became President of the *Staten*. The electoral victory of the VHP was widely interpreted as not only a rebuff for Pengel's somewhat authoritarian political style but also as another indication of the un-willingness of the East Indians (and a number of the Creole upper class) to make any drastic or untimely change in the present relationship with the Netherlands.

Of the small political movements, attention may be drawn to the National Party for the Republic. This party, which so far has only one seat in the *Staten*, is under the articulate leadership of Eddie Bruma, who has been infiltrating the leadership of several labour unions. It has won some support from young intellectuals for its socialist-inclined platform; the party also wants immediate and total independence. In so far as this party's nationalism expresses itself culturally it emphasizes the African heritage, in contrast not only to the European but also to the Asian cultural influences. This has made it less acceptable to progressive Indian elements.

Voices favouring more independence in foreign affairs were raised in Pengel's NPS. The border dispute with Guyana before its recent settle-ment appeared to strengthen their influence, since under the present Charter of the Kingdom (to be discussed presently), its solution lay wholly with the remote Council of Ministers of the Kingdom. The danger of such movements for the country's political stability lies in the fact that they are looked upon with suspicion by the Indians, who seem to prefer the remnants of the *Pax Neerlandica* to any new political experiment as long as they do not have a strong numerical and political minority.[19]

A few words must be said about the Charter of the Kingdom, the constitutional embodiment of the relationship between Holland's former colonies in the Caribbean and their metropolis. This Charter—to which the constitutions of the Netherlands, Surinam, and the Netherlands Antilles are subordinated—designates certain areas, such as defence, foreign affairs, and citizenship, as 'Kingdom affairs'. These can only be dealt with by the Kingdom Council of Ministers, which consists of the Dutch Cabinet plus the permanent Ministers Plenipotentiary of Surinam and the Netherlands Antilles in The Hague. If either of the Ministers Plenipotentiary objects to a particular proposal, the decision on the

---

[19] Cf. Mathews, and Gastmann.

matter is postponed and has to be further discussed in the 'Central Kingdom Council', which is presided over by the Dutch Prime Minister and consists in addition of two Dutch Ministers and two overseas ministers—either the Minister Plenipotentiary and another minister from the same overseas territory, or both Ministers Plenipotentiary. The Kingdom Council of Ministers then decides 'in accordance with the result of the continued consultation' (Art. 12 (51)) in the smaller Council.[20] The Surinam and Netherlands Antilles Ministers Plenipotentiary in The Hague are also members of the Council of State, the highest advisory college of the Crown; they are further entitled to defend the views of their governments on 'Kingdom affairs' in the Dutch parliament. International agreements which may have relevance for the overseas parts of the Kingdom must be approved by their parliaments. All matters not defined as 'Kingdom affairs' are dealt with autonomously by each of the three partners.

In broad terms, the Charter has so far worked satisfactorily.[21] But the overseas partners—especially Surinam—have pressed for greater participation in the Foreign Service of the Kingdom. As a result some Antilleans and Surinamese have been appointed heads of some diplomatic missions in the western hemisphere, for instance in Jamaica, Trinidad, and Chile. Both overseas Kingdom partners are also represented in the Netherlands Embassy in Washington by diplomats of Caribbean origin, who have the personal title of Minister Plenipotentiary. Another point of friction, again felt most deeply in Surinam, lies in the fact that international organizations do not accept Surinam and the Netherlands Antilles in their present status as full members. They participate in the United Nations only indirectly, through the inclusion on the Netherlands delegation to the UN Assembly of a representative of each Kingdom partner. They are wholly excluded from the OAS, a matter which is not only felt as having political significance, but also carries with it certain economic disadvantages, as it constitutes a bar to their participation in inter-American programmes of financial and technical assistance. These disadvantages are only partly counterbalanced by the association of Surinam and the Netherlands Antilles with the EEC. It is in this context that one must interpret the rumblings of dissatisfaction with the Charter in Surinam. As we have seen, however, the internal political situation in that country makes it unlikely that a forceful movement towards complete indepen-

---

[20] The Charter has been published in English in Gastmann and in Inter-Parliamentary Union, *Constitutional and Parliamentary Information*, 3rd ser., no. 21, 15 Jan. 1955. See espec. Pt. II: 'The management of the affairs of the Kingdom'.
[21] See further Mathews, and Mitchell.

dence, backed by a political majority, will emerge in the near future. But it is to be noted that there is nothing in the Charter to prevent swift attainment of full independence if and when this becomes official policy, nor are there any reasons to suppose that the other component parts of the Kingdom would *a priori* object to it.

A generous scholarship policy of all Kingdom partners has brought considerable numbers of students from Surinam and the Netherlands Antilles to Holland. Once there, away from their own country, often united in a struggle against—admittedly mild—prejudice, and slowly losing touch with the many subtle dividing forces in their own society, they arrive easily at the formulation of radical programmes for cultural and structural reform. Once returned to their home countries, however, only a few maintain their original political enthusiasm. In Curaçao several of these young coloured intellectuals—whose social cohesion is strengthened by the fact that many of them have European wives—recently founded a new party, the Antillean Reformist Union, inspired by the Latin American Christian Democrats. On the same island 'happenings' have been taking place, clearly inspired by the 'provo' movement of Amsterdam, which found some ardent missionaries among young Dutch teachers and artists. One of these demonstrations was in favour of renaming the streets after tortured leaders of the great slave rebellion. Incidents such as these had been viewed as insignificant until the May 1969 riots put them in a different perspective.

Not only students, but also labourers from Surinam and the Netherlands Antilles find their way to Holland: the number of Surinamese in Holland increased from approximately 6,200 in 1962 to 10,670 in 1965, and the rate of increase has accelerated even more rapidly in the last two years. The estimate for 1970 is about 40,000. The image, especially of the Surinamese, is not too favourable in the old mother country. The average Dutchman has never had more than scant information on the Caribbean parts of the Kingdom; they were seen as unimportant, quaint, and remote rather than as important and charmingly exotic, as were the Dutch *East* Indies. With the loss of the Asian colonies, the majority of the Dutch would not seem to have minded if the American possessions had been lost into the bargain. And this attitude has remained essentially the same, in spite of considerable efforts by the respective governments.

Nevertheless the willingness to help finance the economic development of Surinam and the Netherlands Antilles is undoubtedly great in Holland. This arises in part from feelings of historical guilt over a colonial past. Another consideration is that, while development aid in general is widely considered a moral obligation in the Netherlands, it is felt to be more practical to extend such aid to the countries with which one has special relations.

Thus the relationship of the Netherlands, Surinam, and the Netherlands Antilles is based on a mixture of moral motives, self-interest, and vague considerations of historical solidarity. It is being maintained within a framework that does not, as does the French one, foster total assimilation or, as does the British one, stimulate the attainment of complete independence—though it does not make it impossible. Essentially that framework leaves future development completely open.

7 Cuba and the Super-Powers

ROBIN BLACKBURN

THE focus of this chapter is on the relation between Cuba's internal social structure and her international relations, both before and after the revolution. Identifying this relation, in however provisional and partial a fashion, is essential if a false abstraction is to be avoided in the study of relations between nation states. A revolution demonstrates this fact in a particularly clear way since the impact of internal transformations on external relations is invariably very great.

Much writing in the field of international relations is permeated by the explicit or implicit assumption that small, poor countries must expect to be dominated by large, rich ones especially where they happen to fall within the latter's traditional sphere of influence. The course of the Vietnamese struggle for independence against Japan, France, and the United States has gone some way to undermine this view but usually in the direction of making greater allowance for the significance of geographical factors. The argument which follows seeks to apply a sociological corrective to any excessive emphasis on size, propinquity to a great power, or level of economic development. By a study of Cuba's relations with the super-powers both before and after the revolution of 1959–60 it can be shown that the nature of the internal social formation is decisive in organizing and distributing the weight of these factors. The social regime which prevailed in Cuba before the revolution was such as greatly to enhance the island's external dependence; that which has prevailed since has enabled Cuba to limit or negate these factors where they threatened national independence. Post-revolutionary Cuba is very far from being an autarchic power, but the intensive domestic mobilization of the society consequent upon the revolution has for the first time alowed her to develop a foreign policy of her own. To be effective, national independence must be sustained internally by a strong and coherent social force, as it was in Europe at the time of the birth of the nation state. Today the underdeveloped bourgeoisie of the third world is rarely able to fill this role, and the realization of national independence can only be brought

I

about by the revolutionary assertion of new social forces.[1] The history of Cuba provides a useful illustration of this thesis.

THE CUBAN REPUBLIC AND THE UNITED STATES

For the first five decades of its existence (1902–58) the Cuban Republic was so totally dominated by its large northern neighbour that at times only formal sovereignty seemed to be denied to the United States. This fact is not often disputed and for that reason it is not usually established with sufficient precision. What has to be explained is how it was possible for Cuba to escape a domination that was so complete. The thesis explored here is that the very completeness of this domination contained a self-destructive potential. Only a closer look at the forms that domination assumed can locate the source of this contradiction.

The Cuban Republic was established by an act of the US Congress after four years of US military occupation, following the Spanish-American war of 1898. Such origins could only heavily compromise national independence right from the outset. Added to this is the fact that the Cuban social order had been greatly weakened by the prolonged and bitter conflict with imperial Spain which raged for some thirty years. At the time of the North American intervention Spain had concentrated a military force in Cuba larger than that which they had possessed on the entire mainland during the Wars of Independence. Those sections of the local élite who initiated the struggle against Spain in 1868 (mainly land-owners in the Eastern provinces) suffered great loss of life and property during the ensuing war.[2] Of course a significant section of the élite sided with the colonial power: landowners from the Western and Central provinces and the church hierarchy, as well as colonial functionaries. Approximately two hundred thousand of the island's inhabitants returned to Spain after the US occupation and the ending of Spanish rule. During this period, when the traditional oligarchy was politically divided and decimated, the source of its economic power was also undercut by the falling prices and fierce competition met by Cuba's sugar exports. Only the largest and most efficient estates survived the rationalization of the sugar industry which reduced the number of mills from some 2,000 in

---

[1] Cf. 'With regard to countries with a belated bourgeois development, especially the colonial and semi-colonial countries, the theory of the permanent revolution signifies that the complete and genuine solution of their tasks of achieving democracy and national emancipation is conceivable only through the dictatorship of the proletariat as the leader of the subjugated nation, above all of its peasant masses' (Leon Trotsky, *The Permanent Revolution* (1965), p. 152).

[2] Ramiro Guerra y Sánchez, *La guerra de diez años* (Havana, 1950), i. 16–33.

mid-century to only 207 by 1894.[3] All these circumstances conspired to reduce or enfeeble those social classes which might have made the new Republic more resistant to US domination. It is significant that one of the first acts of the US military administration on the island was to insist that agreement be reached on disarming and disbanding the independence forces which had been fighting the Spanish. However there was one impalpable consequence of Cuba's Wars of Independence which might have suggested that in the long run Cuba would be an insecure element in the American system; namely the fierce, radical patriotism which had been born out of the struggle with Spain. Cuba, which was to be less independent than most South American Republics, had from the beginning a more intense awareness of national identity, corresponding to her more intense fight against the Spanish.[4] This radical nationalism was quite diffused among the population and was to become part of the official ideology of the Cuban state—even Batista patronized the cult of José Martí, the incipiently anti-imperialist Cuban leader in the war against Spain.

The Cuban élite never made itself the standard-bearer of this radical nationalist sentiment. From 1810 onwards a significant 'annexationist' current had existed within the élite, especially among the slave owners, who wished Cuba to be incorporated within the United States. At one time this prospect attracted such prominent Cubans as José Antonio Echeverria, Miguel Aldama, and other members of the 'Club de la Habana'. The independence movement itself used the United States as its supply base and few of its leaders shared José Martí's distrust of US power and policy. In short the local oligarchy was not only weak but also predisposed to look on the United States as a friendly power. In the political tussles which marked the first decades of the Republic, Cuban politicians did not hesitate to invite US intervention. If we turn to an examination of the economic, military, diplomatic, and cultural dimensions of Cuban subordination we will see that the new Republic had, from its inception, the sort of neo-colonial status *vis-à-vis* the United States which most of the Latin American republics have possessed only in more recent times.

At the time of the outbreak of the Spanish-American War, US investment in Cuba already amounted to $50 m. This investment climbed to $220 m. in 1913 and a staggering $1,525 m. by 1929. By the 1920s Cuba

[3] Guer a y Sánchez, *Azúcar y población en las Antillas* (Havana, 1940), pp. 73, 91.
[4] C. A. M. Hennessy writes: 'The Cuban belief that Spanish power had already been broken by the time the United States intervened in 1898, three years after the beginning of the [second] War of Liberation, gave a keen edge to anti-Americanism, and the coincidence of national independence with a new phase of American imperialism made for an easy transference of nationalist antagonism, from Spain to the United States' ('The Roots of Cuban Nationalism', *International Affairs*, July 1965, p. 352).

accounted for over a quarter of US investments in the continent as a whole, and per capita US investment in Cuba was seven times the average for the other republics.[5] Cuba's economic life was dominated in all areas (trade and banking as well as investment) by *one* power, while elsewhere on the continent British investments exceeded those of the United States until the second world war. Cuba thus lacked the possibilities for manœuvre which some of the South American Republics occasionally possessed.[6]

The form which US investment in Cuba took was as important as its absolute size in subordinating and integrating the local élite. Sometimes foreign investment is intensive in character: that is to say it forms a relatively isolated enclave within the traditional society (mines, oilfields, even plantations). In Cuba, by contrast, it was extensive: almost half of the cultivable land area was devoted to sugar cane by the 1930s and half the cane fields were controlled by US-owned sugar corporations, though the proportion diminished somewhat after the Great Depression. Of course, whether intensive or extensive, exploitation of this type siphons off to the metropolitan country that vital investable surplus which the underdeveloped country needs for development. In Cuba's case the extensive nature of US investment added to the problems created by the competition of European beet sugar and helped to smother those traditional Cuban landowners who survived the wars of independence. In the sugar-cultivating areas most were either expropriated, or reduced to the status of a *colono*, dependent on the credit and purchasing policy of the sugar company which owned the local *central*.[7] As we shall see, the very scale of US economic penetration of Cuba in the long run conspired to enfeeble, indeed partially eliminate, that social force (the traditional élite) which could have been her most effective indigenous ally.

Before leaving the economic aspect of Cuban subordination to the United States it should be emphasized that direct investment was only one form of this subordination, and not necessarily the most important. Perhaps the most striking index of Cuba's neo-colonial status was the prolonged and profound stagnation of the economy in the thirty-five years or so from the early 1920s up to the triumph of the revolution.

[5] R. F. Smith, *The United States and Cuba, 1917–60* (New York, 1960), p. 117.

[6] For a discussion of the ways in which Latin American countries were able to play off rival imperial powers against one another see Vivian Trías, *Imperialísmo y geopolítica* (Montevideo, 1968).

[7] Less than a fifth of the sugar cane was grown on land administered by the sugar companies; the rest was supplied by 68,000 *colonos*, many of whom leased land from the companies. Large independent estates survived in the cattle lands of Camaguey; small independent farms in the tobacco cultivating areas of Western Cuba (see Lowry Nelson, *Rural Cuba* (Minn., 1950)).

Sugar production was half a million tons lower in 1956 than it had been in 1925.[8] As the population had doubled in the same period, it was only because of a modest expansion in non-sugar production that a catastrophic fall in living standards was prevented. But non-sugar production could only expand within very strict limits. The reciprocal trade treaties by which Cuban sugar entered the United States stipulated the preferential conditions under which US industrial products were to enter the Cuban market. Under these conditions Cuban industry could only achieve any development either when US industry was distracted by war, or by becoming the junior partners of US industry. In this way it was the crushing superiority of US capitalism within the world market which was more or less bound to extinguish the hopes of any autonomous capitalist development in a country like Cuba. Cuba's stagnation was thus the result of the very system of imperialism[9] rather than the expression of the interest of the particular companies which operated in Cuba. For example, Cuban public utilities (telephone, electricity, railways, etc.) were US owned; these companies would have made more profits if the Cuban economy had been expanding but then this possibility was precluded by US domination of the Cuban market.[10]

At no time in the history of the Republic did the United States scruple to use the most direct diplomatic and military methods to defend her interests. Cuba was under direct US military occupation from 1898 to 1902 and then again from 1906 to 1909 after political disturbances appeared to threaten US interests. The defence of these interests was also given as the justification for landing marines in 1912 and 1917. It has already been noted that during the first occupation the Cuban Independence Army had been disbanded: during the second a small Cuban armed force was constituted under US military supervision. After the overthrow of Machado in 1933 US naval might was displayed in a show of force which encouraged Batista to abort the threatened revolution. Indeed, throughout his period in power Batista was to receive US military assistance: even in

[8] *Anuario azucarero de Cuba, 1957*, p. 96.

[9] The concept of 'imperialism' is often invoked in a very vague way. It was first used in a scientific rather than a polemical manner in the works of Hobson, Rosa Luxemburg, and Lenin, who concentrated almost exclusively on the economic aspect. The non-economic aspects were given somewhat greater prominence by Lenin's fellow Bolshevik, Bukharin. A useful survey of this literature is provided by Tom Kemp, *Theories of Imperialism* (London, 1967). Recently there have been further attempts to develop the Marxist theory of imperialism, notably by Paul Baran, A. Gunder Frank, Harry Magdoff, and Ernest Mandel. This chapter attempts only to explore the non-economic aspects of imperialism in Cuba, relating them to the political dynamic of the society. See also O. Pino Santos, *Historia de Cuba* (Havana, 1964). Specifically on trade and imperialism see A. Emmanuel, *Unequal Exchange* (London, 1972).

[10] I have discussed these matters more fully in *LA Handbook* (1968), pp. 622–31.

1958, by which time he was coming to be thought a wasted asset, it continued in some forms. When Fidel Castro entered Campo Colombia, Batista's HQ, in early January 1959 he was met by representatives of the US military mission who had stuck with Batista's forces to the very last (they offered Fidel their services, to which he replied that as he had just defeated the army they advised, he evidently did not require their assistance). The attempted invasion of Cuba in April 1961 organized by the CIA, not to speak of many other smaller attempted infiltrations, represented the continuity of US policy towards Cuba from the birth of the Republic until the most recent times. The defeat of these incursions leaves the US base at Guantánamo Bay as the only relic of her military domination of the island.

The notorious Platt Amendment of 27 February 1901, passed by the US Senate at the time of the first occupation of Cuba, gave the US government the right to intervene in the island 'for the protection of life, property and individual liberty'.[11] Historians often regard it as the major instrument by which the United States maintained its hegemony over Cuba. This is not quite the case. It was the existence of the Amendment that probably saved Cuba from outright annexation in 1906. Further, the abrogation of the Amendment in 1934 was almost as interventionist an act as its institution, since it was designed to strengthen Batista's newly installed regime. On occasion the US representative in Cuba simply dictated policy. Thus Cuba experienced already during General Crowder's mission in the 1920s a form of domination that has now become very general in the underdeveloped world: namely detailed financial control of the economy of the debtor nation as the price of continued 'aid'. The special mission of Sumner Welles, a trouble-shooter for President Roosevelt, had a more avowedly political purpose: firstly removing the unpopular dictator, Machado, and then winding up the popular insurrection of 1933–4 which ensued without any loss of US power or possessions. One of the last US Ambassadors to Cuba, Earl Smith, in a much quoted-statement to a Congressional Committee, declared that the ambassador was usually the second most important man on the island and sometimes the most important. However Smith's word on this should not be enough for us; indeed a reading of his own autobiography belies the statement, since he could control neither Batista nor the forces ranged against him.[12]

US power in Cuba was built into the island's situation by history and by economics. This accumulated structural power made its exercise by particular representatives often quite unnecessary outside crisis situations. It

---

[11] D. F. Healy, *The United States in Cuba, 1898–1902* (Madison, 1963), pp. 167–8.
[12] Earl T. Smith, *The Fourth Floor* (New York, 1962).

is this which largely explains the lack of evidence of direct attempts to influence the Cuban government found by Cuban researchers in the captured files of the large US companies operating in the island. There are, of course, some notable exceptions, such as the huge personal pay-off received by Batista from ITT in 1957 in return for a rise in the telephone rates. More usually simple self-interest was sufficient to ensure that the prosperity of US companies which dominated the economy was promoted to the limited extent to which this lay within the ability of Cuban governments. When major problems arose, the place to apply pressure was Washington, not Havana. We may assume that the United Fruit Company, which retained the Dulles family law firm,[13] found more direct and effective ways of advancing their Cuban sugar interests than seeking to influence Cuban government officials.

In its policy towards Cuba the US government was, from the start, faced with options similar to those delineated by Machiavelli:

When those states which have been acquired are accustomed to live at liberty under their own laws, there are three ways of holding them. The first is to despoil them; the second is to go and live there in person; the third is to allow them to live under their own laws, taking a tribute of them, and creating within the country a government composed of a few who will keep it friendly for you.[14]

Of course, the Cubans were not 'accustomed to live at liberty under their own laws', but they compensated for this by their burning desire to do so. Perhaps partly in recognition of this the US government opted for the third of the three methods—the one Machiavelli recommended as the most effective. At least we may see in the Cuban case what distinguishes modern 'overdeveloped' imperialism from more traditional varieties. Already by 1933 US hegemony had become so complete that it had smothered its own most effective local supporters. The character of the Cuban army was significantly changed by Batista's Sergeants' coup which replaced the old officer class. From this time on those who dominated Cuba did not possess any really reliable instrument of class rule. The Batista regime had a strong gangster element within it from the outset. The political parties also became progressively more unstable and corrupt. Fidel Castro indicated the underlying reason for this when he described the post-war Presidents of the 'democratic interlude' of 1945–52 as representatives of the 'lumpen-bourgeoisie'.[15] To be effective a ruling

[13] The many connections between US public officials and private US interests in Cuba are cited by Hugh Thomas, *Cuba: the Pursuit of Freedom* (London, 1970), pp. 686–7.
[14] *The Prince*, ch. 5.
[15] Speech on 1 Dec. 1961. I have explored the institutional weakness of prerevolutionary Cuba in 'Prologue to the Cuban Revolution', *New Left R.*, Oct. 1963.

group needs to believe in itself and its mission to govern society. It is this class-consciousness which the Cuban bourgeoisie fatally lacked—it had been destroyed mainly by the completeness of US domination over the life of the island. This is why the Cuban political parties were unable to prevent or oppose Batista's second coup in 1952; it is also the reason why no effective centre of opposition to Castro emerged after the overthrow of Batista's military regime, since the military were isolated from any effective social base. More remarkable still, it only took a further two years for Fidel to carry out a complete break with the United States, since he was confronted with no serious or coherent internal opposition and was able to count on enormous popular support.

When considering relatively intangible factors like the morale of the local middle class, it is as well to remember the humiliations to which they were subjected. Cuba became a tourist playground very early in her history; a tourism based on brothels and casinos rather than musuems and cathedrals—or even beaches. It was not just US business which dominated Cuba but also the US underworld. The Kefauver investigations revealed that Havana was a major staging post for *mafia* operations.[16] The notorious Meyer Lansky, owner of the second largest hotel in Havana, was a long-standing crony of Batista's. The prevailing image of Cuba in the United States as an adjacent red-light district was scarcely calculated to encourage class pride in Cuba's élite. It should, of course, be emphasized that Cuba had a relatively large and prosperous middle class despite economic stagnation, since this was stagnation at a relatively high level. Indeed the size of this class attracted further US penetration and Cuba became the local centre for the whole Caribbean for US advertising concerns like J. Walter Thompson. A publication of the British Board of Trade, engagingly called *Hints to Businessmen visiting Cuba* (1958), gives some idea of the consequences:

Cuba is a power selling market. The market has been dominated so long by the United States that all sales promotion is on the American standard; large gaudy hoardings, neon signs; radio, press and television are all-pervading. . . . The expression 'No Bill Posting' is unknown in Cuba and every conceivable nook and cranny is occupied by posters of some type. . . . The purchasing power of the population falls into two distinct brackets, that is to say, the 'haves' and the 'have-nots'. The 'have-nots' are not of much interest as potential buyers of imported goods other than staple food-stuffs and cheap clothing. In this bracket not even extensive hire-purchase facilities would have any influence, because those in this class would be unable to provide either a guarantee or the requisite funds for the initial deposit. Most of the 'haves' are to be found in Greater Havana. . . .

Quite apart from advertising, the Cuban communications media were

[16] See Rafael Otero Echeverría, *Reportaje a una revolución* (Santiago, 1959), espec. pp. 128–35.

swamped by US products; films, television series, and the like. In this cultural aspect of US domination we may see not just a contradiction, but an actively self-defeating impulse. This cultural penetration did not just weaken the position or morale of the local élite, it positively encouraged antagonism to the prevailing order.[17] Values of efficiency, public morality, formal democracy, and freedom would all be endorsed by the films, television, or educational material coming from the United States.[18] No doubt this was discordant with prevailing realities in the United States itself, but in a neo-colonial society like pre-revolutionary Cuba the clash would be extremely harsh. Even the anodyne pieties of conventional liberalism would have been consistently violated in Batista's Cuba. In the same way the advertising which drenched the island portrayed life-styles which could only arouse expectations which the dependent economy was quite unable to satisfy. Finally, the commercialized and debauched features of the invading culture antagonized sections of the middle class, as may be seen in the popular Catholic journal, La Quinzena, or in the speeches of Eduardo Chibás, a populist political leader of the postwar period.

The personal histories of Cuba's political leaders are often cited as an index of North American hegemony. It was indeed the case that most of them underwent North American tutelage at one time or another, for example as officials of a US company, like Presidents Menocal and Machado. But many leaders of the revolution have had a similar background, which clearly had the opposite effect on them. Fidel's father was a manager for the United Fruit Company; Raúl Roa, revolutionary Cuba's Foreign Minister, was formerly vice-president of the Cuban section of the Congress for Cultural Freedom, an international front organization for intellectuals which was covertly financed by the CIA. On the ideological level the Cuban revolution has quite explicitly sought to harness the practicality and resourcefulness of North American bourgeois civilization to the political aims and values of the national-liberation movements. Hence Che Guevara's concern with the technique of guerrilla warfare and Fidel's interest in new methods of cattle-breeding and scientific farming. Interestingly enough, it has been the anti-imperialist revolution which has brought a flood of North American textbooks on mathematics, biology, chemistry, engineering, and other subjects into Cuban classrooms. Before the revolution, when Cuba was dominated by the United States, such

[17] Raymond Carr has noted that 'the presence of the United States was psychologically oppressive in Cuba as in no other country, except possibly Panama' ('The Cold War in Latin America', in J. Plank, ed., Cuba and the United States: Long-Range Perspectives (Washington, 1967), p. 165).
[18] In the late 1940s, John Huston made a film, The Insurgents, which was clearly sympathetic to an attempt by revolutionaries to assassinate a Cuban military dictator.

subjects were taught on only a very small scale in Cuban schools and a large number of children never received any systematic education.

Perhaps the relations which used to obtain between Cuba and the United States can be summed up in this way. Cuba's domestic élite facilitated and encouraged US hegemony but in so doing gravely weakened and discredited itself. The domination of Cuba was effected not just via diplomatic representatives or even just through the large US corporations which straddled the Cuban economy but also through the structure of a market which ensured that Cuba could only be a subordinate appendage of the United States with only those resources being developed which complemented the metropolitan economy. Multiple domination in the political, cultural, military, diplomatic, and economic spheres combined to extinguish the strength and spirit of the local élite and even to stimulate forces of rebellion. The structure of US hegemony induced a deadening passivity and inertness in Cuban social relations which became in their turn a sort of mute obstacle to US policy. Other things being equal the North American policy-makers might have preferred a more presentable local ally than Batista and his henchmen but they found themselves in a situation where, as in so many countries of the third world today, they had no choice. The revolution, which was to sweep away every vestige of US power in the island, initially was able to profit from a short period of US 'neutrality' precisely because it promised to deliver US policy from this impasse. There were not a few, even within the revolutionary movement, who thought that the purpose of the revolution was to replace the 'obsolete' military dictatorship of Batista by a dynamic civilian regime, modelled perhaps on that of Muñoz Marin in Puerto Rico. As we have seen, the crucial miscalculation was the assumption that the social forces still existed in Cuba for an indigenous capitalist development. Once challenged by Fidel, despite the small size of the organized forces at his command, the whole imposing structure of US power collapsed like a house of cards. The world's most powerful nation, economically and militarily, was unable to prevent the defection of a tiny island only ninety miles from its shores. The other major socialist revolutions of the century have occurred in countries where imperialism had yet to acquire a sufficiently firm grip on economy and society; they were, in Mao's term, 'semi-colonial', or, in Lenin's phrase, 'weak links' in the imperialist chain. By contrast US economic interests achieved in Cuba a multiple penetration already at the time of the first world war which it was not to approach in most other third-world countries until sometime after the second world war. Cuba's revolution was thus the first to occur within a context of *over-developed* imperialism.

CUBA'S TURN TO COMMUNISM

The dramatic events that led Cuba to become a communist country are well known though not often well interpreted. Cuba's turn to communism was of great importance in setting her experience apart from the radical nationalist movements which at one time it so much resembled; Nkrumah's Ghana, Nasser's Egypt, Ben Bella's Algeria, Sukarno's Indonesia for a time shared a similar rhetoric with revolutionary Cuba. But Cuba has now demonstrated qualitatively greater political stability and dynamism, largely as a consequence of the turn to communism. Two hypotheses which seek to explain this must be considered.

First, it is often maintained, by commentators on both left and right, that the Cuban revolution was pushed into communism by the actions of the United States. It is certainly true that first Eisenhower, and then Kennedy used the crudest power politics in their attempt to force Cuba to come to heel. The reduction of Cuba's sugar quota and later its abolition, the economic blockade, the attempts at invasion, sabotage, and assassination formed a systematic campaign to crush the revolution which was likely to disabuse even the most pro-western of revolutionaries. But it cannot be denied that in the beginning at least imperialism had been offered some provocation. Thus Cuba's considerable oil requirements had always been met by imports at the high prices fixed by the North American (and British) oil companies. In 1959 Cuba stopped paying for this oil, having accumulated a debt of $76 m.[19] They asked the oil companies to refine the much cheaper Soviet oil they bought instead—and when the companies refused, they were taken over. Extensive trade and aid agreements had been entered into with the Russians during Mikoyan's visit in February of 1960; including the sale of 1 m. tons of sugar, the provision of $100 m. in finance for aid projects, and the resumption of diplomatic relations. Earlier US willingness to discuss economic 'aid' to Cuba had been brusquely rejected by Fidel Castro. It is useless to object that such actions were all well within Cuba's 'rights' as a sovereign nation: for that very reason they constituted a serious threat to imperialism as a system. Perhaps the most dangerous aspect in the development of the revolution was that these policies were not just announced and decided from above, but were accompanied by an awakening and mobilization of Cuba's impoverished and oppressed masses on an unprecedented scale. All in all it is surprising that a Bay of Pigs venture was not organized sooner. The instant attempt to suppress the Dominican uprising in 1965 showed that the lesson was not wasted. Any system of domination which is as interrelated as it was in Cuba cannot be dismantled piecemeal. Any serious

[19] See James O'Connor, *The Origins of Socialism in Cuba* (Ithaca, N.Y., 1970), ch. IV.

attempt to challenge one aspect of the system necessarily escalates into a challenge to the system as a whole. The radicalization of the Cuban revolution is to be credited to the determination and skill of the Cuban revolutionaries rather than to the predictable policies of the White House.

Another hypothesis concerning Cuba's turn to communism holds that it was the ineluctable consequence of Cuba's economic, military, and diplomatic indebtedness to the Soviet Union. It is, of course, true that Cuba was only able to break out of the US orbit because of Soviet support. In this sense the emergence of the Soviet Union as a world power after the second world war was an indispensable precondition to the consummation of the Cuban revolution. Despite the fact that the Soviet leadership had opted for 'revolution in one country', it remains the case that revolutions, once in progress, have often been able to draw on Soviet economic and military resources. As a giant industrial country, even if a distant one, the Soviet Union was willing to supply Cuba with a wide range of industrial goods—though significant gaps were later to appear (e.g. sugar machinery). She could buy Cuba's sugar and, as important, furnish Cuba with modern weaponry. On 9 July 1960 Khrushchev announced, possibly in somewhat vague terms, that Cuba had the protection of Soviet rockets. At the United Nations only the Warsaw Pact countries consistently voted for Cuba in the conflict with the United States—in marked contrast to the so-called 'non-aligned' countries. Though the defection of Cuba from the US camp was a great triumph for Khrushchev, there is no evidence that he wished to complete it by persuading Fidel Castro formally to join the Soviet bloc. On the contrary, there is every sign that Fidel's declaration in April 1961 that Cuba was socialist, and his later declaration in December that he was a Marxist-Leninist were a source of some embarrassment in Moscow. The Cuban revolution had not been led by a communist party, nor did the Soviet Union necessarily welcome the greater commitment to Cuban security which its membership of the Soviet camp would entail. Khrushchev may even have wished, in the Camp David spirit, not to antagonize the United States too much. Whatever the exact reason, it took the Soviet Communist Party some time to register Fidel's decisions. On the third anniversary of the revolution (January 1962), one month after Fidel had declared himself a Marxist-Leninist, the Soviet government sent a telegram to the Cuban government which did not mention the word 'socialism', though it wished the Cubans 'success in creating a new society'. An article in *Pravda* of 11 April 1962 seems to be the first mention of the Cuban leader's 'Marxist-Leninist' views, and the 1 May slogans read: 'Fraternal greetings to the heroic people of Cuba, who have embarked on the path of building socialism'.

Reinforcing the view that the Soviet leadership did not wish for formal induction of Cuba into their bloc, there is the evidence of other countries, such as Guinea and the UAR, which have been as dependent, economically and militarily, as Cuba on the Soviet Union but which have not taken the same path politically. The Soviet Union had naturally sought to extract advantage from this but does not seem to have pressed for any formal adhesion to the communist movement. The aim was, and remains, to sponsor a new grouping of pro-Soviet countries rather than seek insubstantial and awkward political conversions.

If foreign pressure was not responsible for Cuba's political evolution, what was the explanation? Obviously the revolutionary government enhanced Cuba's security by its declarations of political commitment to the Soviet camp, but this cannot have been a decisive reason. But what is more important is that the revolution, during a few months after the seizure of power, had expropriated all foreign and most domestic capital. The economy was now publicly owned, and the United States had for the first time been successfully defied in her own continent, with the support of of the Soviet Union. It is not surprising that Marxist ideas and gratitude to the Soviet bloc throve in this context. Cuba's revolutionary tradition, nourished and radicalized during the long years of war against Spain and again during the 1933 revolution, had a strong communist strand. Important national figures like Antonio Mella (a student leader who founded the Cuban Communist Party), Nicolás Guillén (Cuba's foremost poet), and Jesús Menéndez (leader of the sugar workers) had all enhanced the reputation of communism. Between 1938 and 1947 the Communist Party led the Cuban Trade Union Federation. Against this must, of course, be set the confusing impact of the alliance of the PSP (*Partido Socialista Popular*, as the Cuban Communist Party was known at this time) with Batista in the early 1940s (especially retrospectively), and the increasing isolation of the party during the cold war, when membership fell from 87,000 in 1942, to 20,000 in 1952, and to about 7,000 in 1959. Moreover, the party joined Fidel's revolutionary war against Batista only belatedly, and did not revise many of the views it had held with particular tenacity until the *barbudos* were virtually in the streets of Havana.[20] But once the party had joined Fidel, and had been accepted as part of the revolution, its mere existence as a well-organized political force made Marxist ideas more available.

Quite independently of the distinctly moderate position of the leadership of the Cuban Communist Party, the years 1960 to 1961 saw a decisive

[20] K. S. Karol, *Les guérrilleros au pouvoir* (Paris, 1970), p. 112.

shift to communism within the ranks of the mass of revolutionary militants. I was myself in Cuba at the end of 1961 and witnessed the widespread
and evidently genuine enthusiasm for Marxism-Leninism. *The Communist
Manifesto* and *State and Revolution* were sold in editions of 500,000 each in
1961, before Fidel's own pronouncements on the subject; they were to be
found on the many newsvendors' street stalls outselling such other current
favourites as *Lolita*. For the first time Cubans could hope to become masters
of their own destiny; Cuba could now really have an economy, a foreign
policy, and culture of her own. Communism could tell Cubans where they
were going, whereas radical nationalism could only tell them whence
they had come. Conditions were thus entirely propitious for the combus-
tion of Marxist and Leninist ideas among the mass of Cubans.

With Cuba inside the Soviet camp, it might seem to be natural that
Soviet influence would grow rapidly. Clearly the dependent structure of
the island's economy built up over nearly two centuries would require
time to dismantle and replace. Indeed, some commentators have argued
that post-revolutionary Cuba is as much dominated by the Soviet Union
as was pre-revolutionary Cuba by the United States.[21] Before examining
this question more systematically, three specific events which could have a
bearing on it will be considered: the Escalante episodes, the missiles
crisis, and the change of economic policy in 1963–4.

Aníbal Escalante was one of the more important leaders of the PSP. In
1961 he was entrusted with the organization of the ORI—the Integrated
Revolutionary Organization (comprising the PSP, the Student Director-
ate, and Fidel's 26 July Movement). Of the three, the PSP had much the
most organizational coherence and ideological unity; of its some 18,000
members, many had considerable experience. In March 1962 Fidel
denounced Escalante as a sectarian who was seeking to use the ORI as an
instrument of personal power, in the process converting it into a bureaucratic yoke on the Cuban revolutionary masses. Fidel accused him of
placing his own cronies in all key positions—for example every provincial
secretary of the ORI was a former member of the PSP. Shortly after
Fidel's denunciation the Soviet ambassador, S. M. Kudryatsev, was
recalled and a new one, Aleksandr Alekseyev, was appointed. There may
be some connection here but equally there may not. We may well
imagine that the Soviet Union would have been happy for Escalante to be
a power behind the scenes in Havana. The Soviet ambassador naturally
had close relations with him, and from the Soviet view he would certainly

---

[21] See e.g., the comments by Odell, p. 23 above.

have been more tractable to deal with than the wilder revolutionaries of the Fidelista school.

After a spell of involuntary exile in Eastern Europe, Escalante returned to Cuba in the mid-1960s and was given purely administrative employment. Cuban policy on a number of issues was at this time sharply differentiated from Soviet policies. Cuba was giving open and uninhibited support to the Latin American revolutionary movements and assailing those communist parties which rejected armed struggle; in the economic field the views, then freely and prominently discussed in the Soviet Union, of using market criteria and material incentives were openly rejected. Escalante began to form a group within the party and the state apparatus, mostly comprised of former members of the PSP, which was critical of these positions. This so called 'microfaction' exchanged information and materials with one another and contacted officials of the Soviet Embassy and representatives of Latin American communist parties. Evidently the Soviet Embassy was prepared to countenance Escalante's microfaction at least to the extent of conducting these discussions and receiving potentially valuable information from its few highly placed sympathizers. This time the tiny Escalante group was even less of a threat to Fidel's power than it had been before. Nevertheless, in the spring of 1968 Escalante and his microfaction were arraigned before an extraordinary meeting of the Central Committee, expelled from the party, and given various terms in prison for their violation of state secrets.

Clearly the two Escalante episodes show that Cuba's revolutionary leadership is well able to handle any pro-Soviet intrigues coming from the formerly important PSP. The timing of both attacks on Escalante perhaps reinforces this conclusion. On each occasion Fidel Castro was in the process of aligning Cuba closer to Soviet positions when he chose to isolate and defeat internal pro-Soviet tendencies. In 1962 he had just declared Cuba's formal membership of the Soviet bloc and was about to conclude a defence agreement that would lead to the installation of Soviet rockets on Cuban soil. In 1968 Cuba was about to renegotiate her major Soviet economic agreements and was in process of moderating her hostility to the Soviet Union on international questions (Czechoslovakia and other matters, to be discussed below). Apart from the reasons already discussed for the attacks on Escalante, they served to introduce a certain disjunction between Cuban domestic and foreign policy which gave notice that Cuba intended to maintain her freedom of action. In a not dissimilar manner Fidel Castro chose the occasion of Cuba's turn to a more systematic left policy in 1966 (at the Tricontinental Conference in Havana and, later, at the OLAS Conference of July–August 1967) to launch attacks on the Latin American

Trotskyists and the Chinese Communist Party. Here again, abstracting from the particular causes and consequences of these tactics their underlying political meaning was the assertion of a specific Cuban, and perhaps Latin American, political position capable of autonomously generating its own line. As will be seen, revolutionary Cuba has not rejected the notion of close political alliances (her understandings with the Vietnamese and the Koreans will be cited as evidence of this), but she has certainly so far resisted the hegemony of any other power. Fidel's own experience of making the revolution in Cuba, which owed nothing to foreign advice, certainly does not predispose him to accept outside tutelage.

The missile crisis of 1962 provides a rather different instance of Soviet–Cuban relations. By then the Cubans believed they had reason to prepare for the possibility of another US-sponsored invasion, but this time with full support from the US military establishment.[22] Doubtless Cuban leaders were pressing for some Soviet guarantee against such an eventuality, especially as Cuba's defence forces were relatively deficient at this stage, notably in technical arms. Fidel has said that conversations on the possibility of missiles being sent to Cuba began in June. In July Raúl Castro visited Moscow and concluded the agreement which resulted in the construction of missile sites in September and October. The issue in doubt is whether the Cubans asked for these missiles or whether the Soviet leaders made the suggestion. Publicly Fidel has declared that the missiles were requested by the Cubans (as in his speech of 13 April 1963); in private interviews with the journalists Claude Julien (*Le Monde*, 22 March 1963) and Jean Daniel (*New Republic*, 14 December 1963), he let it be understood that it was the Russians who actually proposed the missiles scheme. Clearly the Cubans negotiated for some effective form of defence, possibly even for some form of missile. Once the Russians proposed the missile plan, the Cuban leaders were ready to agree to it. The main Cuban doubts were about the extent of their participation in the command of the missiles stationed on their soil. Whatever the arrangements made (naturally it is impossible to discover what these were), the Cuban government strongly resented the unilateral Russian initiatives made during the crisis itself. Khrushchev failed to consult the Cubans about the withdrawal of the missiles and even gave some undertaking for the US government to have facilities to inspect the dismantling of the sites. These derogations of Cuban sovereignty by her own ally drew a strong reaction from the Cubans, who disallowed any on-site inspections to take place. They affirmed their right to acquire any weapons they deemed necessary for

[22] The US marines planned an autumn exercise in 1962 in which they were supposed to overthrow a tyrant named Ortsac in a Caribbean island ((Thomas, p. 1387 n.)

their defence or for the defence of the revolutionary principles for which they stood, and refused to sign the Test-Ban Treaty of 1963. Only a protracted visit by Mikoyan in late 1962, followed by Castro's visit to the Soviet Union next year, patched up the rift between the two governments.

Cuba's change of economic strategy in 1963-4 is sometimes cited as an example of undue Soviet interference in Cuban affairs. In the early days of the revolution ambitious industrialization plans were announced by the government. In the drive for diversity the area planted to sugar-cane was reduced by one-third in 1962, resulting in a very low harvest in 1963. Cuba was forced to default on her sugar agreement with the Soviet Union. At roughly the same time it became clear that investment resources had been simultaneously tied up in too many unrelated projects. These involved often hastily imported, frequently unsuitable, technologies and raw materials from Eastern Europe, which could not be integrated into the pockets of industrial plant installed by the former American-dominated economy. Nor did the infrastructure, especially in port, storage, and transport facilities, exist to handle this sudden expansion. In late 1963 a new emphasis appeared in economic policy. Industrialization plans were scaled down and an expansion of the sugar industry was projected. The Soviet Union agreed to increase the price from 4 cents per lb. to 6 cents per lb. and to buy an increasing quantity of sugar, reaching 5 m. tons in 1968. Certainly Soviet advice may have contributed to this reorientation. But the economic conjuncture of 1963 left little alternative;[23] Cuba's long dependence on sugar, the consequence of decades of imperialist domination, could only be shaken off by a transitional concentration on sugar exports to acquire the resources for diversification. The Soviet Union was acquiring sugar at a lower price than it could be produced domestically (c. 18 cents per lb.), and yet with respect to both price and quantity the Soviet agreement was more advantageous than the former quota allotted to Cuba in the US market. The advantage, was, of course, partly offset by the fact that the Soviet Union did not pay in convertible currency, and to that extent Cuba was economically dependent. The urgency of the need to produce considerably more than the Soviet Union would buy, which led to a target of 10 m. tons in 1970, was related to Cuba's growing foreign-exchange problems. The failure of the first attempt at industrialization, sustained almost exclusively by imports from Eastern Europe, also made the Cuban government aware of the country's need for imports from other industrial countries.

Some aspects of Soviet-Cuban relations in the economic, military, and cultural spheres emphasize the difference between these relations and the

[23] See 'The Cuban Economy', ECLA, *Econ. Survey Latin America 1963* (1965).

K

former US-Cuban relationship. The Soviet Union accounts for about one-half of Cuba's foreign trade; the socialist countries as a whole for 80 per cent. Between 1961 and 1965 Soviet aid to Cuba ran at about $300 m. a year, a rate which has probably been maintained since then.[24] Assistance on this scale is bound to constitute a serious constraint on Cuban policy. However there is every evidence that the Cuban government has exploited to the full the freedom of manœuvre left to it. The Soviet economic commitment is public and relatively generous—it is therefore difficult to renege on without great loss of esteem in the third world and elsewhere. Cuba's revolutionary leadership seems to have been fully aware of this fact. Despite her indebtedness, Cuba's economic policy has frequently been at variance with Soviet advice, as when Fidel rejected Soviet views on material incentives, etc., on the grounds that it was possible to think one was constructing socialism but to discover that one had rebuilt capitalism.

Fidel's direct influence on day-to-day decision-making in the economic field has been very great. A general theme underlying economic strategy has certainly been the suppression of the spontaneous forces of the domestic market, though planning has suffered from *ad hoc* interventions and has led to severe rationing. The false hopes of the plans of 1962-3 had to be abandoned—but the general revolutionary objectives were not. And despite the errors, Cuba has clearly used foreign economic assistance to widen the base of the economy. She now produces a host of light industrial goods which were formerly imported and agricultural production for domestic consumption has greatly expanded. Cuba now has a considerable fishing fleet and merchant marine where none existed before. The pressures of the international market cannot be ignored but they can be prevented from repressing the potentialities of domestic production. The introduction for the first time of a minimum of economic planning enables Cuba to attempt to concentrate on those lines of production which have strong export prospects (nickel, meat products, etc.). In pursuing these policies Cuba has not hesitated to buy substantial amounts of equipment from non-socialist countries and to plan exports to these countries in the future. The Soviet Union has been unable, or perhaps unwilling, to prevent such development of Cuba's economic strategy. The economies of the two countries are complementary in a number of respects, but this has not led Cuba to concentrate on being a mere supplier of tropical foodstuffs to the Soviet bloc. Che Guevara, speaking in Algiers shortly before he ceased to be Cuba's Minister of Industries, attacked the Soviet reliance on prices established by the capitalist world market when they are dealing

[24] Cf. R. S. Walters, 'Soviet Economic Aid to Cuba', *International Affairs*, Jan. 1966.

with third world countries.[25] Since Cuba also needs to earn convertible currencies to buy goods which the Soviet Union cannot supply, the prices obtaining on the world sugar market are still a major limiting factor. Though unable to evade all the consequences of this, Cuba has been able to mobilize the domestic sector of the economy, and to choose carefully her export priorities. Dependence on Soviet economic assistance in the short run does not inhibit diversification and stimulation of the economy, as did dependence on the United States formerly.

In the first decade of the revolution Cuba's margin of independence was limited rather than enhanced by the relatively high level of development inherited from the pre-revolutionary neo-colonial economy. Unlike a country based on a subsistence agriculture, Cuba was vitally dependent on imports for staple food supplies (especially wheat, rice, and beans) and for her only significant source of energy (oil). Although agricultural diversification, notably the rapid growth of rice production, has reduced reliance on food imports, the amount of oil required has doubled. Only a diversification and growth of exports can make this compatible with economic independence. For some years over half of Cuba's imports have been producer goods, compared with only a little over a fifth before the revolution. Now a third of national income is devoted to investment compared with under 10 per cent formerly. There has been a simultaneous prodigious expansion in technical education and the army of unemployed has been eliminated. Thus, although Cuba has been more dependent economically on a foreign power in the 1960s than at any time in her history, the character of the dependence is different. It relates to trade and credit, not the ownership of resources. It permits, or even encourages, the development of a viable and balanced economy. In the past growth increased rather than diminished dependence: today the achievement of growth would have the opposite effect. The power to make decisions now rests in Havana—Cuban failures in the economic sphere can no longer be attributed to external domination of the economy. Partly because of this it is impossible to know how long it will take Cuba to overcome her present dependence in economic relations. What can be examined is the ways in which the Cuban government has been able to confine this dependence to the economic sphere, and prevent it from invading all other areas of social, cultural, and political life. But first it will be helpful to consider Cuba's military security, the other main source of external dependence.

[25] See S. Clissold, ed., *Soviet Relations with Latin America* (London, 1970), pp. 289–90. Though it should be noted that the price paid by the Soviet Union for Cuban sugar has been, exceptionally, well above the world market price and also a little above the US sugar quota price.

In the early years of the revolution Cuba's reliance on Soviet military support was very great because of the weak military force which had proved sufficient to make the revolution—at the time of Batista's overthrow Fidel had only a little over 1,000 men under arms. Today Cuba is almost certainly the second strongest military power in the American hemisphere. According to a speech by Fidel of 22 March 1970, the Soviet Union had supplied Cuba with a total of $1,500 million of military equipment up to that date. The armed forces have been estimated to number 200,000 and have very modern equipment. They are trained to live hard, to carry out many economic tasks, and to be able to employ guerrilla tactics when necessary. The traveller in Cuba today meets large numbers of soldiers engaged on various economic or defence assignments, and there can be no doubt that their morale is as high as one would expect of a revolutionary armed force. Even without the Soviet nuclear umbrella—whose deterrent value is not in any case wholly credible—Cuba has a most formidable defensive capability which should be sufficient to deter all but the most reckless US administration. Such Soviet influence as exists in military policy derives more from the Soviet training given to many officers and technicians in the Cuban armed forces than from the Soviet ICBMs. Moreover, it should be added that the Cuban military leaders have made a very close study of the Vietnamese methods of fighting and undoubtedly used this to enrich the lessons of their own revolutionary war.

On the cultural and ideological plane Cuba's policies have been quite distinct from those of any other socialist country. With few exceptions the Soviet interpretation of socialist realism has not been encouraged in Cuba. On the whole experimental and *avant garde* art has flourished with official patronage. Before the revolution Cuba's most talented artists lived abroad in New York or Paris. Despite occasional clashes, their return has combined with the inspiration provided by the revolution and the great increase in educational standards to produce an explosion of cultural activity. Certain arts not previously practised have sprung up, notably film-making and modern dance. Despite the economic restraints, a large number of foreign films and books are bought by Cuba but there is no undue emphasis on Soviet products. At the same time the concentration of all cultural life in Havana has disappeared; theatre groups, musicians, and film shows continually tour even the most remote rural areas. Indeed, the evident successes of the Cuban revolution in popular education and uninhibited cultural exploration have much enhanced its resonance in the world. When Cuba convened a Cultural Congress in Havana in 1968 she was able to attract an impressive galaxy of intellectuals from throughout the world.

If one recalls the cultural desert of Cuba in the 1950s, all this is a remarkable achievement.

Experimentation and diversity also have been evident in the more strictly ideological field. It is not just that the conventional Soviet manuals of economics, philosophy, and the like were abandoned as fundamental textbooks in Cuban schools and universities after a brief experience of them in the early 1960s. Instead Cubans were supplied with a variety of orthodox and unorthodox Marxist writings as well as the works of non-Marxist scholars. The younger generation of Cuban revolutionaries has been nourished on a Marxist education whose range (Lukács, Gramsci, Sartre, Althusser, etc.) no other socialist government has permitted since the death of Lenin. Alone of the countries considered to be in the Soviet camp, Cuba published accurate and enthusiastic reportage and analysis of China's Cultural Revolution, and throughout the 1960s her revolutionary leadership was producing a politics of its own which touched on most major issues. This is reflected in Fidel's speeches, in the writings of Che Guevara (notably his essays on Cuban economic strategy, on 'socialism and man in Cuba', and his message to the Tricontinental Conference), and in the work of certain theoreticians sponsored by the Cuban leadership (in particular Régis Debray).

One limitation of this politics should be mentioned: it was not developed within, or related to, Cuba's only political organization, the Cuban Communist Party.[26] Undoubtedly this reflects the fact that the revolution was made without such an organization. Although in Cuban conditions the revolution could be made and consolidated through personal relations between the leaders and the revolutionary masses, this has entailed risks in the short and in the long run. It has proved easier to mobilize Cuba's human resources for particular campaigns and bursts of activity than for systematic, sustained socialist construction. In the future popular participation in the formulation as well as the execution of policies will be necessary for their success. In the past the guarantee of the automomous dynamic of the revolution has been its capacity to arouse and mobilize the mass of peasants, workers, and young people. The immense demonstrations supporting Fidel were what made it possible for him to break with the United States and to defeat his opponents within the ranks of his own movement. This is as true for those who looked to Moscow for assistance as for those who looked to Washington. In the various organizations of the revolution the political force of the masses has already achieved some institutionalization and some permanence (the Committees for the Defence of the Revolution, the organizations for Youth, Women,

[26] The fused revolutionary organizations officially adopted this name in 1966.

etc.)[27] Yet the political centre of this complex of organizations remains *ad hoc* and unintegrated. In times of crisis or of evident large-scale foreign pressure this does not matter so much, as the *rapport* between leaders and masses is stimulated by clear and urgent tasks at such times. However, on an everyday basis it tends to erode the initiative and capacity of the ordinary cadre on whom so much depends. The failure to reach the target of 10 m. tons of sugar in 1970 was the most dramatic instance of this structural weakness in the political order. A tremendous popular mobilization throughout the harvest period led to the production of $8\frac{1}{2}$ m. tons, a record crop but well below the voluntaristic target which had been so much insisted upon. As Fidel acknowledged in his speech on 26 July 1970, the real failure was not so much the fact that 10 m. tons were not produced as that $8\frac{1}{2}$ m. were produced at the cost of 10 m. An appalling amount of popular energy was wasted mainly because, as Fidel also admitted, the masses were the victims of an arbitrary and inefficient administration. When the harvests of 1968 and 1969 had fallen very short of the planned figures, a technical analysis of the agricultural and economic implications of nevertheless aiming for 10 m. tons in 1970 should almost certainly have led to the abandonment of this goal.[28] The 1970 harvest showed that politically and technically it was disastrous to formulate ambitious plans and attempt to implement them without involving the mass of workers, peasants, and technicians in every level of decision-making.

Unfortunately there are major obstacles in the path of such a thoroughgoing devolution and democratization of revolutionary power. Nothing in Cuba's recent history has given the mass of the population experience of actually initiating and controlling social change. The neo-colonial order in Cuba was so weak and corrupt that Fidel was able to topple it with a thousand or so *barbudos*. I have argued that the achievement of national independence was made possible by the preparedness of the revolutionary leadership to launch an uninhibited mobilization of the masses, in huge demonstrations, in the militia, and in other mass organizations. But these organizations did not lay the ground for the incorporation of the masses as an autonomous, self-active force in the new institutions of the revolutionary state.

It has been argued that only the readiness of Cuba's revolutionary leadership to effect a social revolution allowed them to achieve and sustain national independence. The institutional limits to that revolution have in some measure qualified its exercise. By causing economic setbacks, they

[27] R. R. Fagen, *The Transformation of Political Culture in Cuba* (Stanford, 1969).
[28] In *Socialism in Cuba* (New York, 1969) Leo Huberman & Paul Sweezy made out the technical and political case against the 10 m. target before the harvest began.

have made Cuba more economically dependent on the Soviet Union—
they also sap the confidence of Cuban negotiators who are not certain that
they can deliver on time. Fidel Castro's insistence on discussing the
institutional roots of economic failure undoubtedly stems in part from a
realization that it drastically limits Cuba's room for manœuvre internationally.[29]

CUBA'S INTERNATIONAL RELATIONS

This leads us directly to a consideration of the international political
positions which Cuba's revolutionary leaders have adopted. It is characteristic that Cuba's adhesion to the Soviet bloc in 1961–2 was accompanied by
a renewed commitment to the development of the revolution in Latin
America: the Second Declaration of Havana (February 1962) remains one
of the most fundamental and eloquent statements of the Cuban position.
Cuba's determination to break the isolation of the revolution in the
Americas has been more dramatic and public at some times than at others,
but its underlying orientation has been consistent throughout. The major
statements made by the Cubans have always insisted that armed popular
struggle is the only path to a durable liberation of the continent. The
Cubans maintained this even though it meant a public break with the pro-
Russian communist parties in nearly every Republic. The convening of
the OLAS Conference in 1967 and the powerful speech made by Fidel at
its conclusion marked the decisive point in this development. And it is
well known that Cuba's commitment went far beyond words.[30]

Given the history of Fidel's own radicalization, it is not surprising that
Cuba's hopes have not been confined to explicitly revolutionary currents.
On the whole, Cuba has sought to encourage populist and nationalist
developments, even when their revolutionary credentials were dubious:
this is illustrated in varying ways by the Cuban assessment of those
countries which at first resisted US pressure to break relations with her,
and their subsequent evaluation of Goulart and Brizzola in Brazil, of
Allende and even of Frei in Chile, and lately of the Peruvian military

[29] Shortly before the failure of the 1970 harvest a number of foreign visitors to Cuba had
developed critiques of the exclusion of the masses from decision-making, notably Karol;
René Dumont, *Cuba: est-il socialiste* (Paris, 1970); Huberman & Sweezy. Fidel attacked these
writers in a speech on 22 March 1970, but, following the pattern of such speeches noted above,
he was himself to adopt a modified version of this critique in his speeches on the failure of the
harvest a few months later. It remains to be seen whether the institutional impasse can be
overcome.
[30] R. Gott, *Guerrilla Movements in Latin America* (London, 1970), furnishes a valuable
account of revolutionary Cuba's relations with the guerrilla movements.

regime. The Cubans have also been appreciative of those Marxists who rejected armed struggle so long as their tactics seemed to achieve results (for example the Cuban assessment of Jagan in Guyana or Arismendi in Uruguay at the time of the Tricontinental Conference).

If the Cubans have from a revolutionary point of view been over-generous in their assessments, in most of the cases cited this clearly reflects their great desire to find allies in what has been an unequal struggle against imperialism in Latin America. It is not difficult to detect two strands in Cuban policy. As revolutionaries the leaders have sought to encourage and support the creation of a genuinely revolutionary current within the Latin American left. As the heads of an isolated socialist state they have been grateful for any sign that their isolation could be reduced. Despite the possibilities of a conflict of roles, so far the Cuban leadership has managed to inspire a revolutionary cadre in Latin America at the same time as it allows itself room to profit from any favourable diplomatic conjuncture.

But within a framework of continuity there have been some shifts of emphasis. The years 1966–8 saw a concentration on guerrilla strategies which has since then been superseded by growing interest in other paths of political development, and also by a greater concern with internal (economic) developments. The experience of the guerrillas in the 1960s was a succession of defeats and setbacks: in addition to Che Guevara's death in 1967, other crucial leaders of guerrilla movements, such as Luis Turcios in Guatemala, Camillo Torres in Colombia, Luis de la Puente in Peru, the Peredo brothers in Bolivia, and Marighela in Brazil, were killed. However, those still engaged in armed struggle continue to receive support in the pages of *Granma* and *Tricontinental*. The only significant guerrilla column estranged from Cuba in 1969–70 was that of Douglas Bravo in Venezuela; Yon Sosa's movement in Guatemala was again supported by the Cubans after a period of polemical differences in 1965–6. The Cuban press has also welcomed the emergence of new types of armed struggle in Latin America, and in particular the urban guerrillas of Uruguay, Brazil, and Guatemala. But the emergence of nationalist military regimes in Peru and Bolivia and the election of Allende in Chile has altered the overall cast of Cuban policy. This partly reflects recognition of the immediate benefits which would flow from breaking Cuba's isolation. It also reflects the unwillingness of the Cuban leaders to question from an ideological point of view developments which appear promising to them. But despite Cuba's approval of, for example, the regime of General Torres in Bolivia, *Granma* was still publishing the communiqués of the *Ejercito de Liberación Nacional* in December 1970, which was waging a guerrilla war against Torres.

The elements discussed above are also reflected in Cuba's international policy as a whole. Within the context of correct, and usually cordial, relations with the Soviet Union, Cuba has sought to develop a revolutionary position of her own. Meanwhile correct, though not at all cordial, relations have been maintained with the Chinese. Cuba has sought and found her closest allies in the Vietnamese and Koreans. She has been unstinting in her solidarity with the Vietnamese revolution and has resolutely opposed those who advised her to moderate this support in the interests of achieving a *modus vivendi* with the United States. To the extent of her ability, Cuba has supplied Vietnam with medical and even economic support: she has consistently kept the interests of the Vietnamese in the forefront at all international gatherings and in her internal propaganda. Indeed, great effort was expended to strengthen and expand the anti-imperialist struggle. A series of large international conferences were held in Havana with this as their main purpose: the Tricontinental Conference of 1966, the OLAS Conference of 1967, the Cultural Congress of 1968, as well as a number of smaller conferences. In the early 1960s the Cubans seemed to entertain exaggerated hopes in certain 'neutralist' and 'nationalist' regimes. The evident weakness of Nkrumah, Sukarno, and some other leaders led in 1966-7 to a greater emphasis on the need for a genuinely revolutionary perspective and to a growing understanding with the Vietnamese and with political currents inspired by the Vietnamese revolution. But, as Cuba's participation in the Moscow Conference of Communist Parties in 1969 was to show, this was all within the context of Cuba's continuing refusal to break with the Soviet Union. In a speech on 22 March 1970 Fidel was to insist that 'objectively—I repeat objectively' the Soviet Union was a bulwark of the world revolutionary movement because of her economic and military power.

The most problematic aspect of Cuba's foreign relations undoubtedly lies in the relations to the Soviet Union. Fidel's support of the Soviet occupation of Czechoslovakia is often thought to constitute proof that on major issues Cuba must support the Soviet Union because of her economic dependence. This is too simple. Though Cuba will support the Soviet Union on questions that are very important in the eyes of the Soviet leadership (while only marginally significant to the Cuban leaders), the Soviet invasion was in fact also widely supported by the Latin American left, as well as by revolutionaries in other third-world countries, because of a lack of enthusiasm for anti-imperialist struggles on the part of the Eastern European 'liberals'. Whereas most European communist parties condemned the Soviet occupation, all the Latin American parties (except the Mexican) endorsed it. Although the Cubans had been hostile to economic reforms of the Czech type long before the events of August 1968, the greater freedom of communication and the ending of Stalinist controls and police methods were very positively reported in their newspapers before the invasion. The Cuban leaders chose to ignore the fact that the latter were of much greater significance than the economic reforms. Fidel's speech[31] on the invasion was no blanket endorsement. He said more than once that the Czech reformers were not alone in their revisionism, though he chose to interpret the Russian action as some sort of swing to the left. The terms of this speech must have been the least welcome support the Russians received; it was not reproduced in the Soviet press. What counted politically, however, was not Fidel's qualifications but the fact that he made a major speech in which the Soviet action was endorsed—in contrast with the spare three-line communiqué issued by a minor North Vietnamese official.

Cuban participation in the Moscow Conference of Communist Parties in the summer of 1969 indicated unambiguous support for Soviet policy. Neither the Koreans nor the Vietnamese participated. The Cuban delegate was Carlos Rafael Rodríguez, a pro-Fidelista member of the former PSP and the man who had been responsible for negotiating Cuba's economic relations with the Soviet Union. Rodríguez did distance Cuba from Soviet policy on certain points (he urged a more positive assessment of the new movement of revolutionary youth in the advanced capitalist countries) and Cuba did not sign the conference document. Nevertheless, the fact of Cuban presence was, in the circumstances, a political gain for the Russians. But Cuba's alignment with Soviet positions has not yet made her withdraw support for revolutionary movements even when these do not meet with Soviet approval. Thus Cuba, in marked contrast to the Soviet Union, immediately recognized the post-coup Cambodian provisional government established by Sihanouk in Peking.

It should be evident that Cuba's revolution also revolutionized the entire spectrum of her foreign relations. After the revolution Cuban foreign policy generally displayed greater dynamism and inventiveness than that of any other country of comparable size in the world. At long last, six decades after she acquired formal sovereignty, Cuba began to act like an independent state. For no nation, large or small, could this mean unfettered freedom of action. For Cuba, it meant the opportunity to order her own internal affairs, defend her own interests, and further her own policies within the objective limits of a world still dominated by imperialism. I have suggested that the Soviet support, essential to the

[31] See Clissold, pp. 304–6.

survival of the revolution, had its price, though this was quite different from the old structural dependence on the United States. In the past the United States extracted great wealth from Cuba while all but completely determining her external and internal political options. Today the Soviet Union expends great wealth upon Cuba, and exercises undue influence on her foreign policy, but only rarely on her domestic policy.

The evident connection between social revolution and national independence in the third world could also have been demonstrated by an examination of other attempts to achieve independence by Latin American countries. Even to count as attempts at national emancipation they have had to involve some social-revolutionary content: e.g. Mexico in the past or Peru more recently. To the extent that they were incapable of carrying through to the end their social revolution they have failed to secure their objective of national independence. If foreign domination is built into the economy and culture, it cannot long be escaped in politics: that is what is meant by imperialism. If such domination is torn out by the roots, then a host of options open up: that is what is meant by national liberation. The possibility remains that national independence will be compromised but this will be an act of policy, not the ineluctable consequence of economic and social forces.

Perhaps the point being made here can be clarified by a comparison between the different forms of foreign domination to which Eastern Europe and Latin America have been subject. At first sight it might seem that Soviet domination of Eastern Europe has been more absolute and unchallengeable than American domination of Latin America. Yet paradoxically it has been possible for some Eastern European countries to escape domination without a change in their internal regime (Yugoslavia, Albania, Rumania), and even unsuccessful attempts (e.g. Hungary, Czechoslovakia) have been predominantly rival interpretations of socialism rather than attempts to restore capitalism. In fact it is because the remaining Soviet hold over Eastern Europe rests crudely on military force that it is different from the more deeply embedded and potent domination exercised by Western economic imperialism.

In Latin America it certainly seems to be the case that the local capitalist class is not strong enough to win national independence since it has been so weakened by the imperialist relationship. Cuba is the only Latin American country to have achieved a durable independence from the United States, and it is undeniable that the turn to socialism was an absolute precondition of this. It is probable that all social revolutions qualitatively enhance the autonomy of the countries where they occur. Certainly we may conclude this has been the case in Cuba.

8 The Social Structure of Guatemala: The Internal Dynamics of US Influence

BRYAN ROBERTS

My focus in this paper is the interplay between US influence and the internal social structure of Guatemala.[1] My concern is the internal and not the external dynamics of foreign influence in Guatemala. Thus I shall not attempt an extensive analysis of the strategic or economic reasons for the persisting and close attention given by the United States to Guatemala's internal affairs. Guatemala's position in the Caribbean and her proximity to the Panama Canal undoubtedly make her a sensitive point in US vigilance against possible communist infiltration in Latin America. Neither will I be concerned with the intricacies of, and changes in, US domestic policy as they have affected relations with Guatemala. Such factors as the priorities and styles of different US Presidents, the saliency of the anti-communist issue in her domestic politics and changes in governmental attitudes to private monopolies and private foreign investment have all been reflected in the changing orientation of US policy in Guatemala.

These external factors are important for understanding the total context of US influence in Guatemala. I argue here, however, that no matter the reasons for a presence in Guatemala, the exercise of US influence is heavily conditioned by Guatemala's social structure. US policies towards Guatemala vary in the priority given to strategic, commercial, or developmental goals. These policies are also affected by the unforeseen consequences of involvement with a relatively underdeveloped and unintegrated society. The exercise of influence entails a broad involvement with internal Guatemalan affairs that is both disruptive and unpredictable. US influence within Guatemala is an additional and important factor in the social, political, and economic instability of the country.

I shall examine two critical features of Guatemala's internal structure.

[1] I am indebted to Richard Adams for letting me use the unpublished MS of his *Crucifixion by Power* (Austin, 1970). Many of the ideas presented in this paper were stimulated by the reading of this MS and by conversations with Adams. I was in Guatemala from April to December 1966 and from April to September 1968. My research there was made possible by two periods of leave of absence from the University of Manchester and by grants given by the Wenner-Gren Foundation and by the Inst. of Latin American Studies, University of Texas.

Both features reflect problems in the development of an economically, politically, and socially under-developed country. They are (a) the permeability of Guatemala's social structure to external influences, and (b) the low degree of social and political integration in society. By permeability I mean the extent to which US influence is a pervasive feature of Guatemalan daily life. Any under-developed country is likely to be influenced in most spheres of life by the dominant presence of an economically more developed country. The boundaries separating internal from external influences thus become ill-defined. Foreign influences occurring at many points in society are not likely to be neutral to the balance of power in a social structure. They stimulate new groups and strengthen or weaken old groups. By integration I mean the extent of political and economic interdependence between definable social groups. I also refer to the extent of agreement between social groups over procedures for changing or stabilizing the social and economic structure. Where the various groups in a society have few common interests and do not agree on political procedures, then internal affairs are open to the play of foreign interests. Foreign interests may even be encouraged by internal groups to take an active part in internal disputes. I argue in the case of Guatemala that the boundaries separating internal and external influences are ill defined, that the social structure is loosely integrated, and that consequently both the scope and consequences of US influence cannot be easily controlled either by groups within Guatemala or by the United States. Before proceeding to the body of the analysis, a brief historical note may be helpful.

HISTORICAL NOTE

Present-day Guatemala was originally one of the southernmost extensions of the Mayan political and linguistic groups. It was conquered for Spain by Pedro de Alvarado in 1524. It became the most populous part of the Captaincy-General of Guatemala which also included parts of contemporary Mexico (Chiapas and Tabisco), Honduras, Nicaragua, San Salvador, and Costa Rica. After independence from Spain in 1821 the unity of the Captaincy-General was retained for a short period under the name of the Republic of Central America. This Republic was finally destroyed from 1838 to 1847 by regional interest groups. These groups were often encouraged by British and other foreign interests intent on gaining the maximum trading advantage.[2] The reunion of the various parts of the Central American Republic has remained an important political ideal. However, differences in the politics, the economics, and the social structure

[2] Mario Rodríguez, *Central America* (Prentice Hall, NJ, 1965), pp. 73–92.

of the various countries have, up till the present, been powerful barriers to integration. In 1951 a regional organization was established with the aim of achieving integration in the economic and cultural spheres. By the 1960s a Central American common market had been established.

Until 1944 Guatemala was governed by a series of dictators with slight but varying interest in the economic and social development of their country. British interests were influential in the first half of the nineteenth century and resulted in the qualified recognition by Guatemala of British sovereignty over Belice. In the second half of that century, British influence was replaced by that of the United States. US commercial interests secured privileged economic concessions in the late nineteenth and in the early twentieth centuries. Recent Guatemalan governments have also granted favourable concessions to US mining and petroleum companies. Because of their size and the diplomatic support they received from their government, these companies attained dominant positions within the Guatemalan economy. After the overthrow of Jorge Ubico in 1944 by a popular revolution, a government took over whose platform included greater independence in foreign policy and economic reform at home. Despite the attempts of the head of this government, Juan José Arévalo, and his successor, Jacobo Arbenz, to pursue these programmes, the extent of social and economic reform has been small. US influence has persisted as a major factor in determining the direction of Guatemalan internal development. In the most dramatic example of the exercise of this influence, Arbenz was overthrown in 1954 by an army colonel, Castillo Armas, who was supported by US private and governmental interests.[3]

Economically, Guatemala developed as an exporter of certain agricultural products. These, chiefly coffee, were handled by a small number of native and foreign landowners. The vast majority of native farmers were engaged in a mainly subsistence agriculture. Industry had not developed on any scale. In the years after 1944 serious attempts were made to diversify exports, improve agricultural production, and expand industrially. Cotton became an important export, taking second place to coffee. Agrarian reform, and technical and financial aid for smaller farmers, aimed at improving and diversifying production for the home market. Industry, though contributing a very much smaller part to the GDP than agriculture, has been increasing at a rate of about 5 per cent a year. Guatemala remains, however, both socially and economically a highly underdeveloped country. Her estimated per capita income in 1965 was

[3] The part played by the US in Arbenz's overthrow is still denied by official US sources. It is privately acknowledged by almost everyone in Guatemala, including US officials.

$298. In 1964 66 per cent of the population was estimated to live in villages, hamlets and farms; in the same year 37 per cent was literate.[4]

THE EXTENT OF US INFLUENCE

US influence is partly the result of the peculiar historical circumstances of Guatemala's development. These circumstances include the United States' long involvement and interest in Central America. They also include the weak development of a widely shared national culture in Guatemala's highly stratified and culturally fragmented society. US influence is also the result of factors in Guatemala's development common to many developing countries. Guatemala's relatively recent efforts to develop rapidly have followed the visible models of developed countries, and so development has entailed heavy borrowing of techniques, equipment, and even culture.

Two features of US influence that result from the circumstances of Guatemala's development will now be examined. These are: (a) the American dominance among foreign influences; (b) the pervasiveness of this influence in Guatemalan life.

Of the small number of foreign powers that are economically and politically relevant to Guatemala, the United States is easily predominant. US economic hegemony over Guatemala is one aspect of this. In the years after the second world war the concentration of Guatemala's commerce with the United States was sharp, because of the temporary closing of European markets during the war; in 1956 this amounted to approximately 70 per cent of her external commerce. In recent years Guatemala has diversified her trading partners and by 1965 this total had fallen to approximately 40 per cent,[5] but the United States still remained by far her largest single trading partner and was also the source of most annual foreign investments and assets held by foreigners in Guatemala. In 1956, for example, the United Fruit Company's assets represented almost half the total of foreign assets in Guatemala. The number of new firms controlled completely or partly by US interests has increased sharply since the counter-revolution of 1954. In the period before 1954 there were approximately 44 firms in which there was substantial US control; from 1955 to 1964, 60 new US-controlled firms were established.[6]

The importance of US interests in the Guatemalan economy lies in their

[4] Bank of London & S. America, *The Central American Common Market* (London, 1967), statist. app.; Guatemala, *Census 1964 Población* (1966), Resultados de tabulación por muestreo.
[5] *LA Handbook* (1968), p. 206.
[6] AID, *United States Business Directory for Guatemala, April 1st 1964* (1964).

concentration and location. In 1954, 63 per cent of total foreign investment was owned by the United Fruit Company and its subsidaries.[7] This
company accounted for an important part of Guatemala's total exports
and controlled the port and rail facilities. A further subsidary controlled the
electric-power supply. Interests so strategically concentrated exercise
considerable power. These American companies have been accused by
Guatemalans of widely differing political complexion of retarding the
country's economic development.[8] The United Fruit Company has been
accused of failing to develop adequate port facilities on the Pacific shore,
with keeping large areas of fertile land unnecessarily unused,
and with discouraging rival foreign investments. The railroad company
has been charged with orienting its policy entirely in favour of transporting bananas, of charging excessive rates for other types of cargo, and of
failing to develop an adequate nation-wide railroad system. Likewise the
electric-power company is accused of slowing down the development of
hydro-electric resources that could offer competition to its own plants and
prices. Direct financial aid, manipulation of tariffs, and non-co-operation
at critical moments are stratagems that have been used by these companies
to influence Guatemalan governments in their favour. In 1968, for
example, the railroad company was still using non-payment of wages to
its numerous employees as a means of exercising pressure on the government to grant it a more favourable tax position.

These US companies were ready allies of the conservative landowning
and commercial interests that supported Castillo Armas in his overthrow of
Arbenz. In recent years the preponderance of United Fruit and its subsidaries has diminished. A nationally-owned port has been developed on
the Atlantic. Telecommunications are now controlled by the Guatemalan
government. Bananas have lost their position as the second most important
export to cotton. But the decrease in the importance of United Fruit has
not, as has been seen, meant a decrease in total US commercial power in
Guatemala. The strength of US-financed banks, such as the Bank of
America, was the subject of a prolonged controversy in the summer of
1968. Strong Guatemalan opposition was voiced to the government's
allowing further American banks to extend their operations in Guatemala.
It was argued that US and other foreign banks already controlled nearly
half the private banking transactions, represented a potential outflow of
capital, and meant possible foreign control of internal-investment decisions.

[7] Mario Monteforte Toledo, *Guatemala, monografía sociológica* (Mexico, 1959), p. 508.
[8] These criticisms are widespread in press and books. They are discussed extensively in
Monteforte Toledo and mentioned in N. L. Whetten, *Guatemala, the Land and the People*
(New Haven, 1961), pp. 130–3.

THE SOCIAL STRUCTURE OF GUATEMALA 153

With constant world fluctuations in the prices of primary products Guatemala's balance of trade has often been adverse. In the period after the fall of Arbenz many of Guatemala's deficits and development programmes were financed by large-scale US loans which, together with grants, have been estimated to total some $195 m. Along with Bolivia and the Dominican Republic, since the second world war, Guatemala has been the major Latin American recipient of US development grants.[9]

The United States has been equally dominant politically. In the same period diplomats, military attachés, and business men have taken an active interest in the internal affairs of Guatemala that has not been rivalled by any other foreign power. The total US establishment numbers several thousand people dispersed among the various official and semi-official US agencies. The American business community is probably several times larger, and has its own chamber of commerce. No foreign power has the same number of information-gathering agencies in Guatemala. AID, the Peace Corps, USIS, and the various departments of the Embassy make available a body of detailed information concerning Guatemalan internal affairs that is often superior to that possessed by the Guatemalan government. In none of the accusations and counter-accusations of left- and right-wing groups in the political upheavals of the last twenty years has any country other than the United States been assigned a prominent place in the internal politics of Guatemala. Moreover, as a result of US economic dominance, no other power has been able or willing to expend the resources to exercise significant influence in that respect.

Mexico has a degree of economic influence in Guatemala and there is a growing trade between the two countries. Yet relations between them have often been cool, and save for granting asylum to Guatemalan exiles, Mexican governments have shown little active interest in Guatemalan politics or development.

Economic relations between Guatemala and the other Central American Republics have been accompanied by military and political co-operation. On several occasions, for example, Nicaragua has provided military support for Guatemalan governments against dissident left-wing elements. Yet Guatemala's sister republics in Central America remain significant politically mainly as bases for Guatemalans in exile and as possible sources of material support against rival groups within the country. None of her neighbours maintains the same range and quantity of personnel as does the US government.

Two further, though indirect, foreign influences should be mentioned. First, there is the question of Belice, or British Honduras. For the past

9 David Ross, 'The United States and Latin America', *New Republic*, 27 Sept. 1968.

L

thirty years there have been active attempts by various Guatemalan governments to regain this territory. These attempts continue; but the degree to which they become the focus of a public campaign has a marked correlation with the internal difficulties faced by a Guatemalan government. Within governing circles there have been notable and public divisions of opinion as to the utility of Belice and as to Guatemala's capacity to absorb it if it were reintegrated. Belice is not a major source of concern to Guatemalans at middle or lower levels of society. News concerning it has less prominence than that accorded to US domestic affairs.

The other and more important source of indirect foreign influence is Cuba, whose influence is directly opposed to that of the United States. It is exercised indirectly and not materially. There is, for example, very little evidence that Cuba has been a source of military aid to Guatemalan guerrilla groups. Cuba is important as a point of reference for various groups within Guatemalan society, representing a form of economic development radically different from that offered by the United States. Whether Guatemalans be of right or left political tendencies, the image of Cuba influences policy and behaviour. Cuban radio transmitters are powerful and can easily be heard in Guatemala. In one low-income neighbourhood of Guatemala City approximately 60 per cent of those with radio receivers occasionally listen to Radio Havana. Approximately the same number also occasionally listen to Voice of America.[10]

The relatively restricted field of foreign powers influential in Guatemala, and the US dominant position among them, limits the manœuvrability of Guatemalan interest groups in face of foreign influence. These groups cannot lessen the pressure of foreign interests by playing off competing foreign powers against each other. Equally, as will be seen, US influence in economics and politics entails her influence in other fields as well.

THE PERVASIVENESS OF US INFLUENCE

Guatemala has not been able to provide sufficient internal resources for her current development. Thus US private and public agencies have become increasingly drawn into Guatemalan society to provide the skills and resources needed to effect social change. In this Guatemala is little different from any developing society which draws upon more industrialized societies for ideas and skills; but in this respect her dependence is almost complete. In technical and professional fields, outside law, there is con-

[10] Roberts, 'Politics in a Neighbourhood of Guatemala City', *Sociology*, May 1968.

siderable reliance on foreign technicians recruited by industrial or agricultural concerns or brought in under foreign assistance programmes. The largest group of these has come from the United States, which is also host to a large proportion of the professionals and technicians who go abroad to obtain or to complete their training.

As is common elsewhere in Latin America, disproportionate numbers of Guatemalan students graduate in the humanities and legal and social sciences, as compared with natural and applied sciences. For example, from 1955 to 1964, 46 students in the Faculty of Agronomy completed the course, an average of 4·6 per year, while the average first-year enrolment in this faculty was around 60. But the demand for trained agronomists in the nation continues to be high. More doctors and engineers are produced but still not enough to meet the needs of the country. Thus outside the capital there was approximately one doctor for every 23,000 inhabitants in 1954.[11] The situation is equally unsatisfactory at lower levels of the educational system. Guatemala has the lowest percentage of children aged 7–10 attending school in Central America. The majority of this age-group (53 per cent) don't go to school, and there is thus a shortage of persons capable of filling the more highly skilled and supervisory jobs in industry and mechanized agriculture.[12] Many reforms in the educational system have been directly introduced by US technicians and are modelled on North American practices. It is a standard complaint in Guatemala that many textbooks are of US origin and have not been adapted to local conditions. A team from Michigan State University helped in the remodelling of the curriculum of the National University of Guatemala. The influence of these specialists was resented by many Guatemalan students and was cited by them as one of their reasons for opposing the new curriculum in 1968.

Social groups who might be the bearers of native cultural and technical innovation are not readily identifiable in Guatemala. White-collar workers are a small minority of the population (8 per cent in the 1964 census). There has been almost no development of a professional bureaucracy in which these groups can find secure employment. Most remain dependent on personal connections and the goodwill of patrons to maintain or advance their positions. This 'middle class' does not represent a powerful, independent stimulus to political and economic development. Native entrepreneurs have long been reluctant to invest internally, and when they do so they usually invest in traditional forms of industrial or agricultural exploitation.

The large-scale aid and loans provided by the United States and by

[11] Whetten, p. 229.   [12] Bank of London & S. America, pp. 23–24, 43.

various international loan-giving bodies have stimulated the beginnings of a professional bureaucracy. International aid and co-operation in development have strengthened those Guatemalan professionals and organizations overseeing the economic development of their country. The Bank of Guatemala is one such organization and attached to it is a group of highly trained economists. Likewise the extensive construction and road-building programmes, undertaken with the help of foreign aid, have provided steady governmental employment for professional planners and engineers. These various *técnicos* have become in the last twenty years an increasingly influential body within the government and society. No matter the political complexion of a Guatemalan government, these experts and their agencies have remained powerful influences on social and economic policy, an influence often regarded with suspicion and hostility by other powerful groups. As an instance, recent tax reforms have met with bitter opposition from landed and commercial interests and in 1968 the vice-president stated that the country's problems could best be solved by sending economists into exile.

The military and the church, both important institutions, have only recently become interested in promoting development. The military has mainly recruited officers and men from small towns and villages where their parents are farmers or traders. The training of officers in modern military standards and practices only began with the reforms of the military academy after the second world war. These reforms, and the enlarging of the scope of an officer's duties to include developmental programmes in city and countryside, owe much to US programmes of military aid and advice, and almost all the Guatemalan officers undergo further training in the United States. The military have been strengthened by US involvement in Guatemala, and besides training officers the US has provided a range of modern equipment and supplied special advisers to the Guatemalan armed forces. This military interest has been related to a fear of communist subversion and has increased with the rise of active guerrilla movements in Guatemala. As a result, the Guatemalan armed forces have become technically more efficient and more independent of their governments. As noted by Richard Adams, it is significant that the Guatemalan military were prepared to take over the running of their country for the first time in recent history shortly after a highly significant increase in US military aid. Until 1962, aid to Guatemala averaged $0·3 m. a year; in 1962 it shot up to 1·3 m.[13] Next year a military junta took over the government from the elected President and imposed a military administration throughout the country. Previously the military, though

[13] Dept. of Defense, *Military Assistance Facts 15, February 1965* (Washington, 1965).

participating in coups or revolutions, had allowed the bulk of government administration to be carried out by civilians. The suggestion is that the military were able to take over the running of the country at a time when they had the material resources needed for governing the whole national territory.

Stimulated to do so by US military advisers, the army has run its own programmes of rural and urban development, which often compete with those of the civilian authorities. A much-needed enlargement of Guatemala City's water supply has been delayed by the rivalry of army and municipality over who should install the water. A US consultant company adjudged that the municipality's plans were the most practicable, but the army was able to maintain sufficient pressure on the national government to prevent a decision being made against its own project, and the stalemate persisted. US emphasis on the Guatemalan army as an essential cog in the strategy of Central American defence further strengthens the independence of the armed forces and their leaders *vis-à-vis* civilian governments. The Guatemalan military have been sceptical of the capacity of civilian governments to rule effectively. In their public actions and private opinions they have been opposed to any increase in government bureaucracy or state control of private enterprise. In their fight against the guerrillas, they have combined with large landowners in paramilitary reprisals against anyone suspected of left-wing sympathies. This became a matter of concern to the ruling civilian party of Guatemala. In August 1968 the party hierarchy took the unusual step of publicly criticizing the army's lack of effectiveness against right-wing terrorists who had been coercing candidates of the official party in the eastern region of the country.

Throughout 1969-70 the extension of the guerrilla campaign to urban areas by both right and left wing which began in 1968 continued. Among other incidents in 1969 were: in June the murder of the leader of the anti-communist group, Mario López Villatoro, one of the officers who helped Castillo Armas overthrow Arbenz, who had been the target of previous assassination attempts; in December the shooting of three police agents and the murder of a candidate for the mayoralty of Guatemala City, as well as extensive bomb attacks in that city. In January 1970 the associate editor of *Prensa libre* and an officer known for right-wing views were killed, and on 11 March the former chief of the secret police. The campaign for presidential elections on 1 March was marked by numerous acts of violence and terrorism, including the kidnapping on 27 February of the Foreign Minister, Alberto Fuentes Mohr. Communist and revolutionary groups unable to put forward candidates urged voters to boycott the election, the results of which were inconclusive, since none of the three candidates received an absolute majority. The candidates were Colonel Carlos Araña Osorio, leader of anti-guerrilla operations, who stood for the extreme right-wing National Liberation Movement, Mario Fuentes Pierruccini, a former Foreign Minister, representing the centrist Revolutionary Party, and Jorge Lucas Caballeros, another former Foreign Minister put up by the Christian Democratic Party which, though anti-communist, attracted the support of smaller left-wing groups by its advocacy of reform. By the terms of the constitution, it was left to the newly elected Congress to choose the new President; Araña Osorio, who had received most votes in the election, was chosen by a majority and was sworn in on 1 July.

For a long time the Guatemalan Catholic Church was content to provide the formal religion of all Guatemalans and had little sacramental contact with the mass of believers. In rural areas Catholicism combines with indigenous religious traditions. Catholic priests and the formal sacraments of the church have little influence on this rural Catholicism. Politically the church often took a strongly conservative stand. During the regimes of Arévalo and Arbenz the church hierarchy frequently openly sided with the conservative landowning interests that brought about the counter-revolution of 1954. During the Castillo Armas regime the church regained many privileges lost during more liberal regimes and the traditional hostility of church and military was replaced by active co-operation in face of the perceived common enemy of radical dissent.

With changes in the policy of international Catholicism and an awareness that Latin America needed to be 're-converted' to Roman Catholicism, the Guatemalan Catholic hierarchy has begun to place increased emphasis on its pastoral duties. Attempts are made to provide priests for each municipal area and to combat what are considered superstitious elements in local religious practices. Such aims require a body of priests far larger than that produced in Guatemala; consequently the last thirty years has seen the increasing influx of foreign priests. Estimates for 1966 were that of 531 priests only 97 were native Guatemalans. Many of these priests are supplied by foreign missions such as the Maryknoll Fathers, a US order, and the Belgian Fathers. These priests, though formally attached to the Guatemalan hierarchy, have a considerable degree of latitude in their own areas. This has meant the introduction of skills and practices derived from foreign rather than native sources into many areas of the country.

Many of the attempts of the Guatemalan church to provide for the social welfare of its members have depended on foreign aid. That this aid is a further way of extending US influence is illustrated by the relation of the Guatemalan church organization Caritas to Catholic Relief Services, an organization of North American bishops which uses surplus US food in its charitable activities. It channelled its food and financial aid to Guatemala through Caritas. In order to have better accounts to present to the US government, Catholic Relief Services began to put pressure on Caritas in 1965 to improve its bookkeeping. At first Caritas reacted strongly against this interference with its own administration and seemed prepared to forego US aid to preserve its independence. But in the absence of alternative sources of aid, it eventually agreed to conform and to open their accounts to inspection by Catholic Relief Services.[14]

One consequence of the weakening of traditional religious practices and beliefs has been the recent upsurge of Protestanism. Protestants are disproportionately concentrated in urban centres and other areas where the population is relatively mobile. In a sample drawn from two urban neighbourhoods of Guatemala City, they constituted approximately 20 per cent of the population.[15] US influence is strong in their various churches, members of which derived their original impetus from US missionaries, and many of whom maintain strong ties with their parent churches and have directly channelled North American standards of behaviour into Guatemala. This is especially marked among lower-income groups. Protestant churches catering for low-income Guatemalans often hold weekly classes instructing their members in correct social behaviour, including table manners and household budgeting. These churches attempt to protect their members from the social evils they see around them and try to encompass as much of their lives as possible. One consequence is that members are often more orientated to the United States and its way of life than to the problems of their own country. In interviews, Protestants frequently mention their North American 'brethren' and the high quality of life in the United States. On several occasions Protestants in two low-income neighbourhoods told me that Guatemala's political problem could be solved if a foreigner were placed in charge.

In culture, and especially mass culture, the influence of the United States and other foreign countries has been increasing in the last twenty years. In cultural terms too Guatemala has been a dependent society. Although there are writers, artists, and poets of note, the country has relied on foreign cultures, notably French, Anglo-Saxon, and Mexican. With the increase in mass media these foreign cultural products have been placed

[14] This incident is fully reported in Adams, *Crucifixion by Power*, and is based on the description given by Bruce Calder in *The Guatemalan Church*, unpub. master's thesis, Latin American Studies Program, Univ. of Texas.

[15] Roberts, 'Protestantism and coping with urban life in Guatemala City', *Am. J. Sociol.*, May 1968.

within the reach of all. This is especially true, for example, of films, which are shown in city and provinces and are almost equally divided between US and Mexican ones. Newspapers, television, and radio rely heavily on US news agencies and on advertisements and material originally produced for the American market. As has been noted, many of the books used at all levels of the educational system are written and supplied from US sources.

Many Guatemalan families have themselves had direct experience of the United States or have near relatives who live there, and there is considerable migration to the United States. In my sample of two low-income areas of Guatemala City, approximately 6 per cent of families had near-relations there. Fewer families had relatives living in other foreign countries. It is difficult to estimate the effect of such contacts, but they are likely to be further factors strengthening US influence and reducing the cultural distance between the two countries.

US commercial and governmental interests have been influential in opposing certain Guatemalan development schemes. For instance, the building of a road linking the capital to the Atlantic coast was long delayed by the pressure of the United Fruit Company on US national and international agencies. The Guatemalans needed a loan from US financed agencies to build the road but the loan was long in coming because United Fruit owned the only railroad link between the capital and the Atlantic coast and the proposed road threatened its commercial viability. Under the Arbenz regime, US commercial and governmental interests stimulated and helped organize opposition among conservative landowning and industrial groups.[16] However, the relations of the US government with private US companies have varied over time. While the government supported United Fruit in its complaints that Arbenz had not given adequate compensation for expropriated lands, in the same year it filed an anti-trust suit against the company charging it with monopolistic practices.

Through its governmental agencies and commercial and religious interests, the United States influences most areas of Guatemalan life, blurring the boundary between foreign and internal concerns. This is important for understanding the relatively passive reaction of most low and middle-income Guatemalans to the more overt examples of US political and economic intervention in Guatemalan affairs.[17] The pervasiveness of US influence also means that the United States is exposed to Guatemalan affairs in many different areas and through different agencies. In religion, politics, military affairs, commerce, and culture, the United

---

[16] Monteforte Toledo, pp. 317–19.

[17] This lack of strong national feeling is discussed in Manning Nash, *Machine Age Maya* (Chicago, 1958), pp. 110–18.

States is represented by a range of official and privately sponsored personnel, who do not all encounter the same types of problems, and whose attitudes towards Guatemala's internal affairs differ. The extent to which the United States is influenced by their views changes at different times and makes it difficult to pursue a co-ordinated and consistent policy towards Guatemala.

Some examples illustrate the problems of pursuing a consistent policy. The action of US missionaries and non-religious developmental personnel is currently stimulating local community organization and leadership. The establishment of co-operatives and the encouragement of lay organizations contributes to the mobilization of sections of the rural and urban population hitherto marginal to national politics. The impact of these activities varies in form and intent. For example, while some of the earlier US Catholic missionaries had taken a strong anti-communist position, others had favoured extreme left-wing groups. In 1968 two Maryknoll Fathers were expelled from their parishes, being accused of actively assisting the left-wing guerrilla forces operating there.[18] Many of the co-operative programmes financed by US sources have been run by people sympathetic to the Guatemalan Christian Democratic party and have contributed to strengthening the party's rural and urban organization. This organization is an avowed opponent of the established power structure and advocated economic and social reform 'in depth'. Other US developmental programmes have, as has been seen, strengthened the power of the military in rural areas. One reason why two American military attachés were assassinated in 1968 by left-wing guerrillas was the claim that US military personnel were assisting the Guatemalan army and landowners in paramilitary reprisals against rural political leaders. AID is currently lobbying for a tax-reform measure that is being considered by the Guatemalan Congress and is being bitterly opposed by landowning interests.

These examples demonstrate that US influence is an active and pervasive element in current social and political changes in Guatemala. The Guatemalan social structure and its implications for the exercise of this influence will now be examined.

SOCIAL AND NATIONAL INTEGRATION

The exercise of US influence at different points in the social structure has been heavily conditioned by what is termed the low integration of the various sectors of Guatemalan society. This has meant that US interests have found it relatively easy to play an active part in Guatemalan internal

[18] Le Monde, 20 Jan. 1968.

affairs—in fact they have often been spurred on by various Guatemalan groups to do so.

The historical development of Guatemala has ensured that the various social groups in the country have little in common. They exchange services but relations are characterized more by one-sided exploitations than by mutual benefit and interdependence. This results in a country in which common nationality entails little shared sentiment or felt obligations between various social groups.

When the Spaniards conquered Guatemala they found an agrarian society, and despite much exploration, did not discover substantial mineral deposits; consequently Spanish settlement there was, relative to Mexico, sparse. To the Spaniards, Guatemala's most useful natural asset was native labour, and throughout the colonial period the population was organized to provide that labour. This situation continued after independence. The emphasis of various governments on private rather than communal landholdings strengthened concentration of ownership in a few hands and permitted the alienation of land previously held in village units. The large-scale production of single agricultural crops, combined with the scarcity of alternative sources of wealth, was not suited to the extensive development of a middle commercial group. This situation has largely persisted to this day. Land ownership is still heavily concentrated in the hands of a few landowners, some of them foreign. For example, according to Whetten, ·03 per cent of landowners own 50 per cent of total farmland and 2 per cent of landowners control 72 per cent of farm land.

The large landowners depend on other segments of society only for labour. The bulk of their investments are often outside the country. Their children are frequently educated abroad and many large landowners spend much of their own time abroad. There is a middling group of farmers and merchants in most villages and towns that is of Spanish speech and dress. Even in predominantly Indian villages they often monopolize commerce and the larger landholdings. This Ladino element does not intermarry with the Indian population and their mode of interaction with the Indians has been compared with a caste system.[19] The bulk of the rural population, whether Indian or Ladino, continues in subsistence agriculture and as agricultural labourers. There is some local specialization in agricultural products and a regional market system flourishes. To a varying extent both Indians and Ladinos participate in and are affected by the national economy and labour market. Agricultural and manufactured

[19] Melvin Tumin, *Caste in a Peasant Society* (Princeton, 1952). My own observations and the weight of recent scholarly research suggest that there has been no radical change in Indian-Ladino relations since Tumin's work.

products circulate throughout the country and prices fluctuate with national as well as local conditions. Yet these elements of economic inter-dependence must be set against the divisive forces present in the predomin-ance of subsistence agriculture, the low prices obtained for products or labour, and the deep social cleavages between the various sectors of the rural population.

Social and economic factors dividing rural populations are re-enforced by cultural differences, mainly the difference between the Europeanized culture of Ladino sections and the prominently indigenous culture of the Indians with their distinctive language and dress, but there are also cul-tural differences among the Indian population. The Indian *municipios* differ from each other in a variety of ways. There are five main Indian language groups, with a considerable variety of idiom within them. The language groups are not coincident with culture and social organization.

The integration of the various elements in the society has proceeded slowly. In 1950 54 per cent of the population was still defined as Indian, habitually speaking an Indian language and wearing Indian dress. In the 1964 census this percentage had dropped to 40 per cent, though in absolute numbers the Indian population had increased. The change is probably partly due to different definitions of what constitutes an Indian between the census periods. Some of the most dramatic drops in the Indian percent-age occur in areas where the classification Ladino was used more broadly in the 1964 census than in the 1950 census. Indians and Ladinos still regard each other as distinct groups with racially defined abilities and qualities.

The cultural integration that has occurred comes mainly through the migrations of Indians to work in plantations or to reside in urban centres, but this has not made for social or economic integration. In the capital city, there are wide income gaps between manual workers and the upper social strata. In a study of two low-income neighbourhoods there, low-income groups were found to be little integrated either politically or occupationally.[20] In both neighbourhoods almost half the adult heads of households were self-employed in a variety of craft and trading activities. Only a third were employed in large-scale urban enterprises. Less than 10 per cent of these heads of households belonged to voluntary associations of any kind, whether labour unions, sporting associations, or mutual-benefit associations. Though there was a good deal of political activity in the neighbourhoods, few neighbours were consistently active in any of the legal political parties in the city. No matter what their ideological position, these parties were staffed and controlled by middle- and upper-income groups.

[20] Roberts, in *Sociology*, May 1968.

Since Guatemala's industrial development remains limited there are few sources generating wealth in the society besides large-scale agriculture. This means that most sectors of society tend to compete both between and within themselves to exploit the relatively fixed opportunities for economic gain. One of the chief of these opportunities is the government of the day, which is the largest single investor and employer. Office holding and government contracts are a source of economic mobility, but in Guatemala's slowly expanding economy, the benefits gained by one individual from official position or economic good fortune are likely to be at the expense of others. This is a further factor in the low integration of the society. It is a situation that does not generate a sense of national co-operation or interdependence aimed at achieving higher standards for all groups.

Guatemala's social structure can thus be characterized as composed of a series of social groups with a minimum of structural interdependence between them. This helps us understand why foreign influence can be pervasive and yet not meet with a uniformly hostile reaction from all sections of the population. It also means that a foreign power is likely to be drawn into Guatemalan internal affairs as another of the competing interest groups of which the nation is composed.

THE STRUCTURE OF SOCIAL RELATIONSHIP AND US INFLUENCE

The above analysis can be extended to consider the social relationships within and between different social groups, members of which are linked individually. The system of social relationship most nearly approximates a series of vertically organized sets of relationships with little interdependence. Social groups are thus divided by distinctive networks of relationship that include people of different social and economic positions and are based on informal ties of service and aid. This system is receptive to foreign intervention and encourages it as a complement to the competition between various vertically organized groups.[21] It has been seen that Guatemala has little social or cultural homogeneity. Her economic structure rarely groups people in large-scale enterprises in which they share similar positions and are structurally opposed to other social groups.

Families are marginally but importantly differentiated economically and socially. They rely on individual social relationships rather than on co-operation with others of like social and economic position to improve their own lot. In the city, low-income workers are employed in various

[21] R. N. Adams, 'Power and Power Domains', *América Latina*, Apr.–June 1966, 3–22.

jobs, most of which involve personal relationships with an employer or with clients. The situation is similar for white-collar workers in the absence of large-scale enterprises and of a professionalized bureaucracy. Both white- and blue-collar workers thus often depend on having a large number of useful relationships to maintain or improve their positions. Neither their jobs nor the social relationships they develop encourage identification with people in similar positions. In the countryside most Guatemalans are small proprietors trying to improve their position by exploiting their own land with temporary periods as migrant labourers.

The importance of personal relationships is increased because Guatemala lacks a formal mechanism by which available services and opportunities can be secured. Regulations aimed at ensuring impersonal administration of resources such as education facilities, roads, water, and sewage services are largely inoperative. Guatemalan administrators change with each change in government and, given the scarcity of resources and the pressure to redeem political favours, administration is conducted by particularistic criteria. It has long been traditional for local Indian communities to make specific arrangements within their own social organization to have representatives to treat with the national power structure and obtain favours for themselves and their community. Communities and individuals in the city obtain favours by similar relationships.

Sets of personal and group relationships become loosely structured around one or more of the especially powerful and influential groups or individuals. These holders of power do not form a cohesive élite but are fragmented into distinct and possibly competing groups. For example, Adams identifies a series of new and old sources of power active in Guatemala.[22] These include profit-orientated agrarian enterprises, traditional landowners, industrialists of various kinds, bureaucrats and *técnicos*, the branches of the armed forces, the churches, political parties, and labour organizations.

US influences fit in with this predominant pattern and become elements in various sets of vertically organized relationships. The effect of this is to frustrate the intent of much US policy towards Guatemala. The various aid and technical-assistance programmes were designed to stimulate self-help and development in the different communities or organizations where they were applied. Instead, the United States often becomes accepted as a new but permanent element in the set of relationships developed by the community in question. The US agencies involved have come to be regarded as a channel to national and international favours.

[22] Adams, 'Political Power and Social Structures', in C. Véliz, ed., *Politics of Conformity in Latin America* (London, 1967).

The predominance of vertically organized sets of relationships means that the power groups are competing for influence over the same people. For example, both government and landowners attempt to exercise control over the peasantry. Army officers may compete with civilian politicians to obtain the dependence of urban or rural dwellers through patronage or civic-action programmes. This competition is not confined to the normal political process, and it is not easily regulated by constitutional procedure. Under these conditions, the use of outside powers, and especially the United States, to redress the internal balance of power becomes a normal procedure used by governments, military, landowners, technocrats, or any other interest group or section. As noted earlier, the absence of solidary middle- or lower-income groups means that there is no nation-wide basis for national sentiment in opposition to foreign influence that prevents interest groups making use of such influence.

Traditionally the strength of landowners in co-operation with the military or church was quite sufficient to prevent radical social change. The scope and efficiency of the central government and its agents was limited to general police functions. After 1944 several powerful groups emerged that threatened to destroy this traditional structure of power. The growing technical efficiency of various social sectors, whether government, military, or organized labour, have enabled them to challenge their rivals in all areas of social and economic control. The issue has become the survival of interest groups and not the bargains that can be made within a generally accepted and continuing political dialogue. It is only in recent times that the various interests within Guatemala have forced themselves into fluctuating but identifiable groups intent on the protection of their common position. For instance, the large landowners did not create permanent, rationally organized agricultural and commercial associations or political parties until the 1950s.

The hostility of US commercial interests and of Guatemalan landowners to the regime of Jácobo Arbenz can be interpreted in these terms, for his regime was the first that seemed capable of posing a realistic threat to the dominance of these interests in the economy and power structure. Through labour organizations and local political party branches Arbenz and his advisers were erecting an organization that could challenge the existing power structure in every part of the country. Not only the traditional dominance of landowners in the rural areas but also the economic power of the city-based industrial and commercial interests were threatened. The possibility that Arbenz might arm his local committees was the final threat to military, landowners, and foreign interests. What Arbenz was doing was changing the structure of Guatemalan power in a way quite different from any of his predecessors, even Arévalo. These changes posed a threat to the United States because they undermined the traditional bases of power to which the United States was sensitive and of which her diplomats and agency personnel were part. US officials identified communism with the mobilization of sectors of the population that had hitherto been an uninfluential part of the power structure. The actual numbers of communists and their influence were never realistically examined.

Since US interests are present at many sensitive points of the Guatemalan power structure and become involved in the various struggles for power, local conflicts often escalate into national and international confrontations. Thus when Arbenz encouraged organized labour to attack the power of the large landholders and sponsored agrarian reform, these landholders turned to US influence as the only counterbalance to what appeared to be an overwhelming coalition.[23] Arbenz had himself to turn to the only possible counterbalance—the communist bloc. Only the communist bloc could provide the technical and military resources normally provided by the United States.

Because of the prominence of the anti-communist issue in US strategic concerns, this type of escalation usually means that US influence is ultimately used to favour the conservative *status quo* in Guatemala. It was widely believed that the US diplomatic mission had exercised pressure to ensure that the military junta handed over authority to a civilian government in 1966. However, with the wave of political assassinations culminating in those of two US military attachés and of the US ambassador in 1968, the US mission was prepared to accept and assist in the strengthening of military authority in the country, although this militates against other US policies in Guatemala. Financial reform programmes, educational and agrarian reforms desired by AID personnel are currently being delayed by the opposition of conservative groups, whose strength has been increased by the frequent periods of martial law applied at the insistence of the military.

It is thus not surprising that the four years of a civilian government (1966–9) that was heralded as bringing the possibility of moderate reform should end in the electoral victory in March 1970 of a political party dominated by military officers and explicitly continuing in the tradition of Castillo Armas. During the period of civilian authority the country spent almost as much time under declared martial law as under constitutional government. Some economic development occurred, but there was little change in the system of landholding or the organization of the rural or

[23] Adams, in *América Latina*, Apr.–June 1966.

urban economy. Effectively a stalemate has been created in which the military and their allies prevent all but a cautious and government-directed change and in which groups desiring more rapid social and economic reform are driven into violent and destructive opposition. Since the new government came to power the guerrilla campaign has continued. On 6 March the labour attaché of the US embassy was kidnapped and released only in exchange for three political prisoners. On 31 March the West German ambassador, Count Karl von Spreti, was kidnapped. The government declined to pay the price demanded for his release, seventeen (later twenty-five) prisoners and a ransom, and he was assassinated. In this context this must be seen as an extension of the guerrillas' assessment of the dominating role of the United States and her allies: the capture of a foreign diplomat must have appeared as the only available means of negotiating with the government, although in fact it provoked right-wing 'White Hand' extremists to kill a communist deputy in revenge.[24]

Under these conditions many people, especially in the rural areas, reverted to the traditional Guatemalan practice of voting for the political party that seemed to offer the most immediate concrete advantage— whether this is a road or bridge built by military civic-action teams, or the promise of the strict enforcement of law and order. It is unlikely, however, that in such a political climate the kinds of personal commitment needed for social or economic development will be forthcoming. The education of children in skills needed by the local economy, the saving of money, the maintenance of a stable family environment are some of the many decisions relevant to development which will not be taken by rich or poor unless they have more confidence in their country's future than is apparent at present.

In general, the effect of US influence in Guatemala has thus been to perpetuate the traditional power structure. The ways in which military, landowners, and commercial interests have maintained their dominance have changed, but their dominance has not substantially changed. The position of the United States has effectively polarized the political process. Moderate reform becomes labelled communist and is challenged by conservative groups confident that they can bring US influence to bear. In this way, the US presence contributes to the intransigence of those elements in society opposed to reform, encouraging the existing power structure to be inflexible and not to incorporate the new elements of power arising in society. Reform-orientated sectors of society become disillusioned, and this influences them to resort to extra-constitutional means to obtain their ends. The result is not likely to be violent social revolution

[24] *The Times*, 10 Apr. 1970.

in the near future; rival sources of power, such as working-class organizations, are not developed, and there is no source of aid and influence rivalling that of the United States. The present situation is a stalemate in which the existing power structure effectively prevents social reform but is unable to secure the co-operation of the population for economic development.

CONCLUSION

US influence is exercised in Guatemala for a variety of strategic and economic reasons; its pervasiveness and effect are conditioned by certain aspects of Guatemala's social structure, which ensures that no matter what the formal intent of US policies, the US presence is an active element in the power structure. The unforeseen consequences of involvement with an unintegrated and underdeveloped society prevent the United States from exercising a limited and consistent influence. Instead, she has increasingly been drawn into, and has contributed to, the competition between various interest groups in Guatemala. In so doing she is not only safeguarding her strategic and economic interests but is used by various local groups to further their own interests. An important consequence is the conversion of internal dispute into issues of international politics. This has made more difficult the internal resolution of Guatemala's social and economic problem, contributing as it does to the polarization and intransigence of local interest groups.

M

9 The United States and the Caribbean

LINCOLN GORDON

I MUST disclaim any pretensions to being an expert on the Caribbean. Such expertise as I possess on Latin American affairs mainly concerns the larger countries of South America. Moreover, while I was responsible for US foreign policy in the whole western hemisphere, except Canada, during 1966 and the first half of 1967, I have had no active connection with official policy since that time. The views expressed here, therefore, must not be taken as representing official US government policy.

In any event, official American policy toward the Caribbean has for some time been undergoing re-examination in the hope of achieving more clear-cut definition. This is not because of any sense of crisis. It rather reflects the recognition that this region of traditional US interest is in flux, that old European imperial relationships have largely disappeared, that much of the region cannot readily be assimilated into traditional western hemisphere policy, and that the next decade may offer both opportunities and dangers which should be anticipated if possible.

In the United States, all discussions of this topic begin with three basic questions: (a) What is meant by the Caribbean region? (b) Is there a special kind of American interest there different from that in the rest of the western hemisphere? (c) Can American policies in the Caribbean simply conform to the broader western hemisphere policies given formal expression through the inter-American system?

WHAT IS THE CARIBBEAN?

As has been discussed in Chapter 2 of this book, the largest definition of the region includes all countries bordering on the Caribbean and the islands within or near it, from Mexico through Central America, Colombia, Venezuela, and the Guianas, around to the Bahamas and even the Bermudas. The smaller definition includes most of the islands, together with Central America and the Guianas, but excluding Mexico, Colombia, and Venezuela.

Neither the larger nor the smaller region shows any cultural, economic, or political homogeneity. There are obviously certain common geographical features, although even on that score the distances and disparities

are greater than might be supposed from the frequent references to a
'Caribbean region'. Apart from merely geographical association, I believe
that the essential common feature of the larger area is a degree of strategic
and economic dependence on the United States paralleled only by that of
Canada. For the smaller defined area, this exceptional influence of the
United States is re-enforced by the fact of subdivision into non-viable
mini-states or micro-states. They are bound to be dependent on someone
and to be seeking some kind of aggregation—either through association
with one another or, more likely, through attachment to some larger non-
Caribbean country or grouping.

One often hears the Caribbean described as 'a region in search of its
personality' or its unity. I am sceptical about this. Perhaps it should be in
search of a unified personality, but its most outstanding characteristic in
fact is fractionalism. The centrifugal tendencies at the moment seem
stronger than the centripetal. Illustrations come readily to mind: the
traditional friction between the Dominican Republic and Haiti; Jamaica's
aloof posture toward the Eastern Caribbean; and so on down to the
tension between St Kitts and Anguilla.

IS THERE A SPECIAL US INTEREST IN THE CARIB-
BEAN?

Traditionally there certainly has been. This is the region where the
Monroe Doctrine has been given positive application over the decades.
It was the area for operation of the Roosevelt Corollary. Since the beginning of this century, first the project and later the fact of the Panama
Canal has heavily influenced American strategic thinking and actual
foreign policy. The thirty-three American military interventions in the
western hemisphere since 1895 have all taken place within the Caribbean
region (if Mexico is included in the definition). American sovereignty
extends to Puerto Rico and the Virgin Islands, and quasi-sovereignty to
the Canal zone. There are major military installations in Puerto Rico, the
Canal zone, and Guantánamo, as well as minor facilities in several of the
Lesser Antilles. American public opinion tends to take for granted a kind
of paramountcy, an acknowledged sphere of influence, which is quite
different from US relations with the larger South American countries or
with Mexico during the past forty years.

The American presence in the Caribbean is qualitatively of a quite
different order from the degree of influence in a country like Brazil, with
her long tradition of friendly and more or less equal partnership in the
development of the inter-American system, or Argentina, with its

*M

tradition of economic rivalry and political wariness towards the United States. Clearly the psychological wound to American pride from the fact that Cuba turned communist was, for all of these reasons, far deeper than would have been caused for example, by a similar revolution in Chile.

While economic relations in the form of investments, raw-material supplies, and markets have something to do with this attitude, its essential element is strategic. From the security viewpoint, if not politically, the Caribbean is very widely regarded by public opinion in the United States as necessarily an American lake.

It is interesting to speculate whether this notion of a special strategic sphere of influence continues to have any objective justification in the era of supersonic jet aircraft and nuclear missiles. Certainly there is much less reason for it today than in earlier times. The Panama Canal has far less military importance in an age of two-ocean navies and air logistics, even though its economic significance continues to be very great indeed. This reduced strategic importance is just as well, in view of the Canal's vulnerability. Its defence, however, is still generally considered a matter of vital US national interest, so that at least the negative objective of avoiding the control of any Caribbean territory by potentially unfriendly powers will probably remain as one anchor of American foreign policy.

This does not imply another attempt to change by force the character of the regime in Cuba, but it certainly does mean strenuous efforts to avoid the creation of a second Cuba in the Caribbean. Such an event would be politically disastrous to any American administration which could be charged with responsibility for it through acts either of commission or of omission.

IS THE GENERAL LATIN AMERICAN POLICY APPLICABLE TO THE CARIBBEAN?

To answer this requires some definition of general US policy in Latin America. Since the launching of the Alliance for Progress in 1961 (and the roots of that programme go back well before the Kennedy administration), the essential thrust of US policy has been towards international economic co-operation to accelerate the modernization of Latin American economic, social, and political life. A similar line of policy has extended to other less developed areas, such as South Asia, but without the crystallization of special relationships formalized in the mutual obligations and the international administrative machinery of the inter-American system. At the meeting of Presidents at Punta del Este in 1967 this broad purpose was complemented by special emphasis on Latin American economic integration, an objective restated by President Johnson in 1968 when he signed the documents of ratification of the revised OAS Charter.

Thus defined, the wider framework of US policy does not readily accommodate all the Caribbean region. Mexico, Colombia, and Venezuela fit readily. Central America has been doing so increasingly, with the help of the prolonged economic boom coinciding with the early development of the Central American common market (CACM). In spite of the severe political and social problems of Guatemala, Honduras, Nicaragua, and El Salvador—and recently even of Costa Rica—it is impressive to see how the integration movement has created a new tone in Central America's external relations. At the two-week Montevideo Conference of March 1967, for example, in preparation for the presidential meeting, Central American representatives spoke with a degree of maturity and self-confidence quite in contrast to their traditional posture of 'little brothers'.

The broad lines of policy, however, do not readily fit the Dominican Republic or Haiti. Physical integration cannot mean very much to island nations, although it could have some meaning in telecommunications, ocean and air transportation, and 'industrial integration' (as with bauxite or aluminum). The present Haitian regime can scarcely be said to have any kind of active foreign relations, and the Dominican Republic is still recovering from the events of 1965. These two countries feel themselves outsiders in face of the CACM and LAFTA, and are not at all clear that their economic destinies lie with a future Latin American common market, despite their adherence to the Presidential document of Punta del Este. Nor is Panama certain whether she prefers joining the CACM, seeking some special economic relationship with the US, or developing along the line of what some Panamanians call 'Hong Kongization'.

These doubts exist in still greater measure—in progression—with Trinidad and Barbados, despite their recent entry into the OAS, with Guyana (although not Belize, where relations with Guatemala are the critical issue), with the Windward and Leeward Islands, and with the Netherlands and French Antilles. And paradoxically, the two largest Caribbean territories wrested from Spain in the war of 1898 are now at the two extremes: Puerto Rico is modernizing and developing economically with great rapidity within the American flag and customs area, while Cuba is suspended from membership in the inter-American system and has become an unruly satellite of the Soviet Union.

It is the increasing recognition in Washington that this miscellaneous assortment of mini- and micro-states is unlikely ever to fit into a general Latin American policy framework which underlies the various reviews and re-examinations which I mentioned earlier.

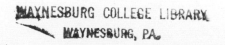

VIABILITY THROUGH ASSOCIATION, BUT ASSOCIATION WITH WHOM?

Economic discussions on the future of the Caribbean centre on some form of special trading and other economic relations with some extra-Caribbean grouping or metropolitan power. There is a great variety of half-formed ideas, few if any supported by economic analysis. Their very multiplicity, however, reflects a broad consensus that the *status quo* cannot endure. Let me mention a few examples.

The Central American bloc has endorsed with enthusiasm the idea of its integration into a broader Latin American common market. This is partly because the limitations of market size for Central America as a whole are becoming increasingly evident. In the Dominican Republic there is considerable interest in a 'Puerto Rican-type economic solution' or some sort of 'special relation' with Puerto Rico as a way-station towards the US market. The political aspects of Puerto Rico's economic union with the United States, however, are scarcely likely to be acceptable to either Dominican or American public opinion. Puerto Rico herself remains divided among the triple long-term choices of 'Commonwealth status', full statehood within the United States, or independence. The plebiscite of July 1967 showed of those voting 61 per cent in favour of Commonwealth status and 39 per cent for statehood; the *independentistas* deliberately abstained but did not account for more than 15 per cent of the total electorate.

Guyana has been promoting free trade and other measures of economic union within the British Commonwealth Caribbean, mainly in the hopes of attracting Negro immigrants to improve the domestic political balance. Trinidad and Barbados decided to join the OAS, partly because it made them eligible for loans from the Inter-American Development Bank and could promote greater bilateral American economic co-operation. Perhaps they also anticipated some system of western hemisphere trade preferences, following on the failure of the proposals in UNCTAD for global trade preferences to less developed countries.

Others of the islands, however, prefer to look towards special economic arrangements with Europe. The French and Netherlands Antilles are apparently satisfied with their association with the EEC, even though they are gradually moving towards greater political and economic independence from France and the Netherlands. Jamaica, continuing her 'lone wolf' tradition of recent years, is apparently the only Caribbean nation which foresees a long-term special relationship with the United Kingdom and a prospect as well of association with the EEC.

There is no indication of a clear-cut US attitude toward any of these possibilities. Notwithstanding the growth of American economic interest in all parts of the Caribbean as transportation improves and tourism becomes a leading industry, it can be said with some confidence that there are insuperable legal and political obstacles to extending the US customs area to the Caribbean region as a whole. The Caribbean might, of course, participate in a general western hemisphere preferential (or ultimately free) trading arrangement. But the very dimensions of this scheme would considerably dilute its advantages to the Caribbean partners.

Sugar poses a special problem. The 725,000 tons of Caribbean sugar now being absorbed into the British preferential market could not readily be incorporated into the American sugar-import quota system. The importance of sugar in the Caribbean economy is demonstrated by the vigour with which the Dominican Republic has sought to secure permanently the short-fall in Puerto Rico's quota supplies in the American market. The adjustments which would be required to absorb Cuban sugar into the western hemisphere system suggest one of those nightmares which each generation of policy-makers tends to hope can be deferred for their successors.

Pending the evolution of a more clear-cut pattern, the United States has been encouraging joint policies with the United Kingdom and Canada for promoting viability in the Commonwealth Caribbean. The economic development and the political stability of this area is a recognized US political interest. Hence support for the Caribbean Development Bank and the Regional Development Agency for the 'little eight' associated states in the Lesser and Greater Antilles. From the American viewpoint, the break-up of the West Indies Federation was regrettable, and the hope persists that prolonged practice in economic co-operation may ultimately lead to some kind of political association.

There is no desire to assume economic responsibilities unilaterally; quite the contrary, there is a strong interest in continued British participation and enhanced Canadian participation. American policy has consistently favoured Canadian membership in the OAS. If the political obstacles to full membership prove insuperable, I believe it would be useful to explore some form of associate membership confined to the economic side.

The role of Puerto Rico is an interesting aspect of the Caribbean scene. While that 'Commonwealth's' formal foreign relations are reserved to the United States, Puerto Rico has shown an active interest in promoting economic development, technical assistance, and cultural relations with both Spanish-speaking and English-speaking neighbours. This has been encouraged by Washington, even to the point of exploring the possibility of direct membership for Puerto Rico in the Caribbean Development Bank.

Some observers, impressed by the success of Commonwealth status in Puerto Rico over the past fifteen years, believe that similar arrangements might be applicable to the Dominican Republic, Panama, and other Caribbean territories. I am sceptical about this idea, doubting that either side would be willing to see the American flag extended to new areas. Any substantial widening of full access to the US market would dilute the trade-creating effects for Puerto Rico itself and would almost certainly raise serious protectionist resistances in a series of American industries, beginning with textiles and clothing. Less ambitious *ad hoc* economic arrangements, on the other hand, not requiring a new system of official preferences, such as joint commercial and investment ventures involving Puerto Rico and the Dominican Republic, might prove quite successful.

The significance of special economic arrangements obviously depends on the nature of economic activity which may be developed in the Caribbean area. Some analysts are apparently persuaded that tourism alone can provide a sufficient base for the prosperity of the entire region. If this were valid, special trading arrangements would be of little importance. The subject warrants careful study, but my own preliminary guess is that tourism alone will not suffice, and that various kinds of labour-intensive industrial activities, as well as more efficient food production, have an important part to play. In this case, special trading arrangements could be of very substantial importance. In addition, unless there is a sharp reduction in rates of population growth, new opportunities for migration will have to be found.

INTERVENTION AND NON-INTERVENTION

Leaving the matter of economic relations in this rather untidy status, let us return to consideration of the political and security relations between the United States and the Caribbean. The experience of the second world war and the Cuban missile-base crisis of 1962 suggest that the Caribbean is still very much under an American security umbrella. The question constantly arises whether that umbrella hides a sword of potential intervention.

Intervention itself is a somewhat ambituous term. It is sometimes used in western hemisphere relations to refer to various forms of economic and political influence as well as armed force. In this broader sense, the American presence in the Caribbean is so great as frequently to lead to allegations of intervention, either by commission or by omission, even if, in fact, official Washington is strictly neutral.

Military intervention is another matter. Action of this type is obviously undesirable and to be avoided if at all possible. Its illegality in the western hemisphere is made clear in the most unequivocal terms by the OAS Charter, except for cases of collective action under the Inter-American Treaty of Reciprocal Assistance.

Nevertheless, the United States has been involved in three cases since the OAS Charter was adopted in 1948: indirectly in Guatemala in 1954; semi-directly in the abortive Bay of Pigs operation in Cuba in 1961; and directly and overtly in the Dominican Republic in 1965. The reality which lies behind these cases—and any others which may arise in the future—is that nations are not isolated sovereign compartments with clearly defined loci of internal sovereignty; they are rather arenas in which international political movements and external influences play their parts alongside of purely domestic ones. In the Caribbean, the studied Cuban policy of active subversion of democratic regimes was an omnipresent fact of life, which could not but help influence the attitudes of US administrations.

The tradition of Latin American political instability gives special importance to the moments of crisis surrounding a change of regime. The planners of coups, whether military or communist, have learned this lesson well. They know the strategic and tactical key points of political crises: the army and police barracks; the government palaces; the radio and television stations; and the national networks of transportation and communications. The inter-American system contains legal obligations to support representative democracy as well as to avoid armed interventions, so that a legal as well as a moral case can be made for collective action against the capture of power through the specialized techniques of coup d'état. Street revolutions in national capitals are not manifestations of genuine representative democracy.

In the Dominican case, whatever the judgement on the unilateral US action in 1965, the final outcome was certainly more compatible with the OAS Charter than the establishment of a regime through civil war in the city of Santo Domingo. The fairness of the democratic election of 1 June 1966 has been certified by outside observers of every political colour.

It seems unlikely, then, that military intervention in the Caribbean can be ruled out in any and all circumstances. As already stated, it should be avoided if at all possible, on both political and legal grounds. If or when it becomes necessary, it should if possible be multilateral rather than unilateral in character. Most retrospective reviews of the Dominican

Republic case, including those which welcome the final outcome, criticize two points: (a) the failure of the American Embassy to mediate between General Wessin and Colonel Caamaño before the military action erupted, and (b) the failure of the US government to consult with the OAS and to seek its endorsement before proceeding unilaterally to intervene. While circumstances never repeat themselves precisely, I have the strong impression that these criticisms have been taken to heart in American official circles.

Obviously, the best way to avoid intervention is to achieve sufficient political stability and economic growth so that regimes are not subject to the kind of crisis which leads to intervention. In my view, the doctrine of non-intervention ought to be complemented by a doctrine of positive interdependence between advanced and developing countries. To explore that theme, however, would take us far beyond the problems of the Caribbean.

CUBA

It is evidently unrealistic to discuss the long-term future of the Caribbean without considering Cuba, the largest country of the area. For the moment, Cuba has taken herself out of the western hemisphere system, both economically and politically. I deliberately use the expression 'taken herself out', in spite of the laboured attempts of some commentators to demonstrate that the Castro regime was forced out by US action. Ever since the crises of 1961 and 1962, the question is periodically raised whether the time has not come for some accommodation between the United States and Cuba, which might lead to Cuba's re-entry into the inter-American system.

If under late-twentieth-century conditions world geography continues to have any significance at all in international relations, surely Cuba's reintegration into the western hemisphere system should be looked for. Perhaps the importance of geography can be exaggerated; the status of Hong Kong is, after all, at least as paradoxical as that of Cuba. In any event, the consistent American official attitude on this issue until mid-1967 (and I have no reason to suppose that it has changed) was declared by President Kennedy in his last official speech, on 18 November 1963. He set forth two, and only two, conditions for restoration of normal relations: (a) separation of Cuba from her military affiliation with the Soviet Union and (b) termination of Cuban efforts to overthrow democratic regimes elsewhere in Latin America. I find it hard to believe that these conditions would be reduced. At present, it also seems to me unlikely that they will be accepted, not because their acceptance would in any sense be bad for Cuba but because they are incompatible with Fidel Castro's conception of the posture required for his own survival.

Notwithstanding their paradoxical aspects, the present arrangements appear fairly stable in the short run. The economic sanctions directed against Cuba by the United States and her OAS partners are largely offset by massive Soviet economic aid and by European and Canadian trade. As the Rhodesian case suggests, moreover, there are severe limits to the efficacy of economic sanctions in influencing the policies of a determined regime. On the other hand, Cuban-assisted subversion is making no visible headway in other countries, even though it is a costly and annoying continuing nuisance in Venezuela, Guatemala, and several other countries, including some of the smaller Caribbean islands. The Cuban revolution seems to have lost most of its former glamour.

In the middle or longer run, however, the situation could easily become less stable. This might occur suddenly through a change of Soviet policy reducing military and economic support or through the death of Fidel Castro. It is not clear how the succession would be handled, since neither Raúl Castro nor President Dorticós possesses the widespread popular appeal of Fidel.

In preparing for possible future changes in Cuban relations with the United States and other neighbours, it appears especially important to avoid so heavy and permanent a dependence of other countries on Cuba's former sugar quota in the preferential American market as to preclude their adjustment to a reintegration of Cuba into the inter-American system. On the political side, if the succession to Fidel Castro were to be hotly disputed—perhaps to the extent of unleashing a civil war—it is not clear that the matter could or would be resolved entirely within Cuba's boundaries. The United States would be extremely reluctant to intervene, but it would also be unlikely to accept quietly any active intervention by forces of the Soviet Union. I raise a question—without suggesting the answer—whether other Latin American countries could or should play an effective role in such a contingency.

CONCLUSION

Let me conclude by bringing together some threads of this rambling *tour d'horizon* of the Caribbean from an American point of view.

The region comprises a scattered group of mini-states in search, if not of a collective policy, at least of economic and political viability. Such viability almost certainly will require some form of aggregation, notwithstanding the centrifugal pressures of domestic politics within each of the political units.

The position of the United States is better described as a posture or set of attitudes than a consistent policy. That posture clearly accepts special responsibilities in relation to the older independent units of the area, i.e. the Latin American states of Central America, Panama, Hispaniola, and— in principle—Cuba, as well as the areas of formal sovereignty, namely Puerto Rico and the Virgin Islands. Towards the newly independent or semi-independent units, however, there is ambivalence in American attitudes. This is true equally of the British Commonwealth Caribbean and the Netherlands and French areas. In the US Congress, for example, the question is often raised why, if external help is needed in the form of aid or special market arrangements, it should not come from the former or present metropoles in Europe rather than the United States.

Against that aloof view, there are factors forcing the development of American policy into a more positive mould than mere watchful waiting. The most important such factor is concern for strategic security. But there are also changing economic patterns tending toward increased American involvement: growing trade, investment, tourism, and to some extent migration. There are also growing cultural interchanges, enthusiastically stimulated by Puerto Rico.

In the Commonwealth Caribbean, the result is an effort to develop a collective policy conjointly with Canada and the United Kingdom. Canada appears almost as a *deus ex machina* able to combine the Commonwealth connection with freedom from the taint of former imperialism and an apparent willingness to place in the Caribbean a significant share of her available aid and technical assistance.

Beyond this, what kinds of aggregation and association should be promoted are more a matter of targets of opportunity than the consequence of any 'grand design' that has yet emerged over the horizon.

Contributors to this volume

ROBIN BLACKBURN is at present preparing a thesis on the sociology of the Cuban Revolution at Oxford University. He recently introduced and edited *Strategy for Revolution: essays on Latin America* (1970), by Régis Debray.

DR LINCOLN GORDON, who was US ambassador to Brazil from 1961 to 1966 and Assistant Secretary of State for inter-American affairs from 1966 to 1967, served as President of the Johns Hopkins University from 1967 to 1971 and is now Professor of Political Economy at the Johns Hopkins School of Advanced International Studies. He is author of *A New Deal for Latin America, the Alliance for Progress* (1963).

DOUGLAS HALL, a Jamaican, is Professor of History at the University of the West Indies (Mona, Jamaica). His publications include *Free Jamaica, an economic history, 1838–65* (1959), *Ideas and Illustrations in Economic History* (1964), and *Five of the Leewards 1834–70* (1971).

COLIN HENFREY is lecturer in the sociology of Latin America at Liverpool University, and a member of St Antony's college, Oxford, while completing a D.Phil. on the sociology of low-income groups in Latin America. His publications include *The Gentle People* (1964) and 'Guyana', in *Latin America and the Caribbean: a Handbook* (1968), edited by C. Véliz.

DR HARMANNUS HOETINK is Director of the Institute of Caribbean Studies and Professor of Sociology at the University of Puerto Rico. He is author of *Caribbean Race Relations* (1971), *El Pueblo dominicano 1850–1900* (1971), and *Slavery and Race Relations in the Americas* which will appear in 1972.

GUY LASSERRE is Professor of Geography of tropical countries at the University of Bordeaux, Director of the Centre d'Études de Géographie Tropicale, and joint editor of the periodical *Les Cahiers d'Outre-Mer*. He is at present preparing a geographical work on Central America, including Mexico and the Antilles.

ALBERT MABILEAU is Director of the Institut d'Études Politiques in Bordeaux, Professor of Public Law and Political Science at Bordeaux University, and Director of the Centre d'Études Antillaises. He is a specialist in political institutions in developing countries.

DR PETER ODELL, who taught at the LSE from 1961 to 1968, is now Professor of Economic Geography at the Netherlands School of Economics in Rotterdam. He is joint author of *Economic and Social Organisation in Latin America: a geographical interpretation* (1970).

DR BRYAN ROBERTS is lecturer in Sociology at the University of Manchester and was Visiting Associate Professor at the University of Texas in 1968. A book on his fieldwork in Guatemala, entitled *Organizing Strangers*, will be published shortly. He is currently working on problems of regional development and entrepreneurship in Peru.

Index

(*Note:* BCC = British Commonwealth Caribbean; CACM = Central American Common Market; SU = Soviet Union.)

Acción Democrática (Venezuela), 25–6
Adams, R., 148n., 156, 165
Affobaka hydro-electric plant, 113–14
AFL–CIO International Affairs Unit, 65
d'Aguiar, P., 15n., 64 f., 67, 71
Ahmadiyya, 116
AID, 161, 167
Alcoa, 52, 113–14
Aldama, M., 123
Alekseyev, A., 134
Algeria, 93, 99, 131
Allende, S., 5n., 143 f.,
Alliance for Progress, 60 f., 172
Aluminium, Ltd., 52
Alvarado, P. de, 149
American Institute for Free Labour Development, 65
Anti-Communist Crusade, 65
Antigua, 7n.
Antillean Reformist Union, 119
Araña Osorio, C., 158
Arbenz, J., 3, 12, 150, 152 f., 157 f., 160, 166–7
Arévalo, J. J., 12, 150, 158, 167
Argentina, 171–2
Arismendi, R., 144
Aruba, 103, 105 f.; political structure, 108–9
Arya Samaj, 116
Association for Cultural Relations with Independent Africa, 79
Association of Antillean Students in France, 98

bananas, 8, 38, 86, 152
Bank of America, 152
Bank of Guatemala, 156

Barbados, 7n., 9, 173 f.
Batista, F., 123, 125–6, 127 ff., 133, 140
bauxite, 26, 44, 52ff., 73, 78f., 80, 113 f.
Bay of Pigs operation, 131, 177
BCC, 1, 7–9, 40 174 f., 180
Belgian Fathers, 158
Betancourt, R., 25
Bethencourt, A., 111
Bhagwan, M., 74
Billiton Mining Co., 113
Blackburn, R., 5, 6, 16, 121–47
Bolivia, 144, 153
Bonaire, 103, 106, 108; *see also* Netherlands Antilles
Booker Bros., 52 ff., 57, 61, 69
Bravo, D., 144
Brazil, 19, 28, 111, 144, 171
British Antilles, *see* individual islands
British Guiana, *see* Guyana
British Honduras, 7n., 23, 29, 150, 153–4, 173
Brizzola, L., 143
Bruma, E., 117
Burnham, F., 15n., 51, 56, 60, 62, 63–4, 71 f., 74, 76, 80
Bustamante, A., 36n, 38

Caamaño, Col., 178
CACM, 31, 150, 173
Cambodia, 146
Canada, 8, 74, 175, 179 f.
Caribbean: dependence on foreign nations, 2; development of US imperialism, 2–3, 17, 21–3, 24–8; foreign investments, 3–4, 5–7, 12, 14–16, 25–6; US military intervention, 4–5, 25, 171, 176–8; foreign

Caribbean—*cont.*
influence, 5–6; regional co-operation, 7–9, 77, 111, 149–50; political associations, 9–10; and decolonization, 10–11; cold-war ideology, 11–12; tourism, 12–13, 27–8; foreign aid, 16–17; definitions of, 18–20, 170–1; European colonialism, 20–1, 23–4; and su, 24; role in Latin America, 28–30; third world, 30; political changes within, 30–1; us sphere of influence, 171–2; and Latin-American policy, 172–3; special economic associations, 174–6; *see also* individual countries
Caribbean Commission, 111
Caribbean Development Bank, 8–9, 175 f.
Caribbean Organization, 111
CARIFTA, 7–9
Caritas, 159
Castillo Armas, C., 150, 152, 157 f., 167
Castro, F., 179; economy and, 24, 138, 143; USA and, 126 ff., 131; approach to communism of, 132 ff., 135–6, 140 f., 143; Escalante episodes, 134–5; missiles crisis, 136–7; *rapport* between people and, 141–2; Czech invasion, 145–6
Castro, R., 136, 179
Catholic Relief Services, 159
Césaire, A., 97–8, 99n.
Chibás, E., 129
Chile, 5n., 118, 144
CIA, 3, 12, 69, 70–1, 126, 129
China, 31, 141
Colombia, 18, 20, 28, 104 f., 144, 170, 173
Colonial Development & Welfare organization (Jamaica), 35
Common Market, *see* EEC
Commonwealth Sugar Agreement, 54
Congress for Cultural Freedom, 129
Conombo, M., 93
Costa Gomez, M. F. da, 109
Costa Rica, 29, 149, 173
Crowther, Gen., 126
Cuba, 1 ff., 5 f., 16, 20, 22 ff., 27, 31, 99, 104, 121–47, 172 f.; Guyana and, 64 f., 144; Independence Army, 125; Guantánamo base, 126, 171; Trade Union Federation, 133; Communist Party, 133, 141; missiles crisis, 136–7, 176; Guatemala and, 154, 179
International relations: Latin America, 143–4; Vietnam, 145; support for su, 145–7
Pre-Revolution us domination: origins, 122–3; economic, 123–5, 127; military and diplomatic, 125–7; 'over-developed' imperialism, 127–8, 130; tourism and advertising, 128; cultural penetration, 129–30; influence on Cuban leaders, 129
Post-Revolution turn to communism: role of USA, 131–2, 178–9; and su, 132–3, 134; communism within Cuba, 133–4; Escalante episodes, 134–5; missiles crisis, 136–7, 176; Soviet–Cuban economic relations, 137–9; military security, 139–40; culture and ideology, 140–1; devolution of power, 141–2
Cultural Congress, Havana (1968), 140, 145
Curaçao, 9, 86, 112; historical background, 103–4, oil industry, 105; tourism, 106; slave trade, 103, 107; common language, 107–8; political organization, 108–9; riots in, 109; Democratic Party, 109–10; role in Caribbean, 111; intellectuals, 119
Czechoslovakia, 135, 145–6, 147

De Kadt, E., 1–17
Debray, R., 141
Defferre, *loi-cadre* (1956), 93, 97
Demerara Bauxite Co., 52, 77
Dominica, 7n, 83
Dominican Republic, 1 f., 22, 25, 104, 131, 153, 171, 173 ff., 177–8
Dorticós, O., 179
Dutch Caribbean, *see* Curaçao; Netherlands Antilles; Surinam
Dutch West India Company, 103

Echeverria, J. A., 123
EEC, 8, 105, 110, 114, 118, 174
Egypt, 131, 133
Eisenhower, D. D., 131
Ejercito de Liberación Nacional (Bolivia), 144
El Salvador, 18–19, 27, 173
emigration, *see* migration
Escalante, A., 134–5
European Development Fund, 114n.

France, 9, 14, 23, 66, 88, 121, 159, 174; *see also* French Antilles; French Guiana
Frank, A. D., 6 f.
Frei, E., 143
French Antilles, 1, 14, 82–102, 173; assimilation policy, 82, 89, 174; social inequalities, 83–4, 96; population, 83–5; economy, 85–8, 92, 94, 96; employment, 87–8, 96; colonial regime, 89–90; departmental status (DOM), 82, 90–3; —modified, 93–4; political malaise, 94–7; public opinion, 97–9; current French policy towards, 99–102
French Guiana, 19, 28, 82; National Centre for Space Studies, 88
Fuentes Mohr, A., 157
Fuentes Pierruccini, M., 158

Garvey, M., 38
de Gaulle, C., 95, 97, 99
Glasgow, R. A., 64
Gordon, L., 3, 170–80
Goulart, J., 143
Grace, J. P., 65
Grace & Co.,W. R., 65
Great Lakes Carbon Ltd., 52
Guadeloupe: riots in, 95, 99; view on assimilation, 98–9; 'Nationalist trial' in, 99; *see also* French Antilles.
Guatemala, 1, 111, 173; and British Honduras, 23, 29; Cuba and, 144, 179
  US influence, 3, 5 f., 11–12, 16, 59, 148–69: historical background, 149–50, 162; economy, 150–3, 160 1; foreign political influence, 153–4;

technical and professional skills, 154–6; the military, 156–7, 161; guerrilla activity, 157, 161, 168; presidential elections (1970), 157–8; Christian Democratic Party, 158, 161; Catholic church, 158–9, 161; and Protestantism, 159; mass culture, 159–60; migration to US, 160; low social integration, 162–4; and social relationships, 164–5; competing power groups, 165–6; opposition to Arbenz regime, 166–7; traditional power structure, 167–9
Guevara, 'Che', 129, 138–9, 141, 144
Guillén, N., 133
Guinea, 100, 133
Guyana, 15n., 19, 22, 49–80, 111, 117, 144, 173 f.; and CARIFTA, 7n., 8 f.; decolonization process, 10–11; UF, 15n., 49, 64 ff., 71, 75; PNC, 15n., 49 f., 62 ff., 72–4; Venezuela, 23, 29; foreign influence, 49–51; colonial background, 51–5; economy, 50, 52–3, 65–7, 77, 78–9; Robertson Commission, 52, 60n., 61 f.; racial categories, 56–7, 64, 68, 72, 79; Labour Relations Bill, 58, 68–70; suspension of Constitution, 58–62; failure of nationalist leadership, 63–4; US intervention, 64–5, 66, 69, 70–1, 73 ff.; TUC, 65, 67 ff., 72; foreign reaction against Jagan, 66–7; riots and strikes, 67–8, 72; general strike, 69–70; Agricultural Workers' Union, 69–70, 72; CIA involvement, 70–1; Sandys Constitution, 71–2; PNC-UF coalition, 72–4; elections (1968), 74–7; Independence (1966), 78–80; 'Co-operative Republic', 77, 78–9
PPP, 15n., 49 f., 65, 71; 1953 electoral success, 51, 56–8; clashes between British and, 57–60, 71; suspension of Constitution, 60, 61–2; split within, 62–3, 64; 1961 programme, 66–7; and riots, 67–8, 72; Labour Relations Bill, 58, 68–70.

Haiti, 1, 104, 107, 171, 173

Hall, D , 11, 32–48
Havana, 2nd Declaration of, 143
Henfrey, C , 10, 11n., 49–81
Hirschman, A. O., 7
Hoetink, H., 9, 103–20
Honduras, 26, 149, 173; see also British Honduras

ICFTU, 70
Inter-American Development Bank, 174
Inter-American Treaty of Reciprocal Assistance, 177
International Commission of Jurists, 79, 80n.
Ishmael, R., 69

Jagan, C., 15n., 51, 56, 59 f., 62, 63–4, 66, 70 f., 74, 144
Jagan, J., 60, 62 f.
Jamaica, 1, 7n., 8 f., 11, 27, 32–48, 118, 171, 174; under colonial rule, 32–6; political parties, 36n.; Federation of West Indies, 36–7; Independence, 37–40; party political behaviour, 40–1, 46; reliance on 'experts', 41–2; economy, 42–6; challenges of decolonization, 46–8
Japan, 8, 121
Jessurun, A., 104
Johnson, L. B., 173

Kennedy, J. F., 131, 178
Kefauver, Senator, 128
Kielstra, Governor, 115
King, S., 79
Khrushchev, N., 132, 136
Korea, 136, 145 f.
Kudryatsev, S. M., 134

Lachmon, J., 116 f.
LAFTA, 173
Lansky, Meyer, 128
Latin America, 1, 7, 20; inter-American system, 28–30, 171, 177; Castro's views on, 135–6; revolutionary role of Cuba in, 143–4, 178 f.; SU and, 145; US policy, 172–3; Caribbean economic integration in, 174; see also individual countries

Lasserre, G., 9, 82–102
Lee, J., 70
Leeward Islands, 1, 8, 173
Lesser Antilles, 19, 83, 103, 171; see also British Antilles; French Antilles; Netherlands Antilles
López Villatoro, M., 157
Lucas Caballeros, J., 158

Mabileau, A., 9, 82–102
Machado, G., 125 f., 129
MacLeod, I., 71, 73
Macmillan, H., 59n.
Manley, N., 36n.
Marighela, C., 144
Marin, M., 130
Martí, J., 123
Martinique: riots in, 95; criticism of departmental status, 98; see also French Antilles
Maryknoll Fathers, 158, 161
Mella, A., 133
Menéndez, J., 133
Menocal, Gen., 129
Mexico, 13, 18, 20, 29–30, 147, 149, 153, 159, 170 f., 173
migration, 9, 23, 43, 88, 96, 105, 112–13, 119, 160
Mikoyan, A., 131, 137
Monroe Doctrine, 2, 171
Monserrat, 7n.
Montevideo Conference (1967), 173
Moscow Conference of Communist Parties (1969), 145 f.
Moutet, M., 90

Netherlands, 9, 23, 117–19, 174; Charter of the Kingdom, 108 f., 117–19
Netherlands Antilles, 1, 103–11, 113, 173 f.; historical background, 103–4; economic development, 104–6; social groups, 106–8; federative structure, 108–9, 110; political demands, 109–10; Charter of the Kingdom, 108 f., 117–18; migration to Holland, 119; see also Curaçao and Surinam.
Newman, P., 53–4, 71
Nicaragua, 149, 153, 173

Nkrumah, K., 131, 145

OAS, 3, 29, 50, 118, 173 ff., 177 ff.
Odell, P., 2, 13, 18–31
oil, 24 ff., 30, 105, 110, 131
OLAS Conference (1967), 135, 143, 145
OPEC, 30

Panama, 173, 176, 180; Canal, 2, 11, 20, 22, 148, 171 f.
Pearson, D., 70
Pengel, J., 116–17
Peredo brothers, 144
Peru, 143–4, 147
Petronia, E., 110
Platt amendment, 2, 126
population: Jamaica, 40, 42 f., 46; Guyana, 54; French Antilles, 83–5; Neth. Antilles, 105, 106–8; Surinam, 112, 114–16
'provo' movement, 119
Puerto Rico, 1, 20, 22, 27, 44, 130, 171, 173 f., 175–6, 180
Puente, L. de la, 144
Punta del Este presidential meeting (1967), 172 f.

Regional Development Agency, 175
Réunion, 82
Reynolds Metal Co., 52, 113
Roa, R., 129
Roberts, B., 5 f., 11–12, 16, 148–69
Rodriguez, C. R., 146
Roosevelt, F. D., 3, 126
Royal Dutch Shell, 105
Rusk, D., 70 f.

Saba, 103, 106
St Eustatius, 103, 106
St Kitts–Nevis–Anguilla, 7n., 171
St Lucia, 7n.
St Martin, 103, 106
St Thomas, 104
St Vincent, 7n.
San Salvador, 149
Sandys, D., 11n., 70 ff.
Santo Domingo, 20, 104, 177; see also Dominican Republic
Schoelcher decree, 89

Sedney, J., 117
Sihanouk, N., 146
Simms, P., 62
Singer, H., 7
slavery, slave trade, 32–4, 89, 103, 107
Smith, E., 126
Smith, R., 52 f.
Sosa, Y., 144
Soviet Union: relations with Cuba, 3, 5 f., 24, 30–1; economic ties, 6, 24, 131 f., 137–9, 143, 179; Soviet support for evolution, 132–3; military aid, 132, 140; Escalante episodes, 134–5; cultural influence, 140–1; missiles crisis, 136–7; occupation of Czechoslovakia, 145–6
Spain, 20–1, 22, 24, 32, 103 f., 122–3, 149, 162
Spanish-American War (1898), 2, 22, 122 f.
Spreti, K. von, 168
Standard Oil (N.J.), 105 f.
sugar industry, 8, 175; Cuba, 24, 122–3, 124–5, 127, 131 f., 137, 143, 175; Jamaica, 32, 34, 37–8, 43; Guyana, 52–3, 55, 57, 58–9, 69, 78; French Antilles, 83, 86–7
Sukarno, A., 131, 145
Surinam, 1, 10, 19, 105, 108, 110, 111–19; as plantation colony, 111–13; Surinam Aluminium Co., 113; economic development, 113–14; social groups, 112, 114–16; political organization, 116–17; Charter of the Kingdom, 117–19; migration to Holland, 119

Tobago, 7n., 8
Test-Ban Treaty (1963), 137
Tricontinental Conference, Havana, 135, 141, 144 f.
Trinidad, 1, 7n, 8 f., 14, 19, 29, 86, 118, 173 f.
Turcios, L., 144

UAR, see Egypt
Ubico, J., 150
UN, 30, 118, 132
UNCTAD, 174

UNIDO, 9
United Fruit Co., 26, 127, 151 f., 160
United Kingdom, 16, 21, 23, 29, 31; BCC and, 8, 175, 180; colonial rule in Jamaica, 32–7, 39, 41, 174; Cuba, 124, 128; Guatemala, 149 f., 153–4, 159
  Guyana, 10–11, 51–73; colonial background, 51–55; pre-1953 Constitutions of, 55–6; and PPP electoral success (1953), 56–7; suspension of Constitution by, 58–62; nationalist leaders compromise with, 63–4; economic relations, 65–6, 74; strikes and riots, 67–8, 70–1; Sandys Constitution, 71–2; and PNC–UF coalition, 72–3; Independence, 75, 77, 80
Uruguay, 144
USA: Good-Neighbour Policy, 3; SU and, 3, 24, 131 f.; Guyana, 11, 22, 50, 59, 64–5, 66 f., 69 f., 73 ff., 77; Puerto Rico, 22; Dominican Republic, 22, 25–6, 104, 177; Venezuela, 25–6; Jamaica, 38; Dutch Caribbean, 104, 106, 113–14, 118; Vietnam, 121
  Caribbean policy: emergence of, 2–3, 21–22; ideology, 3; economic involvement, 4, 16, 25–7, 151–2; military intervention, 4–5, 25, 176–8; sphere of influence, 22–3, 171–2; imperial role, 24–8; tourism, 12–

13, 27–8, 128, 176; Latin America and, 172–3; special economic relations, 174–6
Cuba: pre-Revolution dominance, 122–30, 134, 137 f., 147; post-Revolution, 131–2; missiles crisis, 136–7, 176; Bay of Pigs, 177; current US policy, 178–9
Guatemala, 11–12, 16, 59, 148–69: economic hegemony, 151–3; political dominance, 153–4; technical and professional aid, 154–6; military involvement, 156–7, 177; religion, 158–9; mass media, 159–60; migration, 160; and social relationships, 165–9

Venezuela, 11, 18 ff., 170, 173; Guyana and, 23, 29, 50; oil industry, 25–6, 30; inter-American system, 28; Dutch Antilles, 104 f., 110; guerrillas in, 144, 179
Vietnam, 121, 136, 145 f.
Virgin Islands, 171, 180

Welles, S., 126
Wessin, Gen., 178
West, R. C., 19
West Indies, 9, 23, 105; Federation, 10, 31, 36–7, 175
Willis, R., 70
Wilson, H., 71
Windward Islands, 1, 8, 108, 173

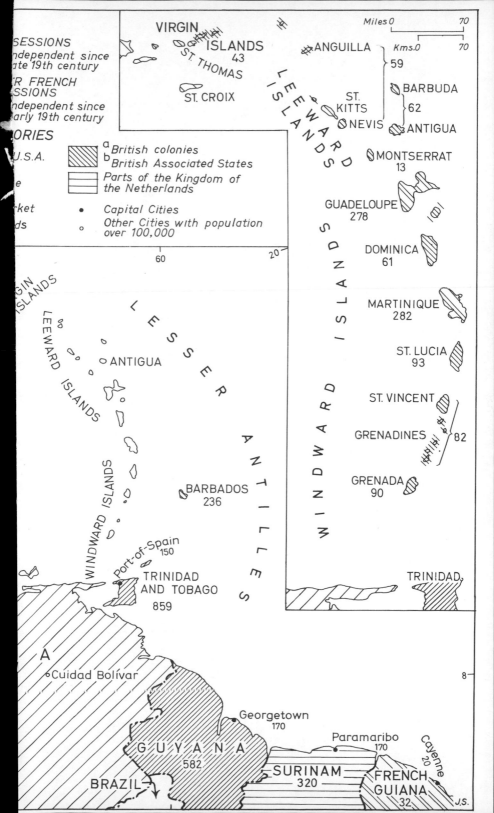

VIRGIN ISLANDS

ST. THOMAS
43

ST. CROIX

L
E
E
W
A
R
D

I
S
L
A
N
D
S

Miles 0   70
Kms. 0   70

ANGUILLA
59

ST.
KITTS
NEVIS

BARBUDA
62
ANTIGUA

MONTSERRAT
13

GUADELOUPE
278

DOMINICA
61

MARTINIQUE
282

ST. LUCIA
93

ST. VINCENT

GRENADINES   82

GRENADA
90

W
I
N
D
W
A
R
D

I
S
L
A
N
D
S

TRINIDAD

8—

SESSIONS
ndependent since
ate 19th century

R FRENCH
SSIONS
ndependent since
arly 19th century

ORIES

U.S.A.

e

rket

ds

a British colonies
b British Associated States

Parts of the Kingdom of
the Netherlands

•   Capital Cities

○   Other Cities with population
    over 100,000

60

20—

GIN
SLANDS

LEEWARD
ISLANDS

L
E
S
S
E
R

ANTIGUA

WINDWARD ISLANDS

A
N
T
I
L
L
E
S

BARBADOS
236

Port-of-Spain
150

TRINIDAD
AND TOBAGO
859

A

Cuidad Bolívar

Georgetown
170

Paramaribo
170

Cayenne
20

G U Y A N A
582

SURINAM
320

FRENCH
GUIANA
32

BRAZIL

J.S.